HOW TO SURVIVE
A KILLER MUSICAL

"I've Been a Bad Boy, Mother . . ." Kit Gill (Bradley Dean) confesses his crimes to the portrait of his late mother, Alexandra Gill (Karen Murphy), in the 2000 Barrington Stage Company production, directed by Rob Ruggiero.
Richard Feldman

HOW TO SURVIVE A KILLER MUSICAL

AGONY AND ECSTASY ON THE ROAD TO BROADWAY

DOUGLAS J. COHEN

APPLAUSE
THEATRE & CINEMA BOOKS
ESSEX, CONNECTICUT

APPLAUSE
THEATRE & CINEMA BOOKS

An imprint of Globe Pequot, the trade division of
The Rowman & Littlefield Publishing Group, Inc.
4501 Forbes Blvd., Ste. 200
Lanham, MD 20706
www.rowman.com

Distributed by NATIONAL BOOK NETWORK

Library of Congress Cataloging-in-Publication Data

Names: Cohen, Douglas J., author.
Title: How to survive a killer musical : agony and ecstasy on the road to
  Broadway / Douglas J. Cohen.
Description: Essex, Connecticut : Applause, 2023. | Includes
  bibliographical references and index. | Summary: "When the young
  composer Douglas Cohen first secured the musical rights to the novel No
  Way to Treat a Lady by William Goldman—the acclaimed author of The
  Princess Bride and Marathon Man—he hoped it would be his big break, the
  first step on a gilt path to artistic triumph and commercial success in
  the form of a hit Broadway musical" —Provided by publisher.
Identifiers: LCCN 2023008879 (print) | LCCN 2023008880 (ebook) | ISBN
  9781493075744 (cloth) | ISBN 9781493075751 (epub)
Subjects: LCSH: Cohen, Douglas J. | Composers—United States—Biography.
  | Musicals—Production and direction—United States. | LCGFT:
  Autobiographies.
Classification: LCC ML410.C7334 A3 2023 (print) | LCC ML410.C7334
  (ebook)
  | DDC 782.1/4092 [B]—dc23/eng/20230224
LC record available at https://lccn.loc.gov/2023008879
LC ebook record available at https://lccn.loc.gov/2023008880

∞™ The paper used in this publication meets the minimum requirements of
American National Standard for Information Sciences—Permanence of Paper
for Printed Library Materials, ANSI/NISO Z39.48-1992.

To Cathy for saying yes,
and Bill Goldman for not saying no.

CONTENTS

AUTHOR'S NOTE

The theater is about euphoric highs and debilitating lows. A show is a hit or a miss, you win an award or you lose, you book a job or you don't, the production runs "now and forever" or closes prematurely out of town. There is plenty of ink devoted to massive hits or notorious flops. The hits produce happy investors and an abundance of T-shirts, totebags, and snow globes. Flops occupy a revered place in discerning hearts and on the walls of Joe Allen, a popular Manhattan restaurant which aims to operate in the black but only celebrates productions in the red. Let's face it: the theater is volatile and built on extremes. If it were embodied in a human being, that person would surely be manic-depressive.

But attention must be paid to the middle ground, which is largely ignored: shows that were publicly lauded, generating nominations and even awards, original cast albums, and licensing agreements, but didn't move to Broadway or extend beyond their limited run. Sometimes they just miss out on the glory due to a leading actor abruptly leaving for a major movie, the detrimental timing of a war or major news event, or a review from an influential critic who favors plays over musicals and attended on a lackluster night.

How to Survive a Killer Musical: Agony and Ecstasy on the Road to Broadway is devoted to the decade-long gestation of one musical, *No Way to Treat a Lady*, for which I wrote book, music, and lyrics. The fact it resides in the middle ground doesn't mean it didn't have its share of backstage drama, often eclipsing the action presented onstage. As these pages will reveal, the emphasis on the word "survive" isn't hyperbole. Larry Gelbart, Tony Award–winning playwright and librettist (*City of Angels* and *A Funny Thing Happened on the Way to the Forum*) is credited for having said, "If Hitler's still alive, I hope he's out of town with a musical." Gelbart knew just how difficult it was to develop a show while under intense public scrutiny as the clock madly ticks away. We view successful musicals as if every word or note was inevitable: We forget or choose to ignore the arduous process that goes into spinning straw into gold. You don't have to place a killer in your musical to know that musicals can be a killer.

When I look at the Herculean task of writing this show and overcoming its many vicissitudes, I can only marvel at how I *did* survive. Perhaps my blind faith and remarkable persistence can be explained in an Oscar Levant song title, "Blame It on My Youth."

But I suspect it's more than that. I knew I had a tiger by the tail and was hellbent on hanging on for dear life, wherever it took me. And we covered a lot of mileage. To date, there have been over two hundred global productions including two Off Broadway, three in the United Kingdom, three in Germany, two Italian tours, and productions in Barcelona, Sweden, Japan, Australia, the Philippines, Amsterdam, Switzerland, and I believe the Czech Republic (my memory is hazy). Although I didn't personally witness all of them, many impacted me in life-altering ways.

Throughout these experiences, I faithfully kept a journal, often the only constant in my mercurial cosmos. William Goldman, author of the original novel on which my musical is based, conceived a protagonist, Detective Morris "Moe" Brummell, who also keeps a diary that he shares with the reader. The juxtaposition of these personal entries against a brutal—and brutally funny—narrative is compelling. Perhaps this influenced my decision.

I wasn't always consistent—there were lapses when duty called, and I focused on rewrites and rehearsals. But these entries capably served as an accurate road map, allowing long-dormant memories to resurface with additional landmarks and rest stops. I have done my best to refrain from significantly editing these entries but rather present them mostly "as is": the private observations and experiences of a somewhat naive, occasionally ambitious, and definitely obsessed young man with a mission. And like Morris Brummell's confessions, they are *italicized*.

For those of you who wish to experience the musical score (and no, I did not write Helen Reddy's hit "Ain't No Way to Treat a Lady"), an original cast album exists of The York Theatre Company revival in 1996 and 1997 (originally through Varèse Sarabande and now through Ghostlight Records). In addition, there are bootleg recordings on the theatrical dark web (a good demo of seven songs from the Hudson Guild production plus live recordings), as well as an original cast album of the first Italian tour, *Serial Killer per Signora*, with terrific, enhanced orchestrations that occasionally pops up on eBay. However, all of this is not necessary for the journey.

Some thirty-five years later, I'm still holding on to that tiger by the tail. And for those of you brave enough to accompany me, I hope you enjoy the ride.

PROLOGUE

A week after my musical *No Way to Treat a Lady* opened Off Broadway in June 1987, I was depressed: Even though the production had been extended, we didn't know if it would transfer to a commercial venue, a move that would lead to a longer New York shelf life and the possibilities of a tour, abundant regional productions, and even a film. More than that, I had made the mistake of reading John Simon's review in *New York Magazine*.

My mother called that Sunday, as was her custom.

"I spoke to Valerie Schor."

Valerie was a dear family friend and the dialect coach at the University of Connecticut in Storrs where I grew up. She spoke in rounded tones.

"How is she?" I asked.

"I told her you were upset with John Simon's review."

"You didn't need to share that."

"Please," my mother reassured me, "it's only Valerie. You know what she said? 'Tell Douglas he is fortunate to have a New York production that is reviewed by John Simon.'"

Valerie was right. Being reviewed or dismissed by John Simon was an honor. It indicated I had achieved something very rare: an honest-to-God production of an original musical on a prominent New York stage. I took it for granted at the time, believing it would be one of many. The ensuing years have taught me otherwise.

I have had other musicals, thankfully, although not all of them have landed on New York shores. Some of them are more emotionally resonant (*The Gig*, 1994), boast splashier scores (*The Big Time*, 2020), take on more relevant themes (*Bridges*, 2016), or challenged me more as a writer (*The Opposite of Sex*, 2006, but you'll just have to take my word on that one since the theatrical rights to the movie on which it was based were unexpectedly withdrawn; another story for another time).

But *No Way to Treat a Lady* was my first foray into professional theater, with a cast of characters comprising leading actors, directors, producers, critics, novelists, screenwriters, music directors, orchestrators, choreographers, designers, public relations directors, and rising and seasoned composers and lyricists of their time.

It outlasted the duration of one "season," to take a cue from William Goldman's legendary book, *The Season*, based on a single theatrical year. In fact, this modest Off Broadway show eventually took me to London with a volatile, Tony-winning director, as well as regional productions in the seemingly idyllic city of Sarasota, Florida (where our leading lady narrowly escaped being murdered), then onto industrial Cohoes, New York, where another leading lady suffered a fall, only to be replaced by the most unlikely of suspects.

Most people helped me achieve my objectives. Others ultimately thwarted the process. But I'm grateful to them all.

I'm even grateful to John Simon. Looking back on his harsh review, he stated my music was an imitation of Sondheim and Marvin Hamlisch—"a sort of sondhamlisch." Rather than a slight, now I feel it's a compliment. Sondheim is the most influential force in musical theater, and Hamlisch wrote catchy tunes that morphed into permanent ear worms. Besides, it makes me sound like a revered member of King Arthur's Court: "Look, my liege, Sondhamlisch approaches."

And so, he does.

1

"YOUR FRIEND, WILLIAM GOLDMAN"

It all began . . . with laundry.

In 1985, I found myself without clean laundry. Fortunately, there were washers and dryers in the basement of my New York City apartment building, so I took the plunge. It was a ritual I painstakingly avoided by bringing dirty laundry home to my folks whenever I could squeeze in a visit. But with no immediate plans to take the train to Hartford, Connecticut, I devoted that particular April Sunday to domestic pleasures.

In between cycles, I turned on my small black and white television, landing on a movie I dimly recalled as a three-minute trailer in my youth. (At ten, my parents felt I wasn't mature enough to see the other one hour and forty-five minutes.) After watching roughly fifteen minutes, I had a "eureka" moment. The movie's premise—a frustrated actor turned killer, Christopher "Kit" Gill (played by Rod Steiger) develops a symbiotic relationship with the lonely, nebbishy detective assigned to the case, Morris "Moe" Brummell (George Segal)—seemed to be rich fodder for a musical. Add to the mix a beautiful love interest, Kate Palmer (Lee Remick at her most beguiling) and a quintessential Jewish mother, Flora Brummell (Eileen Heckart), plus a host of other wonderful character roles representing Kit's potential victims, and you have an entertaining romantic-comedy-thriller musical.

Social media mania in the late 1960s: Rod Steiger as Christopher "Kit" Gill surveys his latest headline in the 1968 film version of No Way to Treat a Lady, *based on William Goldman's novel.*
Photofest

Inspired by the premise and the performances, I went to the piano and started to find melodies as if out of thin air. Composing is often elusive: Sometimes, I go to the piano and no matter how hard I try, the music doesn't materialize. Other times, it's as if I'm seated at a player piano, and the keys are performing independently. Either way, I always had a tape recorder nearby. (Now I use my iPhone.) On that day in April 1985, I hit "record" on my Sony Walkman, and at least seven melodies were created. The lyrics were only half-formed, but the ideas were there.

The placement of the songs was clear to me, as was the tone. As an actor, Kit would sing songs evoking different musical styles, enhancing the disguises he assumes to lure his unsuspecting victims. The songs of Detective Moe Brummell would be more contemporary, but still in a musical theater idiom: With the exception of Liz Swados (*Runaways*), Galt MacDermot (*Hair*), and Jonathan Larson, who hadn't fully emerged, very few composers were

Detective Moe Brummell (George Segal) interrogates "one of the beautiful people,"
Kate Palmer (Lee Remick), in Jack Smight's 1968 film No Way to Treat a Lady.
Photofest

focused on writing truly contemporary scores. Kate Palmer, the
Holly Golightly archetype ready to renounce breakfast at Tiffany's
in favor of brunch at Flora Brummell's, would have a more romantic sound.

Three songs written that day would survive for the musical's
world premiere: "So Far, So Good," "I Have Noticed a Change in
You," and "Five More Minutes." I hadn't chosen these titles yet . . .
in fact, "So Far, So Good" was written to the nondescript place-
holder lyrics "I met a guy/He has a name." (I sing while I write,
and these were the first words to come out of my mouth.)

After composing enough music to fill a whole A side of the
cassette, I called Cathy Kiliper, my girlfriend (and later my wife).
We met during our freshman year at college (Amherst and Mount
Holyoke, respectively) and were steadily dating when I wrote my
first full-length musical as my senior thesis: *Dr. Jekyll and the Mr.*
Hyde Bar, based on my experiences as a pianist-vocalist observing

people's duality. Cathy was well-acquainted with my expanding musical oeuvre, the false starts, the obscure shows that never got produced, the trunk tunes, and the occasional live performances.

"Turn on the TV. There's this film, *No Way to Treat a Lady*. Please watch," I said breathlessly, "and tell me if you think it's a musical."

Cathy dutifully caught the last half hour of the movie and concurred. Definitely a musical and definitely something I could write.

There were no search engines then, so I couldn't find out who wrote the screenplay. More importantly, was it based on a novel? That was a critical distinction, for even though I had never applied for theatrical rights before, I was aware that to musically adapt a screenplay you needed not only the written consent of the writer but also, more importantly, the film studio. A novel, on the other hand, was like one-stop shopping: Earn the approval of the author, and you had a deal. (However, this is predicated on the fact the author retained the theatrical rights.)

I've been a movie buff since the impressionable age of eleven after meeting silent screen star Lillian Gish at the University of Connecticut. My father, the Hillel rabbi at the university, decided on a whim to take me to von der Mehden Hall to hear Miss Gish speak while publicizing her book, *The Movies, Mr. Griffith, and Me*. I only knew of her from an Al Hirschfeld caricature in a theater book my father owned, surrounded by scholarly, biblical journals.

With book in hand, we attended Miss Gish's lecture, which was accompanied by a liberal number of silent film clips and an actual pianist providing a soundtrack. (It was often related to me that Nana, my maternal grandmother, Leah Trabich, a gifted concert pianist, would accompany silent movies.) Whether it was the musical accompaniment or hearing Miss Gish speak of her near demise on an iceberg in *Way Down East*, I was entranced and became a regular visitor to the film festivals curated by two graduate students. Not only did they introduce me to F. W. Murnau's *Sunrise* and Billy Wilder's *Sunset Boulevard*, but also, more importantly, they inspired me to collect memorabilia and film books.

My apartment in New York was small, and few books had weathered the move. So I did what anyone would do on a Sunday when libraries are closed: I called my folks and explained I needed the credits to *No Way to Treat a Lady*. Less than ten minutes later, the phone rang. My father held a large reference book as my mother read, "*No Way to Treat a Lady*. Paramount Pictures, 1968. Produced by Sol C. Siegel, Directed by Jack Smight. Screenplay by John Gay. Based on a novel by . . . you'll never guess?"

"Who, who?" I demanded.

"Your friend, William Goldman," she replied.

My mother always had a knack for inserting "your friend" in front of anyone with whom I came in contact, including famous people I admired but never met. Sometimes it went one step further: Having enjoyed a thriving correspondence with Tony and Emmy winner Jane Alexander, I would frequently hear my mom (quoting her sources from *TV Guide*) report on Jane's next project with, "You'll never guess what your *girlfriend* Jane Alexander is up to."

So "your friend, William Goldman" wasn't exactly accurate. But it wasn't inaccurate either.

In 1983, I wrote the music to a modest revue entitled *This Week in the Suburbs* featuring humorous skits by Norman Kline, manager of the Emelin Theater in Westchester County. My collaborator was Susan DiLallo, a talented lyricist and successful copywriter in advertising. We thoroughly enjoyed each other's company, made each other laugh, and wrote some good songs. We had met at the 92nd Street Y while attending Carol Hall's and Carolyn Leigh's lyric writing workshops. (Lucie Arnaz was also enrolled in the latter class, prompting Carolyn to exclaim, "Oh, Lucie, I did a terrible thing to your mother—*Wildcat!*" referring to Lucille Ball's only Broadway musical.) Those classes gave Susan and me enough courage to apply to the BMI Musical Theater Workshop shortly after its founder and leader, Lehman Engel, died. We were both accepted.

This Week in the Suburbs had a modest run at the Inner Circle in the West Village. It is only notable for four reasons: 1) I played the entire audition with a broken wrist, having just come from a bike accident in Central Park. 2) It marked my professional New York debut (although critics were thankfully not invited). 3) Stephen Flaherty the future composer of *Ragtime*, supplied the vocal arrangements. 4) It featured a game cast of four: our book writer Norman Kline, Ron Orbach, Denise Moses, and Terri Beringer. Terri, a talented, effervescent blonde, had a boyfriend, actor Kurt Zischke.

Through Kurt's friend, Ilene, Kurt and Terri became friends with Ilene's husband, Bill . . . better known as William Goldman.

By 1983, Goldman's celebrated works included *Marathon Man* and *The Princess Bride*. (The latter hadn't been filmed yet but was regarded as one of the most beloved novels of the twentieth century.) In fact, he had enjoyed success in nearly every aspect of show business, as his two Academy Awards for *Butch Cassidy and the Sundance Kid* and *All the President's Men* could attest. A successful career in the theater, however, had eluded him: He and his brother James collaborated on the short-lived Broadway play, *Blood, Sweat and Stanley Poole*, as well as *A Family Affair*, a modest musical notable for marking the Broadway debut of their fellow roommate, composer John Kander. Nevertheless, Bill wrote a definitive, theatrical nonfiction book, *The Season*, chronicling Broadway from 1967 to 1968.

Bill and Ilene were fond of Terri and wanted to support her in her latest endeavor. I was (coincidentally?) devouring Bill's *Adventures in the Screen Trade*. I also knew the night the Goldmans planned to be at our show and brought his book with me.

This Week in the Suburbs was not in danger of upstaging *A Chorus Line* and *Little Shop of Horrors*, two popular musicals originally developed in BMI. At best, it was a modestly amusing show with a sprinkling of good songs. There were times, however, when the show failed to ignite. In fact, of the six performances, five of them were kind of dormant.

The sixth was on the night Ilene and Bill attended. The Inner Circle was a restaurant with a bar which also functioned as an art gallery. When the venue wasn't selling drinks and food, it was displaying oil paintings for sale. One large painting hung just behind the makeshift stage where the actors entered.

On this particular night, David Gaines, our eternally youthful music director, was passionately playing the "Overture." The vibrations from the piano caused the landscape painting directly behind him to shake, freeing itself from its perch and landing with a thud on the floor, still upright, but totally blocking the actors' entrance. The audience started to giggle, then giggles turned to waves of laughter as one hapless member of the cast was instructed to inconspicuously strike the painting. By the time the ensemble entered for the opening number, the audience was in the palm of their hand.

The rest of the show was pure delight. Following the performance, I introduced myself to Bill and Ilene, who couldn't have been warmer. A striking, surprisingly tall man, Bill was an excellent conversationalist, and I didn't outstay my welcome. But I did ask him to sign *Adventures in the Screen Trade*, and he graciously consented. When I got home that night, I read his inscription: "For Douglas Cohen, It was thrilling. God bless, William Goldman."

So . . . while I didn't have a movie reference book on my shelf in New York, I had one inscribed by "my friend" William Goldman.

Oscar-winning screenwriter and best-selling author William Goldman in 1982, the year before our paths crossed. Photofest

Prior to a proliferation of stalkers and inappropriate fans, many well-known New Yorkers were listed in the phone book along with their addresses. Bill Goldman was one such person. But I couldn't just pick up the phone and express my passion for his property. This required a more strategic campaign.

Over the next six weeks, I diligently worked on writing songs for *No Way to Treat a Lady*. "Still," a suspenseful duet sung by Kit in drag and an unsuspecting victim he befriends at a bar, occurred to me while walking to my job as an employment counselor, and I wrote 80 percent of the lyrics commuting that day. Without benefit of a recorder, I went to a phone booth and sang the tune into my answering machine so it would be there to greet me when I returned home. I initially wrote the quartet "Front Page News" as a solo for Kit after he finally receives his first *New York Times* headline. In addition to completing "So Far, So Good" and "Five More Minutes," I also penned an opening number for Kit in his first disguise as a priest entitled "It's a Very Funny Thing."

This number was somewhat reminiscent of Stephen Sondheim's musical voice. And let's face it, while Kit Gill was haunted by his dead mother, I was haunted by the work of the great master. Having seen *Sweeney Todd, Company, Follies, Sunday in the Park with George,* and *Merrily We Roll Along,* I was "under the influence." Sondheim's intelligence, innovative harmonies, fearlessness, and theatricality inspired me, but I was also a child of the 1960s, so Jule Styne, Frank Loesser, Richard Rodgers, and Kander and Ebb were equal partners in crime. The more I worked on *No Way to Treat a Lady,* the more I discovered it was a warped valentine to musical theater. Kit Gill may have been doing his victims irreparable harm, but he was also celebrating the gods of musicals . . . *my* gods.

I also discovered there were significant autobiographical aspects to the property. Even though I left my cloistered world of Storrs for the seductive lights of Broadway (and Amsterdam Avenue), my parents' grip was never entirely released. In addition to the weekly phone calls, there were care packages that accompanied me and my clean laundry back to the city after frequent visits home, weekly letters containing a newspaper clipping of note or a check to help with cab fare and avoid "dangerous" mass transit. Above all, there was the constant nurturing, someone there to help me pick up the pieces wherever they lay. My co-workers, first in development at Lincoln Center and later at M. Luca & Associates, an employment agency, were primarily women, many of whom were older and maternal. Detective Morris Brummell wasn't the only man who needed to come into his own.

I was also Kit Gill in many respects. No, I didn't moonlight as a serial killer, but I did have a yearning—an insatiable thirst—to make a name for myself. I wasn't obsessed with celebrity, but I was determined to express my art and make a mark.

After listening to my beloved Nana performing sonatas, the American Popular Songbook, and Scott Joplin, I had discovered I could "play by ear" at the age of four, picking out "The Sound of Music" on a tiny, portable piano barely two octaves in length. For me, printed sheet music was superfluous, like handing a map to someone with an internal GPS. My parents wasted good money on classical lessons, as my normal course of action would be to imitate music I had heard my sister practice a year or two earlier before the same piece was assigned to me. My exceptionally patient piano teacher, Marilyn Schmidt, would often remark that I performed Bach "by way of Doug Cohen."

That may have been the earliest sign that I was experimenting with composition. But in the fifth grade, I earned my first full-fledged credit. Cast as the Sandman in Engelbert Humperdinck's *Hansel and Gretel*, I was nearly despondent when I didn't land the role of Hansel. My teachers, Mrs. Tuite and Mrs. Murray, assured me that the Sandman's song was the most difficult, and since I had the best voice in my grade, they knew it was in good hands. But it was still a cameo—one scene, one song, and a handful of pixie dust. How could I make a lasting impression?

Then it occurred to me. What the musical was missing was a narrator, a troubadour who could greet the students and give the show a more contemporary setting. I started fiddling on my guitar and came up with a tune appropriately called "Hansel and Gretel." I phoned Mrs. Tuite (who conveniently lived a half mile from our house) and asked if I could play it for her. She graciously shared her Saturday morning and even contributed some lyrics to a second verse which contained the phrase, "The Brothers Grimm wrote this music very rare, sounding like bells in a church yard square." (A rabbi's son would never naturally reference a "church yard square.")

Once the song was complete, my teachers gave it their blessing and allowed me to "open" the show. It probably marks the only time Engelbert Humperdinck collaborated with a writer over a hundred years his junior! And unlike the rest of the opera, my original song was never performed again. But it awakened in me the desire to create music and lyrics, and from then on, I composed at least two to three songs a week.

My music was often the soundtrack to drama unfolding in our house. My father, H. Hirsch Cohen, a reform rabbi, attracted throngs of people every Friday night. It wasn't until I was eight or nine that I realized they weren't coming to see *him* but rather commune with *God*. When he lost his temper or meted out punishment at home, I was never sure if it was being delivered by my father or some higher being. There were additional family tensions, nothing out of the ordinary, but playing the piano tended to obscure competing high-decibel voices.

My mother, Claudia, had entertained as a child in Atlantic City after winning a Shirley Temple look-alike contest and later starred as Jo in *Little Women* on early live television in Philadelphia. She appeared as Uta Hagen and Jose Ferrer's daughter in a war bond rally directed by Broadway veteran Margaret Webster. (Paul Robeson also appeared that night.) My mother always felt I had a flair for the dramatic: "Douglas, the Academy Awards aren't until April," she'd exclaim whenever I overreacted. However, she often gave as good as she got. One time when returning to New York laden with her noodle pudding, I called my folks to let them know I had arrived safely. My mother refused to talk until I had refrigerated her "goodies." "I can keep," she insisted, "the perishables can't."

Too tempting to ignore, I used much of my mother's obsession in Flora Brummell's instructions to Morris in the song "Five More Minutes": "If you don't refrigerate your perishables, Morris, you could take one bite . . . and die. Now I want you to call me as soon as you refrigerate the perishables."

My parents saw just about every show that opened out of town in Philadelphia between 1952 and 1955, the year my sister Debby was born, trading *Playbills* for playpens. By the time I arrived, they had assembled a nifty collection of cast albums, which I listened to in lieu of bedtime stories. They introduced us to musicals at the Cape Cod Melody Tent in Hyannis (apparently, I was so enamored with *The Most Happy Fella*, I didn't touch my ice cream cone) and eventually Broadway musicals, beginning with the Lincoln Center revival of *Annie Get Your Gun* starring Ethel Merman. Other jaunts to the city included meeting my first Broadway star, Kay Medford (best known as Barbra Streisand's mother in *Funny Girl*), whom my parents befriended back in Philly during one of her many out-of-town tryouts that never fulfilled their Broadway potential. Discovering we were both Virgos, I gave Kay a Virgo ring which she wore onstage and television during the mid-1970s.

Determined to adapt William Goldman's novel and not the film, I located an obscure copy at one of the branches of the New York Public Library and dove in with abandon. It was an odd structure for a novel, fifty-three chapters and only 182 pages. Hours later, I wondered why I had been attracted to the source material. Though brilliantly written, it's exceptionally dark. Like the movie, it focuses on Kit Gill, a publicity-crazed, unhinged actor who strangles lonely women reminiscent of his late mother (a celebrated actress) before planting a lipstick kiss on their foreheads. Through perfectly timed phone calls, he confesses his crimes to a slovenly detective, Morris Brummell, who is saddled with his own mother problems and eager to accept clues in exchange for helping Kit achieve media attention. Detective Brummell gains stature in pursuit of a killer while simultaneously pursuing an effervescent socialite, Sarah Stone (renamed Kate Palmer in the movie).

But unlike the movie, Morris Brummell is a pathetic character with horrible facial scars caused by a childhood grease accident and exacerbated by monstrous ministrations from his equally monstrous mother. (Her pet name for Morris: "Goliath from the neck down.") Sarah Stone is—spoiler alert—brutally murdered by Kit two-thirds of the way through the book to make it look like the work of a copycat killer. In fact, much of the book deals with Kit's fixation with an actual copycat, which barely surfaces in the film adaptation. By the end of the novel, Morris's personal tragedies have reduced him to a sadist on par with Kit. As much as I respected Goldman's writing, I now had even greater respect for John Gay, who penned the screenplay.

Now, Doug, you're on your way. Good luck & Keep in touch.

—Dad & Mom

4/10/85

My father's tongue-in-cheek instructions after lovingly photocopying and mailing the entire Goldman novel. Author's collection

The novel left me with serious doubts about the project's viability. But I soon realized it was merely a blueprint: I could find a tone closer to the movie while using part of the book's structure. Also, I was now free to invent new disguises for Kit that weren't in the movie, should the film rights prove unattainable. So instead of musicalizing an effeminate salesperson giving an unsuspecting victim a complimentary wig fitting, Kit was now an Arthur Murray dance instructor bestowing a free dance lesson. The latter had greater theatrical weight while avoiding unflattering stereotypes.

Each character seemed to be grappling with intense loneliness. Kit had recently lost his mother; Morris was lonely for companionship; Sarah, although surrounded by beautiful people, felt strangely alienated from her tribe; Flora Brummell infantilized her son so he wouldn't abandon her. Kit's victims were isolated women who invited him into their apartments to help fill a void. Everyone existed against the backdrop of New York City, Sondheim's "city of strangers," which functioned almost as a secondary character.

It was around this time that an idea occurred to me that put the whole show into focus. Instead of a cast that would include Kit Gill, Moe, Sarah, Flora Brummell, Kit's mother Alexandra, and additional victims, why not have one woman play both mothers *and* all the victims? Kit was essentially killing his mother, and he and Morris were both having mother issues. Why not connect them through the same actress?

This was long before doubling was done ad nauseam in theatrical productions for economic reasons. True, a cast of four was certainly more attractive in keeping costs in check, but there was a psychological justification for this artifice.

My typed letter to Bill Goldman did not give away this delicious discovery. But I reminded him of my previous writing credit, *This Week in the Suburbs*, and told him I'd embarked on an even more exciting project, adapting his novel *No Way to Treat a Lady* as a musical! I related I was eager to play him my songs and hoped he would share my enthusiasm. I even provided my phone number, believing he would read the letter and quickly pick up the phone to ebulliently schedule a meeting.

Every week that passed seemed like an eternity. After waiting a month, I finally secluded myself in the smallest office at M. Luca & Associates and dialed his number.

"Bill? Hi, it's Doug Cohen. How are you?"

"Fine, Doug. Fine."

"Good. I just called because I wrote you and hadn't heard back so—"

"Yes, I got your letter." Here he paused. "I don't know how to respond, Doug. It's such a strange choice. I really don't know what to say."

"I know your novel's dark, but if I can share my vision and play some songs, I'm sure you'll have a very different impression."

After another pregnant pause, he finally said, "Okay. What about tonight?"

"Tonight?!" (It was 3:00, I was at my job, and I hadn't cleaned my apartment in three weeks.) "Okay. What time were you thinking?"

"How about 7:00?"

I was quickly doing the math in my head. Could I leave work early and arrive home in time to get out of my corporate attire, tidy up and clean, grab a bite, warm up my voice, and rehearse the songs?

My boss, Margaret Luca, had attended the High School of Performing Arts (the *Fame* school). Her first husband, Sergiu Luca, was a world-famous violinist. Her mother, Rosina Lawrence, who occasionally helped with payroll, was the beautiful blonde teacher in the legendary *Our Gang* comedies. If anyone would sanction my leaving the office early to play songs for Bill Goldman, it was Margaret.

I gave Bill my address, and Margaret gave me her blessing.

What transpired that night was entered into my journal:

7/23/1985

8:15 p.m.

William Goldman has just left. He spent exactly an hour here as I poured my heart into my six "Moe Brummell" songs. He said he was "fascinated" by my work. ("You know what I already think of your talents.") Basically, I think he still can't quite accept that this dark book (as he said, "It's no masterpiece") could ever be a musical.

"I just don't see it as a musical. It's very dark stuff. I think I even wrote it before Kennedy was shot."

My vision he could see, but he was curious as to how I would handle Morris and Kit's developing relationship primarily on the phone. He liked the idea of using Kit's recurring confession "I've Been a Bad Boy, Morris" as a song title and saw possibly something "patterish." Basically, he's not very proud of his work and is unable to see how it would appeal to me, although he agrees it is passionate. Also, he sees Morris as being somewhat anti-heroic and wonders if he's a likable enough protagonist. Bill said if I make him a thirty-seven-year-old man who lives with his mother, people might think him strange. I explained that I saw Morris as an underdeveloped man with great potential as a human being. As the drama unfolds, he finds Sarah who helps him realize his potential, with Kit acting as a catalyst.

As impressed as he was with my vision, he still has difficulty accepting the notion of a musical but did concede that it may work as a small theater piece with limited dialogue, running an hour and forty-five minutes, plus an intermission. "Nothing Wagnerian."

Bill told me how he came to write the book. He had been blocked with his novel Boys and Girls Together *and had stopped writing after three years and seven hundred pages. One day, he was walking down the street when this idea of a murderer and a copycat came to him: "It was amazing; the idea just dropped into my head. It had never happened before. I thought maybe it was just an excuse not to write the novel, so I gave myself 10 days to complete it, which I did. It was one continuous flow, so much so that I didn't know where one chapter ended and another began. When I gave it to my editor, he said, 'Bill, I don't know what to make of this. I can't edit it,' so he suggested we publish it under a pseudonym because he had big hopes for* Boys and Girls Together.*"*

I would later learn that Bill chose the pseudonym "Harry Longbaugh," a variation of Harry Longabaugh, the Sundance Kid's real name. At the time, he was currently researching the lives of Butch Cassidy and Sundance, which would eventually result in a screenplay that sold for four hundred thousand dollars, an astronomical sum in 1967, breaking all previous records. And *No Way to Treat a Lady*'s many short chapters resulted in actor Cliff Robertson mistaking it for a strangler "treatment" and contacting Bill to rewrite his current vehicle, *Masquerade*, which became Goldman's entreé into film.

Bill said he didn't like to read his own writing. When I mentioned he was prolific lately, he said, "Yeah, no screenplays, but a lot of books." I asked him if he'd ever consent to letting someone musicalize The Princess Bride.

"No," Bill said somewhat emphatically. Then paused. "Well, maybe Sondheim. But I'm not even sure I'd let Steve adapt it." It is the jewel in Goldman's crown.

Bill encouraged me to work on my own projects but said, "If you're enjoying the creative burst, I'd be interested in seeing what you come up with by Labor Day if you're still interested. I don't want to encourage you, but I can't stop you."

His word upon leaving the apartment was "fascinating." Then he disappeared down the hall with a perfunctory, "God bless."

I felt strangely encouraged.

I suspect that is the thing about youth. We selectively hear words which give us positive reinforcement and discard everything else. Bill Goldman thought my show was "fascinating." He could have said, "Doug, there's no way I'm going to give you the rights." But he didn't. To my still evolving, twenty-five-year-old brain, I heard, "Keep going, Doug, and see you in September."

That summer I wrote more songs and played them for Cathy, my folks, my friends. I shared my progress with an assistant at the William Morris Agency, Betsy Lifton, recommended by a former executive who had heard me perform as a pianist-vocalist on Cape Cod. I also made a demo tape of four songs and submitted them to the ASCAP Musical Theater Workshop.

In the 1980s, there were two major musical theater workshops in New York City: the Lehman Engel BMI Musical Theater Workshop, where you learned your craft, and the ASCAP Musical Theatre Workshop where you learned to schmooze.

By schmooze, I mean networking. This observation isn't meant as a slight to ASCAP. You also received invaluable feedback from some of the most brilliant and influential people in the industry. In fact, I owe a great debt to both illustrious institutions, as these pages will reveal.

Lehman Engel, a renowned conductor, music director, and composer on Broadway, created the BMI Musical Theater workshop and wrote a series of "how to" books, which served as the foundation of the workshop. Students admitted in the first year received a series of writing assignments including a ballad for Blanche DuBois, a charm song (medium-tempo and entrancing, like *Oklahoma!*'s "Surrey with the Fringe on Top") for Carson McCullers's play *The Member of the Wedding*, a comedy song for John Van Druten's *Bell, Book and Candle*, and a final aria for Willy Loman. (You haven't lived till you've heard sixteen successive "suicide" songs.) By the time the second year rolls around, you are writing your own musical, which is so early in the process that it almost never comes to fruition. This can be original or an adaptation. My fellow classmates, future Tony winners Lynn Ahrens and Steve Flaherty, nearly proved to be an exception to the rule by adapting the film *Bedazzled* with remarkable promise. They never got the rights, but they got an agent.

By the third year in BMI, it's a little like the iconic television series *Survivor* where certain writers are voted off the island: roughly half the original group remains to join seasoned veterans. I was fortunate to be among them.

In comparison, ASCAP was about receiving constructive critiques and making introductions. You applied with a cassette of four songs and a project. Like BMI, it didn't matter if you had the rights. If selected, yours would be one of four projects presented on a Monday night. A professional panel was selected to weigh in on your two songs: Charles Strouse (who had enjoyed supernova success as the composer of *Annie*, followed by the more earthbound vehicles *Dance a Little Closer* and *Bring Back Birdie*) was the only constant in the equation. Depending on the night, he would be joined by three other panelists often consisting of theater luminaries such as Peter Stone (librettist of *1776*), Howard Ashman (riding high as the lyricist and librettist for *Little Shop of Horrors*), Frank Rich (chief theater critic for *The New York Times*), Patti LuPone (iconic Broadway performer and surprisingly funny and accessible), Carol Channing (equally iconic, very astute, nothing like her Lorelei image), Sheldon Harnick (legendary lyricist of *Fiddler on the Roof* and *Fiorello!*), Jule Styne (legendary composer of *Gypsy* and *Funny Girl*), Biff Liff (renowned William Morris agent), Henry Krieger (composer of *Dreamgirls* and *The Tap Dance Kid*), Stephen Schwartz (acclaimed composer-lyricist wunderkind before Disney and *Wicked* but after *Godspell*, *Pippin*, and

Rags), Marvin Hamlisch (*A Chorus Line*'s composer, and as entertaining as you would imagine), and Martin Charnin (*Annie*'s celebrated director and lyricist who had more recently struck out with the Jackie Robinson musical, *The First*).

Once a year, Charles would be joined by none other than Stephen Sondheim. During these occasions, no one else would join Charles on the dais: Sondheim was so brilliant in his summation that other guests would have been superfluous. Jonathan Larson presented to Sondheim his musical, *Superbia*, a dystopian, futuristic rock fantasy. I vividly remember Sondheim making an astute observation followed by Jonathan sheepishly agreeing, "Yeah, my uncle Dave warned me about that as well." Sondheim and the entire room were charmed.

ASCAP was run by Bernice Cohen, who was in her fifties at the time but seemed older. She always wore a dour expression and began each session by holding up an umbrella or some other recently lost item and asking—nay, demanding—to know who had left it the previous week. Bernice was deceptive, however: she reluctantly revealed a good heart and shrewdly asked me to sign with ASCAP as my licenser long before BMI made a similar request.

Despite some truly illuminating, occasionally brilliant discussions—and the biting, corrosive wit of Peter Stone—you attended ASCAP not only for the nuts and bolts but also the introductions and Danish. After the first two presentations, Bernice would announce a break, and the honored guests would step off the slightly elevated stage and mingle with the masses. You could sidle up to critic Howard Kissel of the *New York Daily News* or Mitch Douglas (a major ICM agent) or if you were really brazen (and I never was) you could join your peers encircling Sondheim.

The teachers at BMI were equally acclaimed: Maury Yeston (composer and lyricist of *Nine*, whose boundless energy and fertile talent seemed well-suited for the title role in *Amadeus*), Alan Menken (gentle and unassuming composer of *Little Shop of Horrors* who was about to embark on his astonishing Disney career), and Ed Kleban (lyricist of *A Chorus Line*, reserved and deeply revered). Richard Engquist (lyricist of Off Broadway's *Kuni Leml*) taught the second-year students. Diligent and fastidious, Richard spoke in a kind of northern drawl: imagine Truman Capote if he'd been born above the Mason-Dixon Line. Skip Kennon (gifted composer of Off Broadway's *Herringbone*) was my teacher for the first year and did a truly skillful job of dissecting our work. Skip spoke at one volume level and seemed to be in a perpetual state of awe (which is ironic, as he was rarely in awe of our nascent talent).

BMI was a completely different experience from ASCAP: We were being judged by our teacher and, worse, our peers. Most people would focus on lyrics, as that was easier to pinpoint when critiquing. As Skip astutely observed, few people know how to talk about composition. He was one of the exceptions, however, and would frequently bandy terms about only true composers could appreciate—terms like "secondary dominant"—that could make most lyricists (and a few composers) feel as if they had entered an English as a Second Language class.

Another significant difference: We weren't allowed to bring in "ringers" or professional singers to perform our work. Every song we wrote in the first year was performed by the musical team that created it. You could ask fellow writers to perform, however, and I can proudly state I was on that short list. In contrast, at ASCAP you could ask performers currently on the boards, although major Broadway performers were a rarity, as we were unknowns without credentials.

From 1982 to 1985, I applied and was selected to participate in the ASCAP workshop three times over three successive years with three separate projects. You don't have to know much about the first two musicals except the most favorable comment I received was Charles Strouse begrudgingly conceding my ballad was "the jewel in the chicken soup."

But *Moe Brummell* (which, fortunately, I would later retitle *No Way to Treat a Lady*) was different. Even though BMI hadn't exactly embraced it when I brought selections to the advanced class, they hadn't dismissed it either. In fact, Alan Menken thought the melody to "So Far, So Good" was first-rate, and Ed Kleban, after listening to the song "Still," announced to the class, "Ladies and gentlemen, there's a writer in the room."

This last comment should have supplied me with enough helium to keep me afloat for a solid year had I not been determined to surpass myself the following week. "Sarah's Touch" landed like a defused missile completely missing its target. In one fell swoop, Ed (correctly) pointed out that it was an anemic love song with contrived references. I was crestfallen.

But only temporarily. In September, I learned that not only had I been admitted to the 1985 ASCAP Musical Theater Workshop but also the first session was to conclude with *Moe Brummell*!

(Why I didn't call my musical *No Way to Treat a Lady* from the outset, I'll never fully comprehend except to say that most musicals based on a novel or play changed their titles to signify a transformation. Thus *Oliver Twist* became *Oliver!*, *The Matchmaker* became *Hello, Dolly!*, and *Anna and the King of Siam* became *The King and I*. Today, they just take the famous title and slap THE MUSICAL after it.)

I was elated with the news and sprang into action by calling Bill Goldman. He wasn't as enthused.

"Doug, I thought I told you to focus on another show."

"Well, technically you said you couldn't exactly *stop* me from writing it and looked forward to seeing what I came up with. Getting into ASCAP is a big deal, Bill. They're very selective. It would be amazing if you could be there."

"When is it?"

"Monday, October 28 at 7:00 p.m."

"Let me see." Seconds passed as I heard him flipping through his appointment book. I imagined potential conflicts included "drinks with Newman and Redford at 6:00" or "fly to L.A. to pitch Paramount." Finally, he said, "Okay, Doug, wrote it down."

I thanked him profusely, then set about to assemble the best cast possible. I always felt I would have chosen a career in casting if I hadn't gone into writing for the theater. I loved scouring my Theatre World books and had an almost encyclopedic memory for names and faces. I knew I wanted Mary Testa for the character woman. I also knew I wanted Jason Alexander as Detective Moe Brummell.

In September 1985, Jason was appearing in *Personals* Off Broadway, written by David Crane, Seth Friedman, and Marta Kauffman, with music by Alan Menken, Stephen Schwartz, and Michael Skloff, among others. (David and Marta, sans Seth, would eventually create the phenomenon *Friends* with Kevin Bright.) I knew the director,

Paul Lazarus, and had penned a song for his thirtieth birthday with my close friend and frequent collaborator, Tom Toce. (The party was attended by none other than Stephen Sondheim, who made a point of complimenting my music, calling it "first rate." It was a very good night.)

Through Paul, I got to Jason who was very intrigued. He loved the movie *No Way to Treat a Lady*, even though if memory serves, he was hoping I'd ask him to perform "the Rod Steiger role." Before long, Jason was at my apartment learning "Five More Minutes." Between his expert comic timing and natural musical gifts, it was pitch perfect casting.

To round out the ASCAP cast, I asked Michael Byers, who later had a nice cameo in the movie *Postcards from the Edge*, to perform "Still" with Mary. Tall and wiry, he was closer to Goldman's description of Kit (modeled after Roddy McDowell, I later learned).

Everything was progressing smoothly. Then, three days before the presentation, I had a minor meltdown.

I remember walking on the Upper East Side when I suddenly experienced a panic attack. What if Monday night was a bust? Not only would I have to weather another very public humiliation (at the hands of some of my idols) but also risk losing the rights if William Goldman witnessed the debacle.

I fumbled for a quarter and called Bill. I explained I was nearby and needed to talk. He graciously invited me over. At that time, he was living in a palatial Upper East Side duplex, boasting a huge foyer and a staircase to somewhere . . . but before I could take it in, I was ushered into Bill's library. It was literally the size of my entire apartment with wall-to-wall bookshelves on three sides climbing to what appeared to be twenty-foot ceilings. Upon reflection, the room probably influenced the dialogue I wrote when Moe Brummell first enters Sarah Stone's apartment: "These are high ceilings. VERY high ceilings. You could play basketball in here."

Bill offered me something to drink. I declined, but I did take him up on his offer to sit on his luxurious couch. As I did, I caught a glimpse of something shiny. When I gazed across the room at the bookshelves, there—dead center—were his two Academy Awards. Talk about an elephant in the room!

"You needed to see me?" Bill asked.

"I just started to think about Monday night. I've been part of the workshop before, and it can be very brutal . . . some of the comments . . . and I have so much on my mind getting all this ready. And I wanted to prepare you, because if the presentation isn't a success, I don't want to blow my chances of getting the rights."

"Don't put that kind of pressure on yourself," he said reassuringly. "My giving you or not giving you the rights has nothing to do with how your presentation is received."

I was kind of relieved to hear that but also felt strangely unsettled. So if it's an unqualified success, it won't *increase* my chances?

I decided it was a good thing and thanked him. We made some additional small talk, and he showed me to the door.

"I'll see you Monday night then," Bill said, ushering me out. "Oh, one more thing—I'd rather you not let anyone know I'm there. God bless."

I nodded and walked stoically toward the elevator. With Bill's ambivalence ringing in my ears, it was just one more detail I had to incorporate into Monday night's presentation.

2

SO FAR, SO GOOD

That Monday night, I sat with the other members of the workshop in the first six rows. At one point, I turned around to see Bill unobtrusively taking a seat near the back of what looked to be a packed room. Bernice welcomed everyone; there were four chairs on the dais which meant *Sondheim was not in the house*.

Charles Strouse took his usual seat house left (nearest the piano) and introduced the very prestigious panel: Stephen Schwartz, Burton Lane, and Frank Rich. It was almost comical. If the stars aligned, this could be the start of something big. If not, it was just one of those things.

Either way, I was performing for four people I strongly admired. Strouse, Schwartz, and Lane are legendary writers in musical theater. Burton Lane may not have had as productive an output as Charles Strouse and Stephen Schwartz, but based on two scores, *Finian's Rainbow* and *On a Clear Day You Can See Forever*, plus his Hollywood contributions, he deserved to be in the same category. I had a history with the work of each titan, having appeared in amateur productions of *Bye Bye Birdie* (music by Strouse), *Pippin* and *Godspell* (music and lyrics by Schwartz), and eventually making my Carnegie Hall debut singing, "Old Devil Moon" from *Finian's Rainbow*. As for Frank Rich, I feel very few people have written so passionately and eloquently about the theater. I didn't always agree with his ultimate verdict, but it's difficult to deny he's a brilliant writer.

23

Listening to Charles's, Stephen's, and Burton's scores growing up made them into deities. Being in close proximity at ASCAP made them more human, but they still were elevated beyond that eight inch high platform. For my first decade as a fledgling writer in New York, I expected one of my childhood idols to mentor me. What I didn't realize was that as commercial producers were becoming risk-averse and the not-for-profit theaters were taking greater risks, both the older guard and the newer guard began to compete for these few precious opportunities for productions. Actors don't compete with actors of a different generation, but the same is not true of writers. Ironically, one of ASCAP's participants that year, Jonathan Larson, was going to change the shape of musical theater, making it difficult for the established guard to remain relevant. This was particularly true when *Rent* and *Big* opened in the same season on Broadway. Venerated collaborators Richard Malty, Jr. and David Shire, who penned *Big*, had about twenty-five years of Broadway and Off Broadway experience, but relative newcomer Larson posthumously won the Tony and Pulitzer, and *Rent* completely eclipsed *Big*.

But at ASCAP that night, I had no way of predicting how the panel would receive *Moe Brummell*, let alone foreseeing the future of the American musical.

The first two presentations fell flat; the panel didn't find much to admire. We broke for Danish and refreshments. William Goldman hung back, preferring to remain anonymous in case one of the panelists recognized him. I briefly spoke with him and asked if he was enjoying himself. He nodded, acknowledging it was fascinating to observe and wished me luck.

The penultimate presentation was written by Paris Barclay, a very accomplished writer who would leave New York about five years later to become one of the most sought-after directors in television. Paris preferred to play his more elaborately produced songs on a boom box, which was frowned upon at both ASCAP and BMI, where live presentations were encouraged. The panel was once again not favorable in their response. And unlike *Moe Brummell*, his project did not offer opportunities for comedy.

It was now my turn. I introduced my musical and set the stage for the first number. Even though I have genuine stage fright when it comes to accompanying my own work, ASCAP forced you outside of your comfort zone.

As Flora Brummell, Mary Testa's booming voice awakened the hall:

FLORA:
Morris, get up! You have to be at the station in a half hour. Kum!

Here, Jason Alexander's Morris Brummell began to slowly awaken, singing the opening of "Five More Minutes":

MORRIS:
FIVE MORE MINUTES OF DREAMING
FIVE MORE MINUTES OF PRECIOUS SLEEP
FIVE MORE MINUTES OF NEVERLASTING BLISS

FLORA:
Morris, are you up? I don't hear you moving . . .

MORRIS:
FIVE MORE MINUTES OF SCHEMING
HOW TO SILENCE THE WAKE-UP CALL.
WHERE'S THE SOMEONE WHO'LL ROUSE ME . . . WITH A KISS?

There were already laughs, and as the song progressed, bigger ones followed. People were listening and enjoying what they heard, especially Flora Brummell's instructions on the "perishables." (Thank you, Mom.) I hoped the panel was sharing the audience's enthusiasm as the number entered the home stretch:

MORRIS:
GOD, PLEASE SHOW SOME HUMANITY
QUICKLY END THIS INSANITY
CAN'T YOU SEE THAT I'M NEAR THE BREAKING POINT . . .
IF IT'S TRUE THAT THE LORD REWARDS THE PATIENT,
HOW MUCH LONGER MUST I WAIT.
WHEN LADY LUCK COMES A KNOCKING

SHE'LL BE FIVE DAMN MINUTES
TOO LATE!

Just as Morris began to exit, Flora intruded for the last time.

FLORA:
Morris, you forgot your gun.

Jason shot Mary a classic look of exasperation and stifled anger,
reached for the imaginary gun, and placed it in his coat pocket
exactly as the number "buttoned"—or in layman's terms, reached
its finish.
   Big applause.
   So far, so good.
   In hindsight, I probably should have presented "So Far, So
Good" as my second piece so the panel could hear a tuneful
charm song between Morris and his love interest, Sarah. But since
the musical is about a cop and a killer, I didn't want to leave the
antagonist out of the equation. And Ed Kleban's incredibly strong
endorsement of "Still"—a cat and mouse song sung by Kit in drag
and Sadie Bellows, an unsuspecting barfly—made the choice something of a no-brainer.

SADIE:
STILL, I FEEL THAT SOMETHING'S NOT RIGHT,
I'LL DIE OF FRIGHT IF I DON'T FIND OUT SOON.
THIS IS NO WAY TO BEHAVE,
BUT HONEY I NEED A REFILL—
AND YOU NEED A SHAVE!

OH, GOD, WHERE IS THAT BOTTLE OF SCOTCH?!
PLEASE STOP THE FILM, I CAN'T WATCH ANYMORE.
LET ME HAVE ONE MORE SHOT THEN PASS OUT,
SEE I PROMISE I WON'T EVEN SHOUT.
LOOK, I'LL STAY VERY CALM IF YOU STAY OVER THERE
HERE'S FOUR DOLLARS IN CHANGE,
OH COME ON, FAIR IS FAIR.
(Kit removes his wig)

SHIT, YOU'VE LOST ALL YOUR HAIR . . .

KIT:
Shh. Still.

The performance was smooth, and there was nice tension and a few chuckles in the right places. I rushed the tempo, so there was a similar manic feel to "Five More Minutes," the preceding song. Not a major flaw. However, if we were rating the evening as an Olympic event, my routine was strong with an impressive dismount, although I lost some points on technicalities.

Again, the applause was strong. I smiled and nodded thanks to my performers, then turned to the panel for their verdict. I knew this routine all too well from my two previous at-bats, which had led to scoreless innings. But tonight, I felt the tides turning. Charles Strouse, rather than starting the conversation, indicated for Stephen Schwartz to go first.

Stephen began, "Well, it's very clever, obviously. And the lyrics are funny and extremely well put together. Musically, I start to find it increasingly wearing, and it may just be the fact that the two numbers were very similar from a musical approach. They're staccato and slightly dissonant, and after a while I just got tired, but it may just be that we've been sitting here for a while which is a little unfair to you."

I had made modifications in the accompaniment I played at ASCAP that night based on what fared better in the BMI Musical Theatre Workshop, favoring an idiosyncratic, post-Sondheim style over a more conventional Broadway sound. The latter rarely went down well with my BMI teachers and peers.

Stephen continued with more observations, including one that touched on Flora Brummell: "The character of the mother is such a cliché that for me it reflected badly on the character I know I'm supposed to root for. He was realer than this woman who was so stereotypical—he would have left long ago, a woman that extreme. And so I wasn't sure what your reality was. This is somewhat nitpicky because, you know, it's very good work."

This was high praise coming from Stephen Schwartz, a writer who was always astute but never gratuitous with compliments. He then passed the baton to Burton Lane, who started by saying he enjoyed "Five More Minutes" and found it "rhythmically interesting." Burton went on to discuss the universality of the characters, particularly the Jewish mother, recalling that Joe Stein, the book writer for *Fiddler on the Roof*, had been amazed to discover during a production of *Fiddler* in Japan that he had written "a perfect Japanese mother."

As for the music, Burton called it "witty, clever but I thought it could be a little truer." And he agreed that "Still" was musically similar to "Five More Minutes." He was clearly from the old school of musical theater writers: succinct and to the point. I can't imagine Irving Berlin pontificating about harmonies or rhyme schemes. The song either landed or it didn't. If Burton were a guest star on the then-popular television show *At the Movies*, I would have earned a thumbs up, with reservations.

He then motioned for Frank Rich to speak. I was suddenly struck by the fact that panels usually included four participants, something I had observed as a child watching *What's My Line?* and *To Tell the Truth*. Now there was some irony in that realization, as I wondered whether this panel would decide if the show was the genuine article.

Frank largely agreed with Stephen as well, "but one overriding thing that is important is that of the four shows tonight, this is the one I'm only interested in seeing, knowing the kind of stuff that Goldman writes and appreciating, if I'm understanding it correctly, that it's a comic sort of schleppy Jewish gumshoe with a fun murder case. It's very unpretentious. I think if it's done well, it could be extremely satisfying." Like Stephen, Frank had concerns about Flora: "No Jewish mother is *that* funny. I can't speak for *all* Jewish mothers." But overall he found the material "very, very clever with a lot of potential. . . . What I really like about the second song was you took something that's dramatic and fun in a detective murder scene—one involving mistaken identity at that—and dramatized it as a song, even though the execution wasn't equal to the concept. It had a potential of being a light, funny version of the kind of thing that Sondheim does gravely in *Sweeney Todd*."

My heart was racing. Frank Rich was not only giving me a positive "review," but it was also happening in real time. It wasn't as if I had to wait for the intimidating sound of *The New York Times* dropping with a thud at a newsstand at 5:00 a.m., Sky Masterson's "time of day." It was happening in the moment, and I recognized then and now the importance of those words and how they were likely to impact my future.

Charles Strouse was the last to speak, and his approval was the one I craved the most. During the previous two misfires at ASCAP, his words had stung. On one occasion, he had politely chided me for not challenging myself and digging deep enough. I knew there was a kernel of truth to that comment and hoped he would recognize that with this project I had taken his words to heart.

Charles began with "Still," which he thought was "*this* close to making it work. One of the reasons it doesn't work is oddly enough you get too much comfort in the song. When you see a movie and the music becomes too dramatic sometimes, you're comforted: You're more frightened if there's silence. I feel that basically you have such a terrific sense of humor, if you don't fill it up so much. Startle us a little bit more dramatically—you would not only get more humor, but you would also seize the moment and make something of the threat. As funny as it is, the threat is implicit."

Like the rest of the panel, he was a fan of "Five More Minutes": "I found it a very amusing idea and I did believe—unlike Stephen—that this man would have a mother like that. There's no explaining sons' love for mothers. . . . It was just a fun and funny song with interesting things to do for the character when he wasn't singing. That's why in the second song you have to have the element of fright."

Then Frank Rich asked the question to end all questions: "Do you have the rights?" I told him I had no idea: I was just working on the show and seeing what came of it. Frank cautioned that it could become "one of those horror stories one hears all the time where someone adapts and finds the rights are tied up forever. You know, it's a 20-year-old novel of his, it's not in hot demand." He advised me to act "now rather than later."

At this point an audience member pointed out the massive labor, potential expense, and uncertainty of success that securing rights entailed, asking how young writers could possibly pull it off:

"If we're unknown, how else can we pursue a William Goldman to give us the rights or sell us the rights until we have written enough to demonstrate to him that we are worthy?"

To this, Stephen pointed out that it was "easier because Bill Goldman is here, he's alive, he lives in New York City, he's listed in the phone book. You can write him a letter."

And, Charles generously added, "You can say you have a good review from Frank Rich."

Fifteen years ago, I remember seeing a movie called *(500) Days of Summer*. For me, the most devastating scene was when the hero, played by Joseph Gordon-Levitt, attends a party thrown by his ex-girlfriend, played by Zooey Deschanel. There is a split screen where you see his "Expectations" on the left side and the "Reality" on the right. He expects he and his ex will quickly reconcile, but in reality, she's distant and reveals to a friend she's engaged to another man. That night at ASCAP, I felt as if expectations and reality had somehow fused, obliterating the need for a split screen. Everything I had ever desired for the show happened in those thirty-five minutes, and William Goldman was indeed "here" and "alive" and in the room where it happened, all thanks to a "phone book" and a "letter."

The room applauded. I turned off my tape recorder (fortunately it recorded) and thanked my performers, who were very pleased. As I gathered up my things, a dark-haired man in his early twenties exuberantly bounded to the piano. He was green but intently focused.

"Hi, I'm Robert Roth, and I just have to tell you that I read and listen to musicals all the time for Ira Weitzman at Playwrights Horizons, and 95% of it is shit. But I loved what I heard tonight, and I want to hear more!"

We exchanged numbers, and I saw Cathy beaming, as well as Peter Filichia, successful columnist and author, who had been complimentary when I performed songs three years earlier to a panel of naysayers. That meant the world to me and got me through a rough patch.

Bill Goldman was standing up now. He too was smiling . . . faintly. I went over to him.

"Congratulations. It went well," he said.

I felt chagrined. He was listening in on a very public conversation where potentially awkward references were made, like Ebenezer Scrooge being teleported and eavesdropping in Bob Cratchit's home.

"Bill, I'm sorry if anything was said that—"

"No, no. It was fine. Give me a call tomorrow," he instructed.

With that, he wished me a good night and added "God bless" as he headed for the door.

Later that night, I wrote in my journal:

10/29/1985 1:05 a.m.

I have just experienced one of the most exhilarating nights of my life, namely a victory at ASCAP. This has been a long time coming, and having been denied dessert for three years, I seemed to have OD'd on sweets tonight. It's amazing, though—I do seem to have perspective, so maybe that's what three years of rejection have given me. I'm not sure. What I am sure is that I feel tonight was earned, that I applied myself and put myself on the line in ways I had earlier avoided. The compliments meant a lot to me because it reinforced in my mind that my vision is right, and lo and behold, others agree.

I feel gratified and exhausted, but I must remember that these feelings come from within, and they are what have sustained me through times when my work was not appreciated.

I don't usually write things of a religious nature, but thank you, God. I pray tonight is just the beginning of the realization of my work. Why is it that suddenly dreams don't seem like dreams?

The next morning, I called Bill. He reiterated I should be pleased with last night.

"Listen, I checked my film contract, and I held onto the theatrical rights. I don't want you to pay for an option. You won't be able to afford it, so we'll work something out on a percentage basis. Have your lawyer give my lawyer a call."

I thanked him and immediately contacted Elliot Brown. A few years earlier, Elliot had secured the theatrical rights for *Nine*, a musical based on Federico Fellini's film *8½*. (I was told he got on a plane to personally meet with Fellini when negotiations started to go south and flew home from Italy with a deal.) He was warm, gracious, and approachable, and always gave me a discount knowing I couldn't afford exorbitant legal fees. I attempted to make it up to him each holiday season with an unusual gift, like brandy with an entire pear magically suspended.

Then and now, Elliot has been a constant in my life, and I have always valued his counsel. There were only two times I didn't heed his advice: when he felt a rights agreement for my musicalization of *The Opposite of Sex* was substandard, and when he warned me of potential problems with a certain director in London—which I'll cover later in this book. On both accounts, he was proven right.

Elliot called Goldman's attorney. Indeed, Goldman wanted to spare me laying out money for the rights, so he requested one-third of my author's share, the revenue I would receive from the show. A third was steep but within reason: Goldman clearly wanted the deal to happen and sensed it could be lucrative and advantageous for everyone involved.

Someone had once told me what a shrewd businessman Bill Goldman was, asking, "How do you think he got his name?" To be honest, if he wanted 50 percent of my share, I probably would have consented. This show was everything to me.

I went to work immediately. Having recorded the ASCAP presentation, I lifted the two songs presented, adding studio recordings of "So Far, So Good" and Kit's "Front Page News" and reached out to Betsy Lifton, my contact at the William Morris Agency. By this time, she no longer worked there, but she recommended I speak with Michael Traum, who assisted superagent George Lane. Michael was one of those Midwestern guys who seemingly let everything roll off his back. As George's assistant, that was probably an indispensable talent. I liked and respected George, but he intimidated the hell out of me.

Michael suggested I send George a cassette, which must have made a positive impression, for a few days later Michael was ushering me into George's office on the twenty-sixth floor of 1099 Sixth Avenue. The sun had just set, and Michael took a moment to call attention to the view and skyline. It was definitely impressive. George, a slim man with a beautifully tailored suit and auburn hair, peered from behind his desk, rose, and shook my hand. He was surprisingly tall.

After a few pleasantries, we both took a seat, and George got down to business.

"So, tell me about your night at ASCAP."

I related the experience in what more closely resembled an elevator pitch—I was at William Morris, after all. Leaning back in his chair as he surveyed me, his hands folded near his face, George looked like he was multi-tasking even when sedentary.

"Very exciting," he said in subdued tones. "And where are you with the rights?"

I explained that Bill Goldman was negotiating with Elliot and, in lieu of my paying for an option, wanted a third of my take. George was unfazed, but his eyes widened: you could tell he thought it was a little excessive. However, if he took me on, George would be representing one person writing book, music, and lyrics. His commission would still be significant.

"I like the tape. We have a room here with a piano. Next time you come, you'll play more of your songs."

I agreed. We set up a time, and a few days later I returned with lyric pages but no sheet music; I can recall music very well but am disastrous at remembering my own lyrics.

We were in a beautiful conference room. In lieu of windows, it boasted a baby grand (in tune!) and atmospheric lighting. I'd performed in many a piano bar on Cape Cod, and this seemed strangely familiar.

I started playing some of the more serious songs: "I've Been a Bad Boy," "I Have Noticed a Change in You," and "One of the Beautiful People." I could tell George was impressed. He smiled, nodded, and listened intently. I also played him some of "I Hear Humming," a comic duet for Flora and Morris when she suspects he has fallen in love with a young woman (Sarah Stone), but he evasively responds with only hums. George was sold.

"I want to represent you. How far along are you?"

"I can probably get a draft done by March." It was November.

"Good. You need a theater to help you develop the material. We'll do some presentations here. Nothing elaborate. Maybe about a half hour of material with four singers. How does that sound?"

It sounded good. I nodded; we shook hands. As I left the building, I started thinking about the song "Front Page News," sung by Kit Gill after his killing spree finally makes the front page of *The New York Times*. A friend from college, Madeline Sanchez, had heard a recording as a solo and encouraged me to think of making it a more expansive song, encompassing the other characters' points of view.

A few steps from the William Morris building, I started to get a tune in my head for Sarah.

"Detective Morris Brummell, will you look at that it's Morris facing front on the front page of *The Times*."

It was a good melody with real lyrics—not "dummy lyrics," or placeholders. I rushed home, singing the tune over and over so I wouldn't forget it. About an hour later, I had Sarah's contrapuntal part added to "Front Page News." I soon added a stanza for Morris and a patter section for Flora:

ALWAYS KNEW MY MORRIS WAS A WINNER,
THOUGH HE'S BEEN A SLOW BEGINNER
I HAD CONFIDENCE IN TIME HE WOULD COME THROUGH.
THIS SON OF MINE ALSO RISES,
LIFE'S A SERIES OF SURPRISES.
SUCH A STORY—IT'S CONTINUED ON PAGE TWO!

George, true to his word, organized our in-house presentations. The cast I assembled was comprised of Jason Alexander, Judith Bro, Mary Testa (Nancy Opel would later fill in when Mary was unavailable), and Stephen Bogardus. I was a huge fan of William Finn and James Lapine's *March of the Falsettos*—Stephen originated the role of "Whizzer" Off Broadway and recorded the original cast album—and he was ideally cast as Kit Gill: His innate charm and vocal chops could seduce even the most circumspect victim—and the audience as well.

Stephen also taught me an invaluable lesson about compensation. Since the William Morris Agency was only providing the room but no stipend to the actors, I wasn't sure I could or should compensate every presentation. Stephen said it was important that the performers get paid. It could be a nominal fee, but a tangible acknowledgment of their services was important. I have remembered that throughout my career. Actors are exploited enough as it is, so it's important to show their work is appreciated.

Watching these four superb performers inches from me was truly an honor. I couldn't believe how they took ownership of roles still gestating and were able to convey the characters' complexities so simply and effectively. I once remarked to Jason that he always seemed to make interesting and often surprising choices, which I found mind-boggling, as there are infinite possibilities available to an actor in a given moment. Jason said he was in awe of writers who also have a myriad of notes and words at their disposal, yet the good ones seem to make it look like there was only one solution.

There were four presentations, but the only one of real consequence was for Howard Rogut, general manager of Jujamcyn Theaters—one of the three theatrical dynasties presiding over Broadway houses in the 1980s. Howard would continue to be a passionate champion of the piece even if he could never quite get Jujamcyn to commit.

George Lane realized the presentations were not gaining traction for the express reason producers wanted finished shows, and we were still in the pupa stage. Therefore, it was important for me to take more time to revise and submit a stronger draft to George.

In the meantime, on June 6, 1986, something wonderful occurred:

Today, it arrived!

"It," of course, is the contract from William Goldman—a piece of paper that I have prayed for ever since I began work on the project, over a year ago.

It's truly amazing that things have turned out exactly as I envisioned. But it scares me to know how easily these dreams could have fallen apart at the seams. What if Frank Rich had not appeared on the panel that night? What if William Goldman had failed to attend? What if I hadn't decided to watch television while doing my laundry? What if I hadn't had such a productive and inspiring session at the piano?

The fact that all the elements came together beautifully again makes me believe some divine being was instrumental. But I also realize I worked harder on this show than I have ever worked before, and the work is not over. So maybe, through my efforts, I did something to help things along. It certainly couldn't have hurt.

Cathy and I had vowed to toast the contract's arrival over margaritas. We chose a local restaurant and after our order, she excused herself to visit the restroom. My eyes started to wander around the room, and I spotted Frank Rich only a few feet away! At first, I thought I was seeing things, but he too glanced in my direction. Finally, he smiled and rose from his table. I walked over, and we greeted one another like long-lost friends.

Frank's first question was if I had any news about *No Way to Treat a Lady*.

"Funny you should ask," I replied, and proceeded to tell him the story and the reason Cathy and I were out celebrating. Frank was delighted and wished me the best. I credited him and ASCAP with playing an instrumental part in my acquiring the rights, but he modestly resisted the compliment.

That brief encounter further cemented in my mind the evidence of serendipity. Now, if only I could find a good producer . . .

Ira Weitzman, who served as an artistic associate for William Finn and Jonathan Larson, invited me to perform songs solely for him at Playwrights Horizons. (Rob Roth, whom I had met that night at ASCAP, was still reading scripts for Playwrights and ferociously advocating they produce *No Way to Treat a Lady*.) I described the musical sequence when Kit as Ramone gives a free dance lesson to Carmella Tocci, employing "Safer in My Arms," a liltingly seductive tune, before she usurps his moment with a strenuous tango, "Dance Until We Drop." I played both songs adding, "Imagine a dance break where the two songs are battling one another, each trying to claim victory." Ira said, "Why don't you improvise something and show me what you mean?" It was tricky, as I'm not a dance arranger, but when the person making the request holds the Golden Ticket, you tap into your inner Leonard Bernstein. I came up with something so good I never was able to replicate it! It didn't matter—Playwrights Horizons ultimately never committed, although they continued to express interest until another theater made us a bona fide offer.

Enter Geoffrey Sherman, a British director with dual citizenship who had recently taken over as producing director of the Hudson Guild Theater, a venue on West 26th Street. Farther west than the American Jewish Theater, it was more than a performance space, offering a wide range of programs and services for the nearby community.

The Hudson Guild was once as indispensable an Off Broadway theater company as Playwrights Horizons, the WPA, and the Manhattan Theatre Club. *Da* by Hugh Leonard, which won the 1978 Tony for Best Play, first premiered there, as did *On Golden Pond* (1978), perhaps its most celebrated tenant before transferring to Broadway and morphing into a multi-Oscar-winning film. Prior to 1986, the Hudson Guild had suffered from poor management and questionable artistic choices. But Geoffrey was hired to change the course, and he wanted a musical to conclude his first season. George Lane sent him *No Way to Treat a Lady*, and he leapt at the opportunity.

I met with Geoffrey at the Guild. It felt more like a daycare center than a not-for-profit theater, but I instantly warmed to Geoffrey. Unflappable, he made you feel secure in his presence. He also had a charming British accent and a tendency to call me "love" and "Sir Douglas." He responded to the black comedy aspects of the piece, as did his associate director, Jim Abar, and literary manager, Steve Ramey. They were a warm, unpretentious trio.

Geoffrey's idea was to submit *No Way to Treat a Lady* for the Richard Rodgers Production Award. If we won, we would receive money to pay for the entire production at the Guild. But he also assured me that they could hopefully make it work without the Rodgers money. It was a win-win.

Their season was already set and announced. For the final selection in May, the brochure read "A Musical TBA."

Mum's the word.

February 1, 1987, 12:30 a.m.

Yesterday, at approximately 12:15 p.m., Miriam, our receptionist at M. Luca & Associates, belatedly gave me a message that "Jeffrey [sic] Sherman from the Hudson Guild" had called an hour earlier. I dialed the number and got Geoffrey out of an important meeting. He told me he didn't have much time and rather casually explained, "Listen, you did not get the big production award from the Richard Rodgers Foundation, but they did give you a development grant to have the show workshopped. Then we'll probably go directly into rehearsals for a full production."

I felt disappointed, as if I had let them down and was a runner-up or voted Miss Congeniality.

"Geoffrey," I asked, "this is good news, though, isn't it? I mean, I know we wanted the big award, but I should be happy, right?"

"Of course, you should be happy, love. Yes, it's very good," he assured me. "I wish I could talk some more, but I have to rush back. We'll speak at greater length next week."

Considering I had just won my first award as a writer, it was a mundane conversation. As much as I liked and respected Geoffrey, he needed direction expressing joyous news. It was only until I spoke to Cathy and later my parents that I realized there was indeed reason to celebrate. Cathy burst into tears when I phoned her. When I told my parents, I followed suit.

I was eating lunch (I treated myself to a Roy Rogers chicken breast in honor of Richard Rodgers), when I suddenly realized I hadn't called William Goldman. When I relayed I had just won a Richard Rodgers Grant, Bill said, "That's wonderful, Douglas. What is it?"

I could barely contain my impulse to laugh. I explained that Richard Rodgers had bequeathed one million dollars toward the development of new musicals, and *Nine*, the Tony Award–winning musical, had formerly won a Production Award.

Bill seemed pleased. "That's just terrific. It's wonderful because it's a reaffirmation of your talent, and it's not just your mother telling you it's good."

I thanked him for having an open mind and allowing me to work on the show.

"I encouraged you to do your own projects, but you stuck with it," Bill said.

He asked me what this meant in terms of a production, and I told him all about the Hudson Guild with our show tentatively scheduled to run May 27 to June 27. I added I hoped to see him there, and he congratulated me once more, ending with his customary, "God bless."

Later that night, Cathy and I celebrated by attending Neil Simon's *Broadway Bound*, which turned out to be a magnificent ending to a near-perfect day. Although we had ordered the tickets a month in advance, it seemed to prophetically coincide with the Rodgers news. Whether it was the play or the emotional rollercoaster I had been riding that day, I was weeping uncontrollably during the last five minutes. Never had a play had such a profound effect on me.

Backstage, we visited Jason Alexander—who had been memorable as Stanley Jerome, based on Neil Simon's brother—and later dined out together. Our diverse topics of conversation included reincarnation, Ouija boards, wedding plans (Cathy and I were getting married on August 9 no matter what productions loomed in our future), . . . and potential directors.

A night to remember: Jason Alexander (right) and Jonathan Silverman in Neil Simon's Broadway Bound. Photofest

3

JACK

Over the next two weeks, there were four major directors being considered: Jack Hofsiss, Tony Award–winning director of *The Elephant Man*; Paul Lazarus, director of *Personals* Off Broadway and *Epic Proportions* at the Manhattan Punch Line, which earned a very favorable *New York Times* review; the Hudson Guild's Geoffrey Sherman; and Robert Jess Roth, a recent graduate of Rutgers with no New York credits but laudatory and effusive recommendations from Ira Weitzman and *March of the Falsettos'* triple-threat creator William Finn.

Jack was George Lane's client, and the idea of working with him made perfect sense on paper. Jack was beloved in the theater community with good reason: he was celebrated, an intent listener, and possessed both a good heart and a wickedly droll sense of humor. While at the height of his success in 1985, Jack had suffered unspeakable injuries when a swimming accident left him a quadriplegic. He had been in and out of hospitals and treatments, hoping for some improvement. Sadly, he did not progress, but he was determined to return to theater. If I chose Jack, it would mark his first New York credit since the accident.

Paul was in his early thirties, very focused, and very driven. While he didn't have a major Broadway credit, he was accumulating an impressive resume and was whip-smart. Although soft-spoken and occasionally intense, Paul often enjoyed a good laugh.

Jack Hofsiss in 1980, shortly after he became the Tony Award's youngest recipient for Best Director of a Play (The Elephant Man). Photofest

Two years earlier, Cathy and I had run into him traveling solo in London and took him under our wing. We were a memorable trio, swapping theater recommendations and enjoying superior fish and chips and shandies on a tugboat, as we merrily rolled along the Thames.

Geoffrey Sherman threw his hat into the ring. He knew he wasn't a serious candidate, but he also loved the piece and had the right sensibility. If directors were like college applications, Geoffrey was my safety school.

The last candidate, Rob Roth, was a real wild card. He had enormous passion and on more than one occasion had inspired my writing. At twenty-three, Rob had all the makings of a wunderkind, but since I too was young, it didn't bode well for *Lady*'s maiden voyage. However, he "got" the material like no one else.

I had meetings with all four candidates. My conversation with Paul was probably the most in depth. He prodigiously analyzed the material and, with two central male roles, correctly identified the protagonist as Morris, grasping the significant work needed to make his journey complete. At first slightly wary of directing another musical after *Personals* (which enjoyed a respectable run of 265 performances at the Minetta Lane Theater), he ended our conversation by emphatically stating, "I really want to direct your show."

I spoke to Jack on the phone. He was complimentary but didn't offer much in terms of an analysis and the work needed. When I asked him who the protagonist was, he answered Kit. "Why?" I asked. "Well, he's your most interesting character," he replied. This was telling for a couple reasons: I disagreed with Jack's assessment (Morris was the classic protagonist), but by Jack choosing

Kit over Morris, I realized I had failed to make Morris sufficiently "interesting."

Much as I loved Geoffrey and Rob, it was really a decision between Jack and Paul. I chose Paul.

In his capacity as the Hudson Guild's producing director, Geoffrey communicated this to Paul's agent. Paul was in Atlanta directing a world premiere, *Bless*, for the Alliance Theatre. It had recently opened, so I eagerly looked forward to his return the following day. I waited, no call from Paul. Yes, Geoffrey assured me, his agent had relayed the offer. Another day passed, still no word from Paul. So, not one to stand on ceremony, I dialed.

The first thing I noticed was how weary Paul sounded. Things had not gone as smoothly as anticipated in Atlanta. In fact, from his description, it was an exceptionally trying experience. He sounded like someone in desperate need of a vacation and just kept referencing how exhausted he was. There was absolutely no mention of the offer to direct my musical. Finally, I addressed the elephant on the phone:

"Sorry it didn't go as planned in Atlanta, but I'm so excited to work with you on *No Way to Treat a Lady*."

This was met with silence. "You do know about our offer, right?"

"No, Doug. No, I don't."

"That's odd. I told Geoffrey Sherman to offer you the job. He said he called your agent."

"When?"

"Oh, maybe three days ago."

"This is news to me."

"Well, you have the job! I'm thrilled we're finally working together."

"Doug, really, this is the first time I'm hearing this. I can't understand why I wasn't told. I need to get back to you. Sorry, I'm just very surprised."

And with that, he said goodbye.

I was in shock. How was this possible? Why was *I* communicating the offer? Geoffrey had assured me he had spoken with Paul's agent who seemed pleased to hear the news. But what worried me most was not that Paul didn't get the memo but that he never expressed any pleasure at hearing the news. None whatsoever.

The next day, Paul called me. He was very apologetic, explaining that the offer had completely blindsided him (although he certainly knew he was in the running). He was tired, so tired that he couldn't contemplate going back to work in a month. He knew the Herculean task of doing a new musical and not only getting a cast and design team in place but also—more importantly—hunkering down with the writer to prepare a suitable draft in time for the Richard Rodgers reading. As much as he liked the material and was honored to have been chosen, he simply couldn't proceed.

To make matters worse, Geoffrey had called Jack Hofsiss two days earlier to say he didn't get the job. In retrospect, Geoffrey probably sensed that doing so before Paul had officially accepted could have serious ramifications, but the damage had been done. However, it was difficult to reject Geoffrey's profuse mea culpas, especially when he liberally injected "so sorry, love."

I immediately went back to George Lane and asked if Jack would reconsider. George said that although Jack was somewhat ruffled by the rejection, he also took things in stride. He would try to persuade him, but there were no guarantees.

On March 16, 1987, in anticipation of future entries in my journal, I started a new "comp book":

I still have no director. It seems that Jack Hofsiss has been offered a show to begin about the time we're scheduled for rehearsals. The particulars are sketchy due to the fact Jack left a message on my answering machine to call him but didn't leave his number!

I wonder if other people have gone through similar ordeals. Sometimes I think there must be some mass conspiracy to frustrate me until I break, or else Rob Roth has sold his soul in exchange for the chance to direct my show. (It will only be a matter of time before even Rob is no longer available!)

I'm just very eager—no, perhaps "eager" isn't strong enough—I'm desperate . . . yes, desperate to begin work on this show. We don't have a director, a cast, a designer, a music director . . . only Danny Troob, the orchestrator, who still thinks Paul Lazarus is the director!

I have this horrible vision that on opening night I'll still be without a director. I hope I'm being histrionic. At any rate, it's getting late, and

I need my rest if I'm to get through another day of tension and anxiety, with the possible exception of therapy and an hour at Jack LaLanne fitness center.

Que sera, sera . . .

Later that day, I heard from George. Jack had agreed to meet with me the next day, face to face. Would it be like Morris finally meeting Kit in the final scene? I felt encouraged: Why would Jack be taking up our time if he wasn't interested?

Maureen Laffey, Jack's indispensable caretaker with bright red hair and an even brighter disposition, led me into his apartment on the Upper West Side. It was spacious, with shiny hardwood floors, southern and northern exposures, and tasteful furnishings.

Jack was seated on a plush sofa, a wineglass precariously perched in his right hand. I was astonished to see he had use of that arm: Although it had limited mobility, he employed it for maximum effectiveness. In fact, looking at Jack in a handsome sea foam sweater, with a full head of striking, jet-black hair, his body serenely positioned like a Buddha, was comforting and not nearly as intimidating as I expected.

We hit it off immediately. Instead of giving me a guilt trip, he was very welcoming, funny, and self-deprecating (albeit some of his jokes were at Maureen's expense). He was also expert at spinning a yarn and making light of his potentially grave situation. I commented on his Tony Award nearby and how it caught the light.

"Oh, yes," he exclaimed. "You enter Tommy Tune's apartment, and he has nine Tonys all under nine separate pin spots!"

We didn't spend a lot of time dissecting *No Way to Treat a Lady*—it was a "getting to know you" kind of meeting. In fact, I would categorize it as a real success if not for the fact I didn't hear the words I was craving: "I accept the offer to direct your show."

I wouldn't hear those words for another twenty-four hours.   •

3/18/1987

On Tuesday when I spoke to Jack, he suggested we meet ASAP. I tactfully asked him what I should tell Geoffrey Sherman, and he said, "Tell him we're beginning work Wednesday if we don't run screaming from the room." Then Jack paused and added, "If you don't run screaming from the room."

A fine example of Jack's macabre sense of humor.

On our first day officially working together, I arrived at Jack's apartment straight from work, wearing a navy suit. Jack commented that instead of dressing down, I was progressively becoming more corporate. I assured him that I did own a pair of jeans.

We tossed around names for casting possibilities. (Morris: Michael O'Gorman, a recent standout in the short-lived Marvin Hamlisch–Howard Ashman musical, Smile. Kit: Kevin Kline, Mandy Patinkin. Sarah Stone: Vanessa Williams.) We discussed the text briefly: Jack felt the book was too long and wanted me to use the word "ladykiller," which presently was not in the text, even suggesting it could be a song. We also discussed the balance between Kit and Morris, and Jack said wryly that he was inclined to say Kit is the main character, "but I'm afraid we'd have to start all over again."

I promised to submit rewrites by Monday along with a possible song.

Geoffrey Sherman connected me with their publicist, Jeffrey Richards, who scheduled my first interview the following week. The casting breakdowns were going out to the various casting directors the next day. Finally, we were gaining momentum. Suddenly, the show had become a reality.

3/23/1987

I had a meeting today with Jack and Geoffrey at Jack's apartment. I came in sweating from rushing to get pages xeroxed and wearing my heavy wool coat. I excused myself and joined Maureen in the kitchen, who gave me paper towels to dry myself. (Jack: "Maureen, help Doug shower off.")

When I returned, Jack and Geoffrey were discussing their respective stints as soap opera directors. I pointed out to Jack that I was wearing blue jeans ("You see, Jack, I take direction well.") Geoffrey, Jack, and I discussed possibilities for a musical director: we all thought Jeanine Levinson was a good choice with her husband, Keith Levinson, on synthesizer. (Jeanine, who later divorced Keith and used her maiden name, Tesori, before establishing a remarkable composing career, was unavailable. But she would eventually sub for our accomplished music director, Uel Wade, on the original cast demo.)

Casting again: I brought up Judy Kaye's name—Danny Troob's choice for Flora; Geoffrey mentioned Dorothy Loudon and Lee Remick for the part (aargh! The latter is wonderful but so miscast! Geoffrey agreed but said, "Can you imagine greeting her every morning as she arrives with coffee?") Mandy Patinkin and Kevin Kline were mentioned again for both Morris and Kit, though they frighten me due to their gargantuan credits (and potential egos). Geoffrey thought they might even trade roles every other night which, I have to say, could be thrilling.

At that meeting, Geoffrey also mentioned a young man from a nearby college would be observing as an intern. When he casually added "He's eager to assist but can't type due to the fact he has only one arm," Jack began to laugh. "They once asked me to direct *The Nerd*," Jack related, referring to the play by Larry Shue, whose career had been tragically cut short by a plane crash. "I figured between a dead author and a director in a wheelchair, how could we lose?"

After Geoffrey left, I played Jack and Maureen my "Ladykiller" song, which thankfully did not register on Jack's "shit detector"— his expression for when he knew in his gut something wasn't good.

HE SLEEPS BY DAY
AND PLAYS BY NIGHT
HE'S LIKE COUNT DRACULA IN SEARCH OF ONE MORE BITE.
HE'S CASANOVA ON THE MAKE,
SO HONEY LAMB, MAKE NO MISTAKE
THE GUY'S A LADYKILLER!

Later, this song, which was meant to be played on the radio showing how fear had gripped the city, would be recorded by none other than original *Dreamgirl*, Loretta Devine, a friend of our choreographer, Chris Chadman. At the Hudson Guild, it also helped to fill a clunky scene change.

When I told Jack of my first telephone interview to promote our show, he referenced his "comeback" experience with the press the previous summer and the *New York Post* headline announcing, "BACK FROM THE DEAD," much to his chagrin. It seemed a natural transition into "the accident," and thankfully he felt comfortable discussing it.

In the summer of 1985, Jack had rented a home on Fire Island and one morning decided to take a quick swim before breakfast.

He dove into the nine-foot-deep pool only to hit his head on a sudden incline where the deep end transitioned into the shallow area. (Unfortunately, *The Post* article implied Jack had been drinking at a boisterous party and dove into the wrong end.) When his body eventually rose to the surface, house guests administered CPR before medics arrived. It was at this time Jack had an out-of-body experience, which he hesitated to publicly disclose due to skepticism surrounding Shirley MacLaine's similar confession in her recent autobiography. Jack admitted on some days he wished he had died. During the past year there had been no improvement: Even a trip to China for acupuncture did not fulfill expectations, although Maureen detected subtle changes. He tried to return to work, which had been his raison d'être. In fact, he emphasized his twelve-to-five work schedule had nothing to do with the accident but was simply when he was most efficient and productive.

I was honored that Jack had chosen to share with me intimate details of his accident and recuperation. I sometimes feel as if meaningful relationships are like the Panama Canal: We are vessels navigating through various locks, and with each one we connect on a deeper level. Some people liken it to peeling back layers of an onion, but for me, it's always been about submersion. We no longer skim the surface but begin to forge deeper and more meaningful connections to people, places, art, and literature. I felt that afternoon we had successfully graduated to the next lock.

I asked Jack what he had in mind regarding choreography, to which he replied, "I do have certain limitations." It may be too soon to tell, but I would say Jack has overcome his limitations in ways I would not have thought humanly possible. But then again, one learns to cope under extraordinary circumstances; life and theater teach us that.

On March 3, Jack, Maureen, and I met at the Hudson Guild to view the space. David Jenkins—our set designer, who had collaborated with Jack on *The Elephant Man*—joined us. His participation was a gesture of friendship, as money was not an incentive. David and Jack said they would be watching the movie *Diva* for inspiration in designing Kit's loft.

When we left the theater, it began to rain, and we had difficulty hailing a taxi: Empty cabs sailed by, unwilling to stop for a man in a wheelchair, even if it meant a potential fare. When one finally did stop, I wondered how Maureen would get Jack into the car while he was seated in a wheelchair. I didn't realize, as I was soon to discover, that wheelchairs come apart and can be reassembled. The magnitude of Maureen's job struck me as I watched her lift Jack into the cab, disassemble the chair, and place the chair in the trunk—all in the pouring rain. I tried to help, but she firmly told me to get into the car; it was her routine, and she performed it better and more expeditiously solo.

It marked the first time I'd seen Jack in a wheelchair, and it brought up painful memories of my beloved Nana after she suffered a debilitating stroke when I was six. An impossibly charismatic woman whose superior pianistic skills enabled her to become the first woman in Philadelphia to earn a musicians' union card, she had survived the next four years with crippling paralysis on her right side, speaking only in vowels and playing unidentifiable etudes solely with her left hand. Perhaps due to this ingrained trauma, suddenly Jack's condition became very real to me. He had tried to shield me from the sight for the past two weeks with one exception: I had walked into his apartment unannounced (the door was ajar) and glimpsed Maureen in the process of wheeling Jack into the room. They told me to wait outside until she had time to position Jack on the couch . . . like a human mannequin. But at the theater, he was exposed, and I had to sort of deal with it all over again.

As for *The New York Times*:

We made the Friday Arts section on 3/27/1987. I had left Jack's apartment at 10:30 p.m., took a 104 bus downtown and grabbed a paper at Broadway and 72nd. I had wanted to open it in the apartment but lost all willpower in front of a "Chirping Chicken." I couldn't believe the headline in Enid Nemy's weekly column: "Director returns with new musical about murderer!" I remember searching for my name and feeling a sense of exhilaration and fear. It was a nice night out, and I must have floated back to my apartment where Cathy and I read it together. I then called Jack, who had asked Maureen to fetch a copy. He felt they made him sound like "Jane Froman" [a famous singer confined to a wheelchair following a plane accident] *and apologized for not mentioning me. I was thoroughly content, however. Jack then said something that echoed my sentiments: "Well, I guess we're really doing it."*

Like Kit Gill, I suddenly sensed the awesome power of The Times.

The night before casting began, I called Bill Goldman to update him on our new director and where we were in the process. He gave me some good advice. I furiously wrote down his words in my notebook, as if he were Confucius:

"Paul Newman said to me during the movie Harper *(1966): 'If the part's right and I'm right for it, I'm worth gold. If not, I'm grossly overpaid.' I say this because you're young, Doug. Just don't get suckered into going for people because they have big names. People will go see Kevin Kline only if he's good, not if he's miscast."*

"Once in a lifetime there's a Lee Remick. Sarah Stone has to be more than beautiful, or it will look like Morris is only after her body. People went to see Liza Minnelli in Chicago *and didn't know who Chita Rivera was. By the end of the show, they were both stars. In other words, go for the best people for the roles."*

But Bill didn't want me to think he was infallible: *"If you had taken my advice, you wouldn't be where you are today. You're talented and stubborn — that's good. The show will succeed because of the material. It's a small musical, but you've given it a large scope."*

We finished our chat with my saying I'd love to have him attend rehearsals, although Bill cautioned, "Better check with your director before inviting me."

4/12/1987

It is Sunday night. Tomorrow is Passover, and then Tuesday we begin rehearsals!

*We've had auditions for the last week. It has been an exhaustive search, yet hopefully it has not been in vain. Through it all, Jack has been a constant source of merriment and stability. He is very sensitive regarding performers. Each actor has performed at least one song in its entirety plus a full scene to read. When the actor or actress is a possibility for Morris or Sarah, Jack asks them to read the Central Park scene. If the actor is an obvious "no" for Morris, Jack asks them to look at the brief telephone call. Jack said the true litmus test for the right Morris is whether the actor pronounces Bernard Bar*uch* correctly. Other gems have included:*

1) Gretchen Wyler (original star of Cole Porter's Silk Stockings*) explaining that she was late due to her meeting with her accountant. Jack's comment, "Don't worry, dear, after this show you won't need one."*

2) Telling a love-smitten Maureen after soap star Christopher Durham's audition, "Maureen! It may surprise you to know the real reason we're doing this show is not so you can get laid!"

3) Instructing two actors to put two chairs together to form a bench: "There, that's the most directing I've done in a year."

4) My favorite: After mistaking the Chef Antonio DeGnocchi scene (Kit disguised as a chef to lure Sarah Stone) for the Carmella Tocci scene (Kit masquerades as Ramone, the dance instructor), Jack exclaimed, "God, I've got to read this play!"

Liz Callaway auditioned, and I admit I was over the moon. My wife and I had attended backer's auditions in 1981 and 1982 for *Baby*, the show for which Liz eventually received a Tony nomination; Though we were far from qualifying as potential backers, we were invited due to our enduring friendship with the lead producer's niece, Julie Auster. I can count on one hand the number of times I've been in a room and felt that incredible rush of discovery. Liz was probably all of nineteen at the time, but her voice shimmered. And David Shire and Richard Maltby Jr. wrote a song, "The Story Goes On," that Liz not only hit out of the ballpark but may have overshot the Big Dipper. I had a similar rush seeing Jessie Mueller in *On a Clear Day You Can See Forever* and sixteen-year-old Timothée Chalamet perform at LaGuardia High School and later star in *Prodigal Son* Off Broadway.

Other than Liz's audition, perhaps the highlight of the day (and I'm being facetious) was when Howard Hensel (one of the four rotating Don Juans in Peter Brooks' Carmen*) auditioned as Kit Gill and asked me if the show was "my maiden voyage." When I answered yes, he added he thought as much, as it "takes you a long time to get to the point." To bolster my sagging confidence, Jack later suggested we write, "cc: Howard Hensel" on the bottom of all the rewrites!*

I began to recall all the times I've been up for a part and the horribly intense feelings that accompanied these auditions. Now, literally having been on the other side of the table, I realize more than anything that the creative team wants to be dazzled by the next person who walks through the door. We are praying for that perfect candidate to appear—like Mary Poppins answering Jane and Michael's advertisement—and it is indeed magical when it happens.

I am thinking now of Peter Slutsker, who auditioned thanks to Jason Alexander's recommendation. In many ways, Peter was our last hope since I knew in my heart of hearts that Michael O'Gorman could not sing the part, even after spending an hour and a half coaching him on "So Far, So Good." Somehow, I sensed Peter would win the role, and my predictions were confirmed Friday when he strode through the door with great authority, explained that he came with and without hair, and demonstrated by ripping off his toupee! Everyone was charmed. It was like a fairy tale where ten previous suitors had all tried but failed. Finally, like King Arthur in The Sword in the Stone, *this unassuming, balding ball of fire arrived to claim the role.*

The rest of the casting went smoothly, although Liz Callaway kept us on tenterhooks for a day before finally accepting. June Gable won the role of Flora, Alexandra, and the victims over Mary Testa. Mary had been amazing in her audition and had contributed mightily at the ASCAP and William Morris presentations and on demos. However, Jack really preferred June and shared a history with her at the Public Theatre. Steve Bogardus really had no competition for Kit (despite David Carroll singing brilliantly). Kay McClelland (who would have been offered the role of Sarah had Liz declined) was terrific: beautiful and winning. Whenever these performers read or sang, a twinkle appeared in my eye.

The most poignant experience that week was Alice Playten's audition . . . as Sarah. A gifted performer, she was no longer an ingenue and perhaps was never right for Sarah. Essentially, Alice was a character actress (she'd been an original cast member of *Hello Dolly!* and *Henry, Sweet Henry*), and knowing this, I asked Jack if we could suggest she also read for Flora Brummell. He sensitively pointed out, "She got dressed this morning with the knowledge she'd be auditioning for the part of a beautiful, free-spirited young woman, and to ask her to suddenly read for the *mother* might be damaging. These suggestions can be made through her agent if we want to call her back." He then quoted Sondheim: "First you're another sloe-eyed vamp, then someone's mother, then you're camp."

The cast we assembled was not satisfactory to everyone: Those who auditioned had particular strengths and weaknesses, and we generally favored performers who were talented actor-singers, not just amazingly gifted in one area. But I remember experiencing a sense of loss for the people I'd never get to see in the role, although they might have been interesting choices. My only consolation to those gnawing "what ifs" was realizing I didn't have the ultimate decision: Jack did. And now it was up to him to validate these choices.

4/14/1987
Our first read-through.
Briefly, I didn't sweat profusely, but this could be due to the fact the room was unusually cold. However, the reading was not as momentous as I had hoped. Peter and June haven't gotten a hold of their characters yet, but June was more successful as the lush Sadie, and Liz gave a nice first reading as Sarah. Steve was strong as Kit, but he's had more time with the role.

I keep telling myself not to jump to conclusions. But I somehow sense the reading did not meet with Geoffrey and Jack's expectations. Of course, it was only a first reading, but initial impressions loom large in the theater.

I hope their doubts are not confirmed.

P.S. Liz remembered me from somewhere. (She thought we might have worked together.) I jokingly told her I'd played opposite her in Baby. *She said, "Oh, that's right. Didn't we have a child together?"*

After just four rehearsals, I noticed significant changes in both the show and the cast. Peter had come a long way: Although he wasn't similar to Jason Alexander in type, he had an equally special persona and was a pleasure to work with. At one point, we compared bad back sagas: After Peter related that his troubles stemmed from running up a wall eight times a week—performing "Make 'em Laugh" as Cosmo in Twyla Tharp's Broadway production of *Singin' in the Rain*—I decided he won the competition hands down.

Liz astutely questioned her character's place in the scheme of things. Was Sarah only "the girl" or did she carry greater weight? I talked to Jack later, and he decided we should tell Liz that her scenes with Morris give the story a *healthy* perspective.

Discussions frequently centered on our own upbringing. Peter and I seem to have been raised by the same mother, similar to "Flora" in their somewhat overly maternal approach. Jack had an

"Alexandra Gill" for a mother; she sat him down when he was eighteen and told him he wasn't talented enough for the theater. Later, when he was nominated for Best Director for *The Elephant Man*, his parents asked for tickets to the Tony Awards. Jack said *No Way to Treat a Lady* is really about the effects of love on the psyche: too much (Morris) or too little (Kit).

With his direction of the Morris/Flora scenes, Jack eschewed the obvious, encouraging Peter and June to use their bickering as an expression of affection. He pointed out that cooking breakfast is very important to Flora since it's a tangible expression of love for her son.

Jack also continued to demonstrate he was a shrewd judge of character and how actors work. When I told him I didn't care for the voice June was using for Flora, he pointed out she had a myriad of characters to play and was dealing with that pressure by making obvious choices, such as varying her voices. He believed once June settled into the role, she would discover other ways of establishing character aside from vocal pitch and dialect. And he was proven right.

Everyone felt free to make suggestions, and I was receptive to their critiques. Most significantly, we pared down the Sadie/Kit scene and moved the spilling of her drink in "Still"—which takes Kit by surprise and causes him to abandon his faux falsetto voice—to the middle of the song. This injected greater tension and a reason for Sadie to be genuinely alarmed.

It was also what the ASCAP panel had previously indicated: There needed to be breathing room in the number. Stephen Schwartz had perceptively noted that things happened too quickly; there was more delicious fun to be had. I'm very grateful to the actors and Jack for helping me discover this in rehearsal.

Jack concluded rehearsal with a funny story of working for Joe Papp at the Public Theater during Joe's "Rabbinic" period. One day, Joe summoned Jack to his office. A crestfallen Papp: "Jack, I just found out you aren't Jewish. Why didn't you tell me?"

4/20–4/21

We made progress with the Sarah and Moe relationship. Jack pointed out that Sarah is privy to things Morris wouldn't reveal to anyone else, such as his "Thing" speech late in Act 1, based on Goldman's original material, when Morris attempts to describe his calls with the killer.

MORRIS: He really likes talking to me. I know that sounds strange . . . but I think he really enjoys our chats. The other day we had some choice words, and he hung up. He told me it was my fault *The New York Times* hadn't put the case on the front page—like I'm some big shot in PR. But a couple minutes later he called back—get this—to apologize. And all of a sudden, I got upset. I mean, here's this crazed THING running around killing people, and you hate him. You hate him because he's just that, a THING. But when the thing shows you its face, and it's a human face . . . well, it kind of got to me.

Eventually, that entire speech was cut in favor of something that hinted at Morris' obsession and desire to know Kit better:

MORRIS: I guess I wouldn't act this way except I know he's up to something.

SARAH: Bronski? *(Referring to Morris' assistant)*

MORRIS: No, the killer. God, I wish I knew his name so I wouldn't have to call him "the killer" all the time. It's so—

SARAH: Impersonal?

MORRIS: Yeah.

SARAH: It might also help you solve the case.

MORRIS: What?

SARAH: If you knew his name.

MORRIS: *(Lost in thought, not really getting the joke)* Oh right.

Meanwhile, the new lyrics to "So Far, So Good" seemed to work nicely.

I wrote no less than five different drafts for "So Far, So Good." An early version of Sarah's verse seemed to indicate she fell for Morris hook, line, and sinker:

WHAT DO YOU KNOW?
JUST WHEN LIFE SEEMS HOPELESS
SOMEONE WALKS IN,
OFFERS YOU A SMILE.
THEN ALL AT ONCE
EVERYTHING LOOKS ROSY
AND YOU'RE MARCHING IN TIME DOWN THE AISLE.

This verse eventually became,

NOT MUCH ON LOOKS,
NOT MUCH OF A DRESSER,

HIS EVERY MOVE LACKS A KIND OF GRACE.
HE'S NOT AT ALL LIKE THE GUYS I'VE DATED . . .
(*Considers this and smiles*)
WHAT A PERFECTLY NICE CHANGE OF PACE.
In the chorus, I traded . . .
HE'S KIND OF SWEET,
AS PROSPECTS GO.
WHO'D GUESS THAT HAPPINESS
IS JUST A THING CALLED "MOE"?
. . . for the following, which humorously acknowledged our
follicly-challenged leading man:
HE'S KIND OF SWEET,
WELL, FOR A COP.
HE HAS A CERTAIN GLOW
ESPECIALLY ON TOP.

*The most significant change occurs at the end of the play. We're think-
ing of keeping Sarah's survival somewhat ambiguous to create tension.
The audience may in fact believe she has been strangled. It means a lot of
rewriting and losing a charming last scene, but then again, "the play's the
thing" (not my quote).*

4/27(28)/1987

12:50 a.m.

*Well, it's morning, and our first public performance in conjunction
with the Richard Rodgers Grant is in twelve hours. Ordinarily, I'd be
afraid, but I'm looking forward to it. Now, maybe I'll live to eat those
words, but I find the piece entertaining and extremely well-acted. Yes, it
is long. (Why do I write to excess?) And yes, I'm sure there will be lines
people don't find as amusing but . . . I enjoyed it tonight. It was* dramatic
*and intensely theatrical. I'm not sure I feel a link between what I saw
onstage and what I spent hours working on to and from work and the
Saturday mornings sprawled out on the living room rug. I can't exactly
define the feeling as pride. I've become more of a spectator now, and as an
audience member, I'm having a good time.*

*More and more, I realize it's important for the writer to do as much
work* before *a show is ever produced. The pressure has not exactly inspired
me to greater heights, so I'm thankful that the piece is in as good a shape
as it is. The two years were well spent. (Listen to my self-confidence! By*

tomorrow night, I'm liable to be tearing these pages out along with what's left of my hair!)

More than as a writer, I feel I'm growing in my instincts as a musical director and a director. For once, I'm not always asking, "Do you think . . . ?" I'm beginning to gain confidence in my own opinions.

While I was discovering previously untapped fortitude, I noticed Jack had lost some of his fighting spirit. He didn't seem preoccupied in clarifying the story through staging, and I rarely observed him giving notes to the actors. Certainly, it was needed. I found a solution by covertly giving Jack directorial suggestions. For instance, following Morris and Sarah's first date in Central Park, I whispered, "Jack, don't you think Sarah and Moe should kiss? After all, he *does* make the first move due to Kit's influence." Jack's response was we shouldn't get too involved with stage business. But a minute later he suggested, "Peter and Liz, how about trying a kiss there." Among other things, I was learning to become a diplomat.

5/4/1987

Well, so much has happened since my last entry, it's hard to know where to begin . . .

The Richard Rodgers readings were well-attended (50 percent of the audience were my friends, plus a couple of foes thrown in for good measure). The 3:00 p.m. performance (attended by Sondheim!) was long and not particularly smooth. The first twenty minutes were quite magical, however. "I've Been a Bad Boy" was so powerful that I dissolved in a veritable sea of tears. I'm not sure if this is due to the fact the number is well-written and performed or because I was sitting next to my parents. Whatever the reason, I was drained. What followed, however, was not exactly memorable.

Flora Brummell quickly outwore her welcome, and the Central Park scene with Moe and Sarah was interminable. Liz gave a tight performance, displaying little of her kittenish, coy qualities that made her so attractive in rehearsal. However, I know I have a lot of work to do to give an enigmatic character more definition.

After the reading, Jack suggested I write more songs for Liz. I composed two new pieces: one, a kind of interior musical monologue when Sarah first meets Moe; the other, a song titled "Out for the Kill" focusing on her planning to seduce Moe with a home-made, romantic dinner. To her credit, Liz listened to both songs and said basically, "I'd rather Sarah perform fewer songs and have those songs truly contribute to how she functions within the show." When you have a superior vocalist like Liz, audiences are happy even if she sings the phone book. I nearly asked her to do just that with those gratuitous compositions, but thankfully she helped me realize Sarah needed to be developed beyond Liz's vocal prowess.

The 8:00 performance (which Mrs. Richard Rodgers attended) went considerably better. The cast raced through the lengthier scenes, and even though the piece is flawed, it has energy. June got carried away in her Carmella Tocci scene and started grabbing Steve's leg during "Safer in My Arms." Because she comes up to his waist, she was also grabbing his inner thigh while holding her script and singing into his crotch! Steve did his best not to break character, while the audience was in hysterics. I kept thinking about Dorothy Rodgers (in the third row) having attended the opening night of Oklahoma! *with its famous dream ballet. Now, instead of experiencing Agnes DeMille's tour jetés, she was witnessing the battle for the bulge! I left the theater that night at 11:30 feeling totally drained but almost comforted in knowing I was still needed at the Hudson Guild.*

The next day, the "reviews" came in. Everyone had an opinion and went to great lengths to share it with me. Peter Filichia felt the show needed a lot of work but said it was in better shape than most out-of-town tryouts. Jason Alexander gave me many helpful comments over dinner. One helped to clarify why Moe and Sarah didn't sleep together until the last ten minutes of the show: Morris felt unworthy of Sarah, but it needed to be emphasized in the scene preceding her big song, "One of the Beautiful People," where she renounces her friends and former lovers in favor of Morris. Later, I rewrote that crucial scene to illustrate his inferiority complex:

MORRIS: Sarah, I'm Moe Brummell, remember? And you're a beautiful woman with a sparkling personality and social graces and money and all the things Flora Brummell reads about while under the dryer—

SARAH: And why the hell should I waste it on some good-for-nothing Jewish cop who's tied to his mother's apron strings?

MORRIS: Well, I wouldn't have put it that strongly, but that's the general idea.

Friends Susan DiLallo, Daena Title (Jason Alexander's wife), Howard Rogut, Nancy Pines, Stephen Flaherty, Tom Toce, Margie Kaplan, Eric Kuttner, Wendy Lamb, and Rob Roth all called with valid points, suggesting edits, some structural changes, and their opinions of the final scene, which didn't reach an exciting climax and denouement. My bosses, Margaret and Bernice, fortunately gave me the day off after offering *their* critique.

I called Jack Hofsiss at 11:00 a.m. as promised, but he didn't return my call. I tried several times that afternoon, as we had made plans to meet at 5:00 p.m., finally reaching him at 7:00. We arranged to meet at 2:00 p.m. the following day.

The next day, I returned to my day job as a personnel counselor. The night before, I had been up until 3:00 in the morning, tossing and turning. I felt like a kid returning to school a month early from summer vacation: I simply wasn't ready. At work I kept thinking, "What am I doing here?" It seemed warped that I had a show desperately in need of repair, and here I was telling applicants about jobs. I couldn't wait for my 2:00 p.m. appointment with Jack, which he postponed until 3:00 p.m.

At 3:00, I finally sat down with Jack, who briefly spoke of the reading. I shared what I had learned from the experience, how I needed to be more vigilant about overwriting and never allow anything to distract from the central relationship between Morris and Kit. I also had new ideas about the ending. He smiled faintly and then mentioned he had spoken to George Lane about having the Tony-winning book writer of *A Chorus Line*, James Kirkwood (also a William Morris client), come in and give us his "opinion"—which was code for rewriting the book. Jack reasoned that, after all, Kirkwood, like Kit Gill, was the son of a famous actress (Kirkwood's mother was a silent screen star, Lila Lee), so this would be in his wheelhouse.

"What does he expect in return?" I asked, wondering if he preferred money and/or partial credit.

"I think he'd be doing it as a favor," was Jack's reply.

I was dubious. My journal reveals I was also less than enthusiastic.

Jack is not allowing me to do my work. He's pushing the panic button. It's as if I were on a plane experiencing engine trouble and looked up to see the pilot with a parachute strapped to his back. Suddenly, I'm beginning to see how wasteful we had been with time. No wonder I had been cocky about the show—Jack made few demands on me, so I believed we were in good shape. And now that I am perceptive enough to handle the flaws, he's bringing in Kirkwood!

Soon after Jack dropped this minor bombshell (by the way, I resented the fact he had discussed it with our agent without first talking with me), Chris Chadman, a seasoned dancer/choreographer who had collaborated with Bob Fosse on *Dancin'* and *Big Deal*, came over to discuss with Jack his possible involvement in the production, signaling the end of our conversation. Again, I felt angry. How could Jack get his priorities so screwed up? If the book was in trouble, the whole day after the readings should have been spent in intense discussion.

Rob Roth called when I got home and even though I was in relatively good spirits, I told him what had transpired. He, too, was angered and rightfully felt if anyone should be brought in to offer guidance, it should be Rob. I couldn't argue with that reasoning.

Rob was instrumental in inspiring me to write Morris's contrapuntal section to "I Hear Humming," the manic jazz waltz "Killer on the Line," and fleshing out and focusing the writing. He's one of the smartest people on the planet who has never properly received his due, despite the fact he would go on to helm the world premiere of *Beauty and the Beast* and encourage Disney to gamble on Broadway.

That night, I called Geoffrey Sherman to voice my frustration. I felt somewhat better, but by 11:30 p.m., I was in a deep depression and physically drained. A call from my parents only seemed to aggravate the situation, as my mother proceeded to tell me "the show did not live up to your fine outline." (I couldn't blame them; they meant well. Rotten timing, though.) My father instructed me on how it might be possible to get Sarah in the loft in the climactic scene, and I thought, "My show is in serious trouble. Why care about Liz and the damn loft?"

2:00 a.m. 5/8/1987

Quick update:

Rob has been working on the show since Jack gave his initial approval last Sunday! The three of us met in Jack's apartment to ostensibly go over the script line by line, but as per usual with Jack, David Jenkins came over about three hours later, so our meeting abruptly ended. Most of the time was spent hearing Rob talk about the piece. He reminded me of a lawyer preparing for his first day in court—he had notes upon notes and nervous energy to spare. Jack was Jack: watchful, pensive, and inscrutable. Eventually, Rob asked me to leave so that he and Jack could get better acquainted. (Rob: "Doug, how about going around the block for some gum?") I half-worried that upon my return, Jack would be nowhere to be found, and Rob would greet me with "Doug, meet your new director."

Rob liked Jack but also found his lack of communication somewhat unsettling. In fact, many of the things I felt about Jack were apparent in Rob's first meeting.

But working with Rob in his official capacity as assistant director/dramaturg that first week was a joy. I felt as if the piece's true potential was finally emerging, and my writing was flowing—it's so much easier when you know your objective before you begin the writing process. The only drawback was having to attend rehearsals, something I usually relished but found time-consuming when dealing with deadlines.

One of the first things Rob taught me was to lose anything that didn't advance the story. That lovely passage in William Goldman's novel of Morris carving his initials in his own park bench like Bernard Baruch? Does it advance the plot? No? Lose it. Rob was merciless, and although there may have been some rich details lost along the way, they were filigree. In a play, it's a touching moment. In a musical, it eats up precious time.

Rob encouraged me to develop Morris's fixation with the case so that Sarah feels as if she's always in competition with Kit. Morris's obsessive nature first ignites in "The First Move," which Rob encouraged me to further develop as a trio, giving Sarah a "voice" in this unusual ménage à trois.

During this time, I rewrote the verse of "The First Move" to illustrate Morris's dichotomy on his first date with Sarah:

CONVERSATIONS ON THIN-ICE .
SO, LET'S QUICKLY ABOUT FACE.
NOW MY EYES ARE ON HER BREASTS . . .
BUT MY MIND IS ON THE CASE!

On the first day back last Tuesday, Rob was virtually ignored. We were all assembled when Jack finally said, "Oh, this is Robert Roth. He's here to help Doug with the revisions." Of course, what was Jack supposed to say? "Here's Rob—he's doing the job I should be doing?"

The two new scenes, the opening, and Sarah and Moe's first encounter were generally well received. Rob made the mistake of telling Jack what other scenes/songs we were working on, and Jack's eyes began to glaze over. I told Rob we must never play all our cards but judiciously know when to reveal our hand. That way, we'll successfully go the distance and won't meet with resistance.

The second day, Wednesday, was even more frustrating when Rob and I brought in revisions of the Kit/Carmella scene. Immediately, June looked at the scene and said to Stephen Bogardus, "Oh, Steve, we've lost some of our best lines." When it came time to read the scene, she read her lines as if she were an automaton. Since Jack didn't intervene, I felt it was incumbent on me to defend my work. I made a speech essentially saying that I want the audience to laugh as much as anyone, but I want the laughs to be earned, not a response to an actress calling upon her tricks of the trade. If Carmella does not emerge as a credible figure, other victims will lose their credibility, and the show will be inconsistent in tone. One scene must be an integral part of the whole. Nothing is written in stone: every change should at least be heard, and if not successful, discarded, just as actors are encouraged to experiment. June kept maintaining that I was cutting my *best lines, and I kept maintaining that that was my prerogative, and we could always return to the original. But I needed everyone's cooperation if the rewrites were to proceed. Chris Chadman said I put it well, and it was obvious to June and everyone else that she was in error. Jack remained stoic throughout.*

Which brings me to an interesting point: Jack's health. I go through a rollercoaster of emotions. Sometimes I don't see his accident as a liability, and other times I can't fathom his predicament. It saddens me that he can't tap his toes to my music. Occasionally in rehearsal, I fantasize that suddenly Jack's feet will begin to move in time with the beat, as if the songs contain special healing powers. Other times, I find myself wondering how he goes to the bathroom, eats, bathes, or experiences any kind of sexual gratification. Mostly, I don't want to know these details. I hate myself for resenting Jack's inability to fulfill my expectations, but it is my show, and I have to be protective of it. As I said to George Lane the other day, I'm finally allowing my intellect to override my emotions. This isn't easy.

And we haven't even started previews.

HUDSON GUILD THEATRE

GEOFFREY SHERMAN, *Producing Director* JAMES ABAR, *Associate Director*

presents the world premiere musical....

NO WAY TO TREAT A LADY

Book, Music and Lyrics by   *Based upon the Novel by*

Douglas J. Cohen   William Goldman

Directed by

Jack Hofsiss

Choreography by Christopher Chadman

Musical Direction by Uel Wade

Orchestrations by Danny Troob

with

Stephen Bogardus, Liz Callaway, June Gable and Peter Slutsker

Set Design by	*Light Design by*	*Sound Design by*
David Jenkins	Beverly Emmons	Aural Fixation

Costumes by	*Stage Manager*
Michael Kaplan	John M. Atherlay

May 27 – June 21

The word is out: the original 1987 postcard announcing a world premiere musical.
Author's collection

4

"DID DOLLY LEVI DIE IN THE END?"

Two weeks passed before I found time to return to my journal. Two weeks in most lives is inconsequential, but when a show is approaching its first week of previews for a New York world premiere, it's an eternity.

5/22/1987 1:00 a.m.

When I got to the theatre, Jack began by apologizing for his criticism of the final scene with Sarah and Morris. He had read it last night and liked it. All right, I accepted it. We then watched the finale when Morris tries to save Sarah. Staged by fight director John Curless, "A Close Call" features Morris and Kit singing as they duel with rapiers. Peter Slutsker asked why Sarah had to live, to which Jack wryly replied, "Did Dolly Levi die in the end? Did Hello, Dolly! run long enough for you, Peter?"

That's the thing about Jack: He's so damn funny and charming that you can't fault him for occasionally doing a lackluster job. But until tonight, I never got a glimmer of what genius lay beneath the surface.

It was about 10:30, the end of a long day. We had staged everything up to and including Kit's death. I was feeling a bit uneasy due to the fact Steve Bogardus asked me point blank why Sarah survives. I made up some lame excuse that Kit needs her as a pawn to get Morris to the loft (even citing that the Bolsheviks used Nicholas and Alexandra for bartering!). Plus, he's driven to kill women who resemble his mother. And yes, I believe musicals with happy endings are usually more popular. The last reason I didn't admit out loud, yet I privately felt it might be a motivating factor for keeping Sarah alive. After all, Kit does sing in "I Have Noticed a Change": that "every romance must end. Kiss her . . . goodbye." Why not kill Sarah and invite Morris over? Also, how do we structurally follow Kit's demise? I wrote a good final scene for Sarah and Morris, but as soon as Peter and Liz read it out loud, I knew it was wrong. After Kit's moving death, everything seems inconsequential. And the visual of Liz Callaway being wheeled out, bound and gagged in a chair, might elicit laughs.

Liz suggested Morris finds Sarah in the bathroom. June suggested Sarah dies. Steve suggested Kit, gravely wounded, admits he didn't kill her. Rob Roth thought a blackout on Kit and Alexandra followed by lights up on Morris consoling Sarah might work. Jack pensively sat, taking it all in and saying nothing (which happened all too frequently). Finally, he said, "I have a suggestion, but I first want to think about it overnight."

I sat down, feeling rather perplexed. It was hard to bring in Sarah, and it was hard to justify her being alive. Rob's idea was okay, except it reminded me of the movie *The Right Stuff* where John Glenn is almost burning up in space due to a faulty heat shield. Now, we know he lives—he later ran for president—but because the scene is so damn suspenseful, we want to know: HOW DID HE GET OUT OF THIS FIX?! But we're robbed of that satisfaction because the next shot is of the New York ticker-tape parade; there is a whole scene missing.

As I sat next to Jack contemplating all this, I turned toward the makeshift playing space in the rehearsal room. My last image of the actors was June (Alexandra) cradling Steve (Kit) in her arms, his head resting in her lap. As I turned back to look at the space, Liz was seated where June had been, stroking Peter's head as it rested in *her* lap. The image almost knocked me out. It was so beautiful and lyrical and moving and seemed to answer all my questions and none at the same time. But it felt complete, and the ambiguity was perfect. Let audiences arrive at their own conclusions. I felt totally satisfied in just taking in the image.

I told Jack I thought it was brilliant. I said it so many times and so enthusiastically that he countered, "Well, I do have a few good suggestions. Why are you so surprised?"

But I am, Jack. For five weeks, we looked to you for results and often came back empty-handed. Maureen said tonight we must all learn to trust each other in our jobs. But tonight's miracle only makes me thirst for more from you, Jack, and makes me wonder why you've held back. Should I be happy that this means the possible start of great contributions or sad because it's taken this long?

After this momentous night, I became laser-focused on rehearsals, rewrites, and meetings. I also started to rely more on Chris Chadman, who was becoming our de facto director. I discovered Chris had chosen to collaborate with Bob Fosse and originate the role of "Fred Casely" in *Chicago* over the character Greg in the world premiere of *A Chorus Line* (even though the latter role had been based on his own life experiences). He was deeply impressing me with his musical staging of such numbers as "I Hear Humming," "Once More from the Top," and "I Have Noticed a Change in You." In fact, it was hard to know where Jack left off and Chris began. Rather, they worked seamlessly together.

Final tableau: Jack Hofsiss's brilliant solution—Liz Callaway cradles Peter Slutsker while June Gable cradles Stephen Bogardus, Hudson Guild 1987.
Photo by Bob Marshak

I wasn't surprised that a couple years later, director Jerry Zaks chose Chris to choreograph the legendary 1992 revival of *Guys and Dolls*. Chris's Tony-nominated work had verve, panache, and theatricality, significantly contributing to that production's success. He was also dealing with a race against time: there were rumors his pronounced weight loss was due to AIDS. On May 3, 1995, as I walked to a meeting to discuss casting for *The Gig* at Goodspeed, I turned down a street in the West Village and actually saw *The New York Times* on the sidewalk directly in front of me with Chris's photo facing up: It was his obituary. He had died on April 30 at just forty-seven.

In 1987, it's amazing that the specter of AIDS didn't significantly impact our cloistered world at the Hudson Guild.

Rob's influence continued to impact my writing. We both had admired the movie *Tightrope* starring Clint Eastwood as a detective in search of his alter ego, a killer with similar predilections. Rob and I believed it would be intriguing to have Morris identify so strongly with Kit, they are almost colluding with one another. In response, I wrote this very lush, pseudo-operatic piece entitled "Whose Hands Are These?" as Morris surveys Kit's handiwork.

MORRIS:
WHAT KIND OF HANDS WOULD TAKE A HUMAN LIFE?
WRAPPED AROUND A NECK
OR WRAPPED AROUND A GUN, IS IT THE SAME?
AM I TO BLAME FOR, OH, THESE HANDS?
WHOSE HANDS ARE THESE . . .
AND WHY AM I SO AFRAID TO KNOW?

Definitely an interesting song, very much influenced by Goldman's novel. But there were two things wrong. One, my performer, Peter Slutsker (who later changed his name professionally to Peter Marx) was tremendously charming, funny, and endearing. As a singer, he had a big voice with a specific timbre. When Sweeney Todd sings "Johanna" or "Pretty Women," it's coming from a dark place with a richly trained bass-baritone sound. Peter's voice simply wasn't well-suited for this song.

Secondly, "Whose Hands" was too dark for a production that needed an engaging protagonist. I recalled Frank Rich's comment at ASCAP: *"It's a comic sort of schlepply Jewish gumshoe with a kind of*

Adversaries or alter egos? Detective Brummell (Peter Slutsker) exploits his only line of communication with a killer (Stephen Bogardus).
Photo by Bob Marshak

fun murder case. . . . It's very unpretentious. I think if it's done well, it could be extremely satisfying."

Well, we were violating Frank Rich's initial observation, and you could feel the audience retreat. And this is where I discovered an important lesson with previews: You may think you have ten full days before critics are invited (an incredible luxury for a struggling not-for-profit theater), but it's deceptive. Even if you want to cut a song, you must rehearse the cut with the actors and the crew. Once previews begin, union rules dictate you can only rehearse with your cast up to five hours a day, and you don't have a full crew unless they're called. On Wednesday, Saturday, and Sunday, you *can't* rehearse because you have matinees. Mondays are out—that's the day off. So basically, that leaves three days (Tuesday, Thursday, and Friday) to make changes. You need to prioritize what major issues you wish to address in that small window. Every department makes requests, and there are notes to be given and incorporated before each rehearsal. If you have a new scene or song, you need to hear it, rehearse it, stage it, and tech it.

I remember realizing my new song's darker tone was bringing the show to a complete halt. After a Friday night performance, I implored Jack and Chris Chadman to cut it, but then stood by help-lessly while the number was performed twice on Saturday and once on Sunday before finally implementing the change the following week.

Aside from "Whose Hands," however, we were starting to ignite. For the first time, I was feeling encouraged.

William Goldman had volunteered to see the show after a week of previews while there was still time to offer advice. He was wait-ing for me near the far lobby wall shortly after the show. I walked up to him, feeling a little like a patient hoping to hear a good prog-nosis from his doctor.

"It's good, except for your opening number and your ending." My heart sank a little, as we only had four days before critics were invited and five days before *The Times* was attending.

Then Bill said something that I never thought I'd hear in my lifetime: "Let's go back to my apartment and work."

5

MASTER CLASS

On the cab over, Bill shared more positive feedback: he thought we had a strong cast. He loved Steve in "the Steiger role" and thought Liz's voice was spectacular, particularly on "One of the Beautiful People." He didn't love Morris's number "A Killer on the Line"— he felt exhausted for the actor: Peter would get beet red trying to get out all the words. But Bill was also a realist and knew that coming up with another number within the next couple days wasn't in the cards. He assured me such gaffes weren't fatal, especially with a strong opening and closing.

I had only seen the study-library when I'd visited Bill's apartment nearly two years earlier. This time, he ushered me into his screening room. Yes, long before streaming and flat screen televisions, Bill had an actual screening room! In addition to the expansive screen, there were rows of seats so you could invite your friends over and watch your latest masterpiece or have your own film retrospective. Maybe he even screened D. W. Griffith's *Orphans of the Storm* starring Lillian Gish on an iceberg. He offered me a seat in the back and my soda of choice. We were there to work.

Bill was energetic and jumping from topic to topic. He felt it was "counterproductive to go through the show line by line. No time for that shit. We have to get safely to shore." We needed to identify the larger issues.

As for "Whose Hands Are These?" "Critics don't give a shit about alter-egos." He continued, "There's too much Morris vocalizing. There's a big drop towards the end of the first act." So "Whose Hands Are These?" was history. "Story is everything," he emphasized.

"I HATE the fuckin' backdrop!" he bellowed, referring to the life-size version of *The New York Times* that opened Act Two. Instead of showing a major headline focusing on the killer, it read "NEW YORK STUDY OF POLICE FINDS NO WIDE MISUSE OF DEADLY FORCE," which was also confusing as it referenced "police" and "deadly force" yet had *nothing* to do with the Strangler. In a much smaller panel off to the side was a lesser headline, "SERIAL KILLER ON A RAMPAGE," not even bolded!

I told him the original *Times* front page inexplicably didn't have *any* mention of the killer, something I shared at the dress rehearsal with my uncle Arthur and my paternal grandfather, "Zadie," in attendance. The next day, Zadie generously donated five hundred

All the news that's fit to print if you squint: (Counterclockwise from left) June Gable, Peter Slutsker (kneeling), Liz Callaway, and Stephen Bogardus in front of the problematic New York Times panels William Goldman detested, Hudson Guild Theatre 1987.
Photo by Bob Marshak

dollars to the Hudson Guild so they could buy another panel. Bill had a sense of what I was up against.

"Years ago, I spoke to Paul Newman's agent, and he said, 'Everyone has his own cocksucker, and I'm Paul's.' What I'm saying to you, Doug, is you have to be your own cocksucker." No one had ever put it that way to me before, but I gathered it was Hollywood speak for "You have to have your own back." Profane and profound.

He then jumped to our opening number, which began with a moody instrumental prologue showing Kit Gill's mother Alexandra enveloped in ghostly fog (that also enveloped Uel Wade conducting the five-piece band in the wings). It culminated in a short preview of "Five More Minutes" performed by Kit, seated in front of a makeup mirror donning a priest's outfit:

KIT:
FIVE MORE MINUTES TO PLACES
FIVE MORE MINUTES TO LEARN MY CUES
TELL THOSE BUTTERFLIES THAT THEY'D BEST BE GONE.
ONLY FIVE MORE MINUTES!
(Spoken): I'm on . . .

Kit exits in his priest habit, as his dressing room disappears, and the set of Flora and Morris's apartment comes into view. In this scene only Flora's arms and hands can be seen; June Gable was already in costume for her next scene.

MORRIS:
FIVE MORE MINUTES OF DREAMING
FIVE MORE MINUTES OF PRECIOUS SLEEP
FIVE MORE MINUTES OF NEVERLASTING BLISS . . .

The song progressed as it did at ASCAP, although I had rewritten a C section which encapsulated Morris's dream of his future. Instead of hoping to go to night school and becoming a lawyer, his current dream was closer to his chosen vocation:

MAYBE RENT AN OFFICE,
FAR AWAY WHERE MA CAN'T PRY.
OOH—THAT WOULD BE SOMETHING!
THERE UPON THE DOOR READS
"MORRIS BRUMMELL PRIVATE EYE!"

Morris sees his name in lights and is momentarily lost in reverie, then returns to his morning ritual. The lights dim and come up on Alice Sullivan (June Gable) in her apartment when an unexpected visitor knocks on her door.

After Mrs. Sullivan admits Father Fitzgerald (Kit in his first disguise), she invites him to "tea and Christian sympathy." Father Fitzgerald starts laughing inappropriately when she references her husband's recent passing, explaining it reminds him of a joke. Kit then proceeds to sing "It's a Very Funny Thing," which has autobiographical overtones:

KIT:
IT'S A VERY FUNNY THING, MRS. SULLIVAN,
IT'S A JOKE I HEARD FROM SISTER BERNADETTE.
NOW IT SEEMS THERE IS THIS PRIEST
AND HIS MOTHER IS DECEASED
SO HE SPENDS HIS TIME IN SEARCH OF DEAR OLD "MUM."
THOUGH I KNOW THE JOKE BY HEART,
IT KEEPS TEARING ME APART
PLEASE EXCUSE ME, I'M COMPLETELY OVERCOME!

Kit then compares Mrs. Sullivan to his late mother, noting how their hairstyle, eyes, and smile were similar, culminating in a "filial" embrace which strangles Mrs. Sullivan. The lights fade and come up on Morris answering his phone at home and learning there's a murder from his colleague, Bronski, at the station.

By this time, June Gable has successfully transformed herself into Flora Brummel and delivers her "perishable" instructions. But instead of Morris finishing the number as in the ASCAP presentation, I had rewritten Morris's final stanza so Kit (leaving Mrs. Sullivan's apartment) could join him:

MORRIS AND KIT:
FIVE MORE STEPS TO THE DOORWAY,
FIVE MORE FLIGHTS AND YOU'RE FREE AT LAST.
CAN'T YOU SEE THAT I'M NEAR . . .
MORRIS:
THE BREAKING POINT?
KIT:
THE STARTING POINT!

Bill admired what we had tried to achieve but got right to the point.

"What would happen if Morris's 'Five More Minutes' is gone?"

"You want to cut 'Five More Minutes'?! It's the song they embraced at ASCAP. It's probably the reason I got the rights."

Bill agreed. "I don't know if it's the staging or the performances, but it's not working. The story is getting smudged. I'm in the audience, and you can feel the energy escaping the room."

He was right. And as wonderful as June Gable was in her many astounding creations, her first appearance as Flora Brummell wasn't landing, including my mother's "perishable" speech.

"Maybe if I rewrite it—"

"No," he said emphatically. Seeing my crestfallen face, he softened. "It's a good song, but okay, what if the show opens with the priest? Just like my book and the movie." (He had his novel nearby for easy reference.) "You have him singing that song—"

"'It's a Very Funny Thing.'"

"Right. Steve's voice is terrific, just terrific. And with that song, the audience doesn't know how to respond, but that's good. It throws them a little off balance. He kills her. It's jarring—"

"There's a final A section to the song that we cut so we could finish with 'A Very Funny Thing.'"

"Perfect," Bill exclaimed. "What is it?"

I rummaged through my script and found the excised stanza:

IT'S A VERY FUNNY THING, MRS. SULLIVAN

IT'S SO FUNNY THAT I HAVE TO SAY FAREWELL.

I'M AWARE IT'S NOT POLITE,

BUT THIS COLLAR IS TOO TIGHT:

IF YOU'D ASKED ME, WELL, I MIGHT HAVE STAYED FOR LUNCH.

BUT I'VE OTHER SEEDS TO SOW,

SO I'LL END THE JOKE AND GO . . .

MRS. SULLIVAN—

(*Her lifeless arm drops*)

YOU'VE BEAT ME TO THE PUNCH!

Bill loved the lyric.

"He kills her, sings a final chorus, sips his tea. Lights out. Boom! Lights up on Morris standing over the body." It's almost as if he were storyboarding it.

"But 'Five More Minutes' is Moe Brummell's 'I want' song," I protested, employing one of BMI and Lehman Engel's most celebrated terms. They were huge proponents of the idea that every successful musical needs to have an "I want" song for the protagonist(s): "Something's Coming" for Tony in *West Side Story*, "Wouldn't it Be Loverly" for Eliza Doolittle in *My Fair Lady*, "I'll Know" for Sarah Brown and Sky Masterson in *Guys and Dolls*.

"It's economical, Doug. Cinematic." (Then Bill delivered the final coup de grace.) "And it's good storytelling."

I had to admit, having Kit murder Mrs. Sullivan followed by Morris discovering the body was kind of brilliant. Very theatrical and expeditious.

Without the "I Want" song, however, it fed into Jack's original take that Kit Gill was indeed the leading role, even though he's the antagonist.

Bill continued, "And the thing of it is, you and I know it's gone, your family will know and maybe a couple friends, but for the audience—no one will know it's missing."

Like a deft film editor, he suggested a cut and splice to eliminate the offending footage. The perfect crime. Maybe it wasn't coincidental we were in his screening room.

Then Bill said something that may have been the most perceptive advice in an evening of indispensable pearls of wisdom: "Not only do you cut something that's weak, but you improve the material that remains." This became obvious to me once the cuts were implemented.

Later during the Hudson Guild run of *No Way to Treat a Lady*, Richard Maltby attended a performance and congratulated me, having heard an earlier demo. "I'm impressed—you're able to drown your babies," he said, welcoming me to the club with an affectionate pat on the back. That marked the first time I'd heard that perverse expression: People also say "kill your darlings," which now as a father, I prefer. But either way, I learned how to do the deed from Bill. I can only imagine how many "darlings" he had to dispatch in his lifetime.

"Now, your ending—" Bill had already moved on. Mission accomplished, check the box. If I was to keep up with him, better go along for the ride. "You're nearly there, but not quite. You need a 'killer' surprise ending."

The ending in Bill's novel was far too sadistic: Kit is gravely wounded by the copycat killer and Morris, avenging Sarah's death, allows him to bleed to death. To be theatrical and more accessible, I went in a different direction: Our disarmed cop and deranged actor duel with rapiers, Kit's "weapon of choice," while singing "A Close Call."

Kit is obviously skilled with a sword—no doubt his theatrical lineage and training give him a distinct advantage. So how do we explain Morris delivering the fatal blow? True, he distracts Kit with psychological tactics, but how should that all play out?

As staged by John Curless, Kit kicks Morris, sending the hilt of Kit's sword into Morris's face. Although Morris manages to recover, Kit grabs him by the foot and sends him over on his back. Kit then points the sword at Morris's neck.

KIT: Shame I have to kill you, Morris. Just as we were becoming close friends—

MORRIS: We have nothing in common!

(In Goldman's book, Morris calls Kit "an afterbirth that walks like a man.")

Bill started animatedly walking around the room, trying to come up with a solution, assuming the roles of both cop and killer. He liked to think on his feet: maybe that explained why he needed such a large study.

"Okay, so Morris is cornered, on the floor, about to meet his maker, the rapier a few feet away. How does he overcome his opponent?"

"Well, I have him retrieving the rapier and running Kit through when he momentarily turns away."

"Yeah. Do you buy it?" he asked.

I had to admit it was contrived.

Bill reasoned, "We need to buy more time for Morris to get to his sword . . ." He started pacing again. "So, you're Morris, you're injured. I'm Kit, before I kill you, I bring in Sarah."

"Where was she?"

"Tied up in the next room. She can have her hands bound, her mouth gagged."

I was trying to visualize Liz with these restrictions. Would the audience laugh? I decided they wouldn't, especially if Kit removes the gag.

"Maybe Kit says something like 'etiquette dictates ladies first,'" I suggested. We were now functioning as an improv team. I used to play piano for TheatreSports, an Off Off Broadway improv group, so my years of training were beginning to pay off.

"Morris distracts Kit . . . mentioning his mother . . ." Bill countered.

"She can appear—in his mind . . ." I chimed in.

"Distracting Kit and giving Morris just enough time to reach for his sword . . ." Bill said, grabbing an imaginary object in the air. He was on a roll and probably a sugar high.

I watched his face as inspiration struck. "He lunges, delivering a fatal blow, declaring, 'Meet the ex-captain of the Brooklyn College Fencing Team, *schmuck!*'"

It was 1 a.m. and hearing Bill Goldman come up with this line—punctuated with the word *schmuck*—was pretty damn funny. We both howled. Could we get away with it?

The next day, I handed the rewrites to John Atherlay, our stage manager. Rob Roth was champing at the bit for details on the night before. I slyly said Bill and I were very productive and a song was cut. Rob was aghast when he found out it was "Five More Minutes" but realized it was the right move.

The changes went in that night, and they proved to be effective. After three performances, we asked Peter Slutsker to drop the word *schmuck*, but the rest of the changes remained.

The new opening also had a significant impact on Flora Brummell's first appearance, which was now delayed until midway through the first act. Morris first references his mother on his first date with Sarah in Central Park, pointing out his building:

MORRIS: I was just trying to see if Flora was up.

SARAH: Flora?

MORRIS: My mother. We . . . occupy the same space. Yeah, see that building on Central Park West. The one that's totally dark except for that one corner window that's lit. (*waves to her*) Don't wait up, Ma!

In the next scene, the following morning, Morris is in love and making his own breakfast, a ritual usually performed by his "Ma." Flora enters and gives him guilt about coming in after 10:00 p.m., demanding to know where's he's been. He's evasive, but then the telltale sign gives him away: he's humming!

FLORA:
I HEAR HUMMING, MORRIS,
AND IT'S COMING, MORRIS, FROM YOU.
ALL THAT AWFUL PURRING
TELLS ME SOMETHING'S STIRRING, SO NU?

She eventually weasels a confession out of Morris, but not before employing outrageous histrionics and threatening to call Morris's boss at the station to verify his whereabouts. The song was always well-received, but losing Flora at the beginning of the show somehow gave this scene greater impact. Chris Chadman and Jack came up with wonderful business for June and Peter, who at one point wards off his mother by fashioning a ladle and spatula into

Flanked by two Bills: William Finn, Douglas Cohen, and William Goldman attend the first performance of Cohen's The Gig *at Goodspeed at Chester, August 1995.*
Photo by Diane Sobelewski

a makeshift cross. The applause at the end of the number, usually appreciative, was now thunderous.

As the astute ASCAP panelists had warned, don't overplay the Flora card. Less is more.

Bill Goldman was right—once you properly identify and eliminate a problem, it helps to fortify the material that remains. But cutting is a very delicate procedure: Like surgeons, in our effort to remove the offending matter, sometimes we lose some good stuff in the process. But it's worth it in the interest of a longer shelf life.

Four days later, Bill returned to admire our handiwork. Again, he greeted me after the performance. This time, he was beaming.

"I never thought I'd say this," he sheepishly admitted, "but it's a fucking musical!"

6

"YOU CAN CONTROL THE EFFORT, NOT THE RESULT"

There was another significant visitor during previews: Ed Kleban, *A Chorus Line*'s lyricist and the first teacher in BMI to acknowledge the merits of *No Way to Treat a Lady*. Several months earlier, Ed, diagnosed with mouth cancer, had a significant part of his tongue removed. He sat in the last of the Hudson Guild's twelve rows with a pen and pad. After the performance, he gave me his blessing and read off the only lyrics he couldn't decipher so I could alert the cast. (They did not have the benefit of microphones, but their voices usually carried beautifully.) Ed knew the value of hearing lyrics for the first time and how important it was—especially with comedy—to make sure they were intelligible. I was very moved by this tangible form of support.

The name Al Francis may not be familiar to many who read these pages, but at one time he was a Broadway general manager and an original producer of *The Shadow Box*, which won the 1977 Tony for Best Play. He also attended *No Way to Treat a Lady* twice, offering help in reaching out to prospective producers and leaving me with these parting words at the last performance, "If you let this show die, I'll never forgive you."

There were other artists I respected who attended. Judd Woldin, the composer of *Raisin*, a remarkable score, attended twice. James Lapine came toward the end of the run. It was the first time I'd met him, although our paths have crossed many times since, and he's been incredibly supportive. On that warm June night, James was courteous but inscrutable. When I later asked my agent (who also represented James) what he thought, George said, "James liked it. But you have to understand that he used similar staging with doors in *March of the Falsettos*."

Upon reflection, between the red floor and the black ubiquitous door frame, Jack's concept was probably influenced by James's classic staging.

Another legendary visitor was an older, bearded man who brought along a pad and pencil, not to critique the show but rather to draw. Our publicist Jeffrey Richards had labored to get iconic caricaturist Al Hirschfeld to attend and sketch June Gable for Enid Nemy's Friday column in the Arts and Entertainment section of *The New York Times*. We all speculated that it would incorporate June's multiple roles, but it was simply June as Alexandra Gill, and Hirschfeld based it entirely on a publicity photo taken two months earlier. Still, it was a thrill to have him capture one of our leads for posterity.

Jonathan Larson, another ASCAP veteran, attended to show his support. We had become friendly through the workshop, and occasionally he'd walk back with me from ASCAP to my building where he'd catch his downtown train at West 72nd Street. Jonathan, who often proudly proclaimed he wanted to change musical theater by fusing rock scores with the musical theater idiom, was hard at work on *Superbia*, which eventually won a Richard Rodgers Development Grant.

Lynn Ahrens and Steve Flaherty came to see the show. That year, they too had won a Richard Rodgers Development Grant for their musical *Lucky Stiff* (later receiving the Production Award) and befriended Rob Roth through Ira Weitzman, who had already taken a healthy interest in their work. They asked me if I thought Rob would be a good choice to direct their Richard Rodgers reading at Playwrights Horizons, and I wholeheartedly concurred.

In fact, many of my colleagues from BMI and ASCAP attended and were mostly supportive, at least to my face. That's the nature of theater—you never know what people really think. (Of course, now we have social media and online forums so people can destroy you anonymously.) My college friend Denis Markell (now a successful young adult author and Douglas Bernstein's writing partner on Martin Charnin's *Upstairs at O'Neals'*), always employs the seven-block rule: Don't discuss a show until you are outside of a seven-block radius from the theater. By that time, anyone directly or indirectly related to the show will no longer be in danger of over-hearing. This rule has saved my family and me many potentially embarrassing snafus.

One of the most humorous stories about peers who attended *No Way to Treat a Lady* was related to me years later by Peter Filichia. He said two fellow unnamed participants from the ASCAP work-shop ran into each other in a gay sex shop in Los Angeles. One of them was out, the other closeted. Needless to say, it was an awkward moment. The "out" writer broke the ice by walking up to the "closeted" writer and said, "So what did you think of Doug Cohen's *No Way to Treat a Lady*?"

As satisfying as it is to be accepted by one's colleagues (and I'm sure I garnered mixed reviews, despite appearances), it's vitally important that critics like the work. No, make that *really, really* like the work. The theater is maybe the only place I know where a B+ is potentially a failing grade, especially for shows that must transfer to a commercial venue to survive.

I like to think of it this way: You buy a lottery ticket and get all six numbers right. Huge win—multi millions. But get only five numbers right, and it's only a small fraction of the winner's take. That's kind of what happens in the theater.

Of course, you could get only four numbers right, but if one of those numbers is a rave in *The New York Times*, well, that trumps just about everything.

I don't think I was quite aware of the odds for success when making my theatrical debut. I just assumed that when everyone works their butts off and presents a solidly entertaining, well-crafted, beautifully performed show that tells a good story, you're going to succeed. But as Frank Gilroy (the Pulitzer Prize–winning playwright and screenwriter of *The Subject Was Roses* and *The Gig*) told me in one of our last conversations, "You can control the effort, not the result."

I wish I had known this going into the home stretch when the critics started to attend; it would have saved me a lot of heartache and therapy bills. But even if Frank had related this to me at that time, I probably wouldn't have comprehended. I guess that's what comes with experience.

6/13/1987 4:30 a.m.

It is the morning after opening night.

I am in something of a stupor. At around 2:00 p.m. yesterday, just hours before our official opening night, Geoffrey Sherman called me to say Jeffrey Richards had advance word on the verdict from the critics: a rave from Clive Barnes in The Post, *a pan from Howard Kissel in* The Daily News, *good reviews in* The Bergen Record *and* Associated Press, *and bad reviews in* Woman's Wear Daily, WINS *radio, and John Simon.*

And the verdict was out on The Times.

Geoffrey does not differentiate between good or bad news. Somehow, everything sounded negative, and I started to sweat profusely, even hyperventilating. I kept thinking, "This is not the way I had envisioned this. Please don't let this be real." Suddenly, I knew just how badly I wanted good reviews. I kept thinking, I've done everything I could—there's my best work on that stage and most people embraced it. And now because of a few critics, no commercial producer will touch the show. It will die in a week, without even the benefit of an extension. There will be no recording, no one will remember my songs. I'll have to start all over.

I called Cathy, but nothing she said offered the consolation I was seeking. I tried working on the computer but ended up staring at a blank screen. Again, I kept thinking, "This can't be happening. It must be some horrible, sick joke God is playing on me." I was being punished, but I wasn't sure why.

I know it sounds like a lot of self-pity, but who else was I going to pity at that point?

It seemed ironic that I was buying roses and champagne bottles for a cast and crew that would soon be saying their goodbyes. I comforted myself knowing the general public embraced the show. But with only 135 in attendance per performance and no advertising budget, the run will have concluded by the time word of mouth kicked in.

I went to therapy, coincidentally scheduled that night. Anger and hurt came pouring out. I couldn't stop crying—I kept feeling a death had occurred, and I needed my parents to comfort me, but they weren't there, which made me even angrier.

My therapist had suggested I read Moss Hart's legendary best-seller, *Act One*, while in rehearsal. It's a brilliant memoir, but I kept thinking how Kaufman and Hart finally solved their third act problems with their first collaboration, *Once in a Lifetime*: Hart wrote a key, intimate scene based on one insider's perceptive comment that there needed to be a respite from the never-flagging energy. All during the previews for *No Way to Treat a Lady*, when significant cuts and changes were made, I had felt a similar process was taking shape, culminating with Bill's input and contributions. As I poured my heart out on my therapist's couch, I proclaimed "but this isn't what happened in *Act One*," as if I was following a "how-to" guide which had suddenly betrayed me.

I knew I loved the theater too much to abandon it, but I feared I couldn't go through this experience again; the reception from the press was taking too much out of me. I left therapy feeling somewhat cleansed, if only because I had unburdened myself.

Opening night's performance was magical, and I sat there reveling in the pleasure of the moment since I knew it would soon end abruptly. George Lane attended looking somewhat optimistic. Hoping there were future prospects, I asked him if The Alley Theater in Houston was still a "go": Pat Brown, the Alley's artistic director, had previously committed to producing *No Way to Treat a Lady* after receiving George's submission and learning of our world premiere. She later attended a week before opening night which coincided with the Tony Awards. Very few people came that night, and who could blame them? Most were glued to their television sets witnessing *Les Misérables* winning Best Musical and *Fences* winning Best Play. We begged her to come another night, but she was adamant. She would later renege on producing my musical months after announcing the regional premiere to the press—which no doubt helped the Alley's ticket subscriptions—claiming we had changed the show significantly from the version she had previously read (which was over three hours long!).

Following the enthusiastic opening night curtain call, we all banded together in the Art Gallery for a champagne toast. I remember talking to Peter Slutsker's father when Geoffrey Sherman tapped me on the shoulder and asked if we could speak alone. I knew it meant *The Times* was in. He led me to the door and read from a small piece of paper the last line of *The Times* review: "*No Way to Treat a Lady* marks the arrival of a significant young musical theater talent."

I haven't known ecstasy many times in my life, but whether it was the champagne or the review or both, I felt an amazing surge. I had the approval of *The Times*.

In retrospect, I feel it shouldn't matter what a critic says—Jane Alexander once warned me "You'll either get a swelled head or a battered ego." But after listening to Friday night's audience (the night *after The Times* review appeared) rolling in the aisles and applauding madly, I was more convinced than ever that many people react according to the voice of authority. Critics are patriarchal/matriarchal figures, and audiences often acquiesce to their opinions.

I was levitating. I called over Cathy, who was in mid-sentence, and asked Geoffrey to read the quote once again. She squeezed my hand; we both needed confirmation that we weren't dreaming. By the time I made it over to George, he was laughing as well, and we continued to drink champagne as sweat trickled down my brow.

As I later wrote in my journal, *there's no doubt about it—I have known happiness, and it has known me.*

Cathy, Rob Roth, and I left the party and took a cab to Rob's apartment on West 57th Street where we picked up The Times *and* The Post. *We went up to his place and simultaneously turned to the same page as we both announced out loud, "Ready, set, go!" Eyes fell to the page—I read the review as if I had just finished the Evelyn Wood speed-reading course, only to go back to read the last paragraph of* The Times *again and again. We then grabbed* The Post, *found the page, and started to read. What euphoria! By this time, I couldn't contain myself any longer. I went to the phone and read the reviews to Mom and Dad. Then I called Bill Goldman, only to find out that he was en route to Santa Fe, so I was given a number there and dialed. Ilene, his wife, answered. Bill wasn't in, but she was overjoyed at hearing the news, and I told her of the upcoming Houston production as well.*

Cathy, Rob, and I decided to go to Jason Alexander's party. Right outside of Rob's apartment, we ran smack into Jeffrey Richards, who was chatting with Eleanor Reissa, starring in Jule Styne's Bar Mitzvah Boy *at the American Jewish Theater. They had received a negative review from*

Mel Gussow in The Times *and were anticipating a quick demise. (I felt bad, but I admit I thought "better them than us.") Jeffrey asked us if we wanted to walk together. He was curious what reviews we had seen and said* The Daily News *was much better than anticipated. He suggested we buy a copy "near that building that kills aspiring actors." (A young actor had tragically been killed by a falling beam only a week before.) He bought us a copy of* The News, *and sure enough there were plenty of quotes from Howard Kissel that could be used in advertising copy, especially the first line.*

That night was a wonderful crash course in public relations. Jeffrey asked Cathy when we were getting married and later reported to the *Daily News* that we became engaged on opening night! (Jeffrey was not only astute in publicity but also in producing: Less than fifteen years later, he would become one of the most successful producers on Broadway—including *August: Osage County* and *Spring Awakening*—and the recipient of eight Tony Awards.)

We went to the tail end of Jason Alexander's party at the Zulu Lounge. He looked dapper in his white coat. Daena, his wife, looked great as well. It was nice to be able to celebrate both our successes. (Soon after his starring role in *Broadway Bound*, Jason was cast in a television pilot . . . no, not that one.)

At 4:00 a.m., Cathy and I returned home exhausted but no less elated. Reflecting on that night a scant two days later, I was worried I would fail to meet people's expectations. But having had more than a glimpse of the alternative, I happily embraced the outcome.

Due to many favorable notices (including excellent reviews in the Associated Press and United Press International), the Hudson Guild run was extended three weeks. Liz was already committed to doing *Sunday in the Park with George* regionally, so Kay McClelland subbed for a week. She was equally memorable and had her own unique take on the role. Jeffrey Richards, working tirelessly, finally got a commitment from Frank Rich to attend that week. Frank greeted me warmly at the theater, explaining he would have reviewed our show but felt "responsible," having been a major catalyst. I never was to learn what he thought of the production—as well as his reaction to the conspicuously absent "Five More Minutes"—but I was very pleased he came.

Howard Rogut called me at work to congratulate me on the reviews and reinforce that "we're still very interested at Jujamcyn. Can you tell me who else is interested in moving your show?"

"Howard, why should that be important?" I asked. "If you like a suit in a store window, you don't go inside and ask who else is interested in buying it."

"I know, Doug," he explained, "but that's not the way things work in the theater."

There *was* other interest, but nothing tangible—not enough to get Jujamcyn to make "the first move," to quote one of my show's song titles. The Weisslers scheduled a meeting to see me. I didn't get Fran and Barry, but rather two employees who primarily wanted to know what else I was working on. I felt like saying, "I'm twenty-eight. I just devoted the last three years to this major musical. Sorry, but I've been otherwise engaged."

And I was engaged—to be married, on August 9. So, another major production loomed in my future . . . or should I say a *co-production*, as my fiancée (and my mother) had done much of the groundwork while I was distracted by this little show. We invited Bill, Jack, Chris, Rob, and the cast of No Way to Treat a Lady. Only Peter and Steve could attend, but it was great to see them from the bimah of the former Emily-Dickinson-church-turned-synagogue in Amherst, Massachusetts. I wrote an original song for my wife entitled, "Ten Short Years," alluding to our lengthy courtship. The bridge referenced No Way to Treat a Lady:

WE HAVE A FIRM FOUNDATION
ON WHICH WE'LL START TO BUILD.
WHO ELSE WOULD SIT THROUGH
THIRTY-FOUR CONSECUTIVE PERFORMANCES
AT THE HUDSON GUILD?

Speaking of performances, my other Lady could have run through the summer, but to extend again would have meant a significant increase in everyone's salaries. So, on July 7, after playing five weeks to packed houses, we closed. There was a nice party on the stage. At one point, Jack Hofsiss's caretaker Maureen Laffey took me aside and playfully shook me. "Now aren't you glad Jack directed your show?"

I told her I was. And I think I meant it. Now, in hindsight, I feel fortunate Jack got the gig. As much as I respect Paul Lazarus, I have a feeling we wouldn't have been as good in the foxhole together. Jack recognized his deficiencies, and he magnanimously allowed both Chris and Rob to collaborate. Even though he knew he was my second choice, he was the consummate professional. In fact, we never exchanged a harsh word.

Jack had made Tony Award history as the youngest director to win Best Director of a Play for *The Elephant Man* when he was just twenty-eight. I was twenty-eight when *No Way to Treat a Lady* opened Off Broadway. In both cases, we were ambitious young men in the theater, eager to establish ourselves. I can't attest to Jack's journey, but decades later, I feel I may have done Jack a disservice in my journal. I certainly didn't apply the Atticus Finch

Final curtain: The Hudson Guild concludes its run. (Back row from left) Maureen Laffey, Christopher Chadman, the author, Peter Slutsker, Liz Callaway, June Gable. (Front row) Stephen Bogardus, Jack Hofsiss.
Photo courtesy of Stephen Bogardus

dictum: "You never really understand a person until you consider things from his point of view." In other words, until you're in his shoes.

Jack had impossible shoes to fill. He was returning to the New York stage after an accident that very few people could survive physically and emotionally. The fact he never hinted at the profound psychic toll is to his credit. He also created a loving atmosphere and filled it with talented professionals who could help carry out his vision. Jack exuded intelligence, wry humor, and taste.

Not long after *No Way to Treat a Lady* closed, I was introduced to Mario Fratti, the original librettist on *Nine* who also was a critic. When he heard I had written *Lady*, he exclaimed, "Oh, that was a wonderful show! Very fast, very elegant." And that's the point: not every director is great with actors but intuitively knows how to support them and help them find their performance—or in Jack's case, "fast, elegant" performances. There was a style to our production that was undeniable, and well, classy. That was Jack. A class act.

7

A CLOSE CALL

With no imminent plans to move *No Way to Treat a Lady* or future regional productions on the horizon, Jeffrey Richards and I worked on a full-page ad for *Variety*. It was very impressive: we had great quotes even if the actual *Times* review had been mixed. You wouldn't know it to look at the ad.

Richard Hopkins of Florida Studio Theatre in Sarasota was the first to respond. He asked George Lane for materials and committed to a production the following season. Within a year, I was at auditions and having meetings with Richard, who was also directing. Richard was an excellent dramaturg and welcomed additional rewrites. We had a memorable session one night in my apartment, deconstructing the Sadie (barfly) scene when she invites Kit (in drag) into her home. Richard correctly felt it should reveal more about Kit and his relationship with his mother. So we made Sadie a mom with an estranged son "right out of Normal Rockwell, except daddy is God knows who, God knows where, baby is shipped off to boarding school, and mommy is left holding the bottle."

We also made her an actress, albeit not as celebrated as Kit's mother, which horrifies Kit, and explains why he's unable to kill her. It was a huge improvement and contributed to a more layered second act.

Richard returned to Florida to begin rehearsals. We had an excellent cast: Though not as seasoned as our New York cast, it boasted Scott Burkell as Kit (who grew up doing summer theater with besties Jonathan Larson and Marin Mazzie), Kate Cornell (Sarah), Mary Baird (Flora, etc.), and Adam Grupper (Moe), who was making his professional debut, thus earning his Equity Card. Kate, Adam, and Scott were also cast in Cameron Mackintosh's *Tomfoolery*, based on the songs of Tom Lehrer, which was scheduled to open first, followed by rehearsals for *No Way to Treat a Lady* the next day.

A couple weeks later, I was composing at the piano when Richard called. I blithely asked how rehearsals were going. "Terrible," Richard replied. "Kate Cornell has been stabbed."

I was in shock. So was Richard. It appeared Kate, Adam, and Mary all shared the ground floor of a house about two hundred yards from the theater. Adam was invited to go out, and Kate stayed behind to help Mary acclimate (she had flown in that day) and run lines. Kate was alone in the kitchen when she was suddenly surprised by a drug addict brandishing a knife, having entered Adam's room via a screen window. He demanded money; Kate remained calm and handed him all her cash, mostly in one dollar bills. He wasn't satisfied and started to slash at her. She tried to fend him off but was cornered.

To distract him, she asked, "What have you done with Mary?" When he instinctively turned in the other direction to investigate, Kate made a beeline for the door, ran outside, and started screaming. Other theater personnel came rushing to her aide as the assailant escaped into the night through the screen window.

Initially, the knife wounds on Kate's chest appeared to be superficial. But her pulse kept dropping. After the ambulance rushed her to the hospital, they discovered the knife had pierced her pericardium. There was internal bleeding that could prove fatal! As if by divine intervention, a cardiology convention was underway in downtown Sarasota. Specialists were summoned, they operated, and Kate's life was saved.

Richard related all this to me on the phone. It was a lot to process.

"She'll survive," he assured me.

"Thank God."

"We're still committed to doing the show, but we need to find a replacement."

The question was . . . who could come down at a moment's notice to start rehearsals the next day? We looked over our casting list. Judith Bro's name appeared. She had always wanted to perform the role after doing the William Morris presentations. She hadn't been Richard's first choice, but she was now.

"Call her," he said. "See if she can be in Florida tomorrow to begin rehearsals."

I made the call, and after her initial shock, Judy said she would drop everything to do the role. She loved the part and welcomed the opportunity, even though we all wished it wasn't under these circumstances.

Judy arrived in Florida the next day. Everyone was relieved and grateful . . . except Kate. She got wind of it from her hospital bed and said no one was going to perform "her role."

I'm not privy to what transpired between Richard, Judy, and Kate, but within seventy-two hours, a crestfallen Judy was flying back to New York and Kate was preparing to resume rehearsals. One heart broken, another on the mend.

Kate Cornell with co-star Scott Burkell in Florida Studio Theatre's 1988 production, directed by Richard Hopkins. Photo courtesy of Florida Studio Theatre

With newspaper headlines like, "It's no way to treat an actress," one couldn't help but feel life was mirroring art, or a reasonable facsimile thereof. The run sold out, reviews were mostly excellent, and everyone came to see Kate's scar partially disguised by surgical tape.

The rewrites worked for the most part, although they didn't mask all the problems. During the run, Richard put together a comprehensive outline based on *The Hero with a Thousand Faces*, Joseph Campbell's classic analysis of the archetypal hero's journey in myths that can be found in narratives from *The Odyssey* to *Star Wars*.

In Richard's analysis, Morris answers the "call to adventure" and leaves his "ordinary world" behind. With the help of "mentors" and "allies" (Richard called them "helpers"), he continues his quest, facing his greatest challenge which he must overcome to achieve his objective. Richard showed me which steps in Morris's journey were in place and which were conspicuously absent, which songs were effective and which failed to fulfill Campbell's thesis. It was both fascinating and instructive, and I hoped there would be additional opportunities to answer my own personal "call to adventure."

Within months, the call came . . . from London.

8

A MAN NAMED VIVIAN

7/5/1989

In a couple of weeks, I am to leave for England! I have to keep knocking on wood because of the bitter disappointments I've faced over these past two years: a near-fatal stabbing of an actress playing Sarah, the cancellation of the Alley Theatre production in Houston, the cancellation of the GEM Theatre production in California due to lack of funds, the cancellation of the show in Tampa this past spring (there seems to be a pattern emerging!). Hopefully, we were just three times unlucky, and the England booking will prevail (knock on . . . you know!).

I had George Lane to thank. He submitted my show to Showpeople, a producing entity best known for mounting Sheldon Epps's *Blues in the Night* on the West End, which ran a year and was something of a hit. Showpeople (comprising three individuals) envisioned a similar game plan for *No Way to Treat a Lady*, although they originally wanted to bring my show into the Donmar Warehouse, a Fringe theater. Then they decided it would be better to premiere at a West End Theatre and pursued the May Fair Theatre within the May Fair Hotel. But the theater had recently been converted into a lucrative conference center, and the owner was reluctant to use his space again for theatrical purposes.

For an eternity (in reality, more like two months), the May Fair's owner kept us all waiting on pins and needles while he went duck hunting. Eventually we fared about as well as the ducks, and the idea was bagged, if you will. Weeks, even months would go by without a word from George or the producers, and they weren't exactly on the best of terms. Of Showpeople's producers, Barbara Bonfigli and the actor David Kernan (Tony nominee for *Side by Side by Sondheim*), only Barbara spoke with George. David always referred to George as "that horrible manager of yours," which stemmed from George's reluctance to grant them world rights. Barbara seemed to be the more pragmatic of the two, and as I was to find out later, the one who controlled the purse strings.

After the May Fair fell through, Barbara and David called to say they were still keen about the show but needed more time to find the right venue. They decided to try a co-production with a repertory theatre in a hamlet called . . . Leatherhead.

Contrary to being an S&M bar, Leatherhead is a picturesque town southwest of London which boasts a regional theatre dubbed the Thorndike, after actress Dame Sybil Thorndike, no less, who even co-starred with Marilyn Monroe in The Prince and the Showgirl. *The news couldn't have arrived at a better time: only an hour earlier, I had informed my bosses, Margaret and Bernice, that I was leaving M. Luca & Associates.*

Looking back, I'm astonished I left a job before I had the certainty of a production. I must have felt after five years that I was ready for a change. However, in hindsight, as a newlywed planning a family, this move seemed a bit reckless.

With an uncertain future, I was relieved when George Lane called later on the same day I gave notice to report that Leatherhead (or as he called it, "Nottingham Forest") was a go. Soon after, the check covering the option came in (twelve hundred pounds), and we were on our way.

Well, almost. We had everything but a director. David Kernan had given the show to a man who had recently directed a successful West End staging of Noel Coward's *The Vortex*. He returned it adding, "I hate musicals." In fact, it seemed everyone David thought of either passed or was busy.

Finally, David suggested Martin Connor, a young director who had gained some prominence with his recent direction of a semi-successful revival of *Wonderful Town* starring West End star Maureen Lippman. Lo and behold, Martin was just hours away directing at the Goodspeed Opera House in Connecticut. When we spoke on the phone, he was charming and witty.

The following week, Martin was every bit as delightful in person when we met at the Times Square restaurant Barrymore's to discuss the script and tape the William Morris Agency had messengered. But he informed me that my show presented a conflict: Goodspeed had asked him to direct an all-Black revival of the Gershwin musical *Oh, Kay!*, scheduled to go into rehearsal in September, the same month *No Way to Treat a Lady* was to open in Leatherhead. I was tempted to say, "Why do you want to go and waste your time on that old thing? Sure, the Gershwins could write tunes, but talk about your dated librettos!" I listened sympathetically as Martin explained there was no new book writer assigned yet, and he was flummoxed as to how to make it work as a Black musical. "So Martin," I thought, "what's to decide?"

The trouble was Martin was being seduced—by New York, by the Nederlanders (one of the largest operators of theaters which extend beyond Broadway), by the lure of big money and questionable promises. He was privileged enough to be working outside of the United Kingdom, and I don't think he planned to go back.

After a brief but semi-productive meeting over carrot cake, he shook my hand and told me it was a pleasure meeting me.

"With or without me," he said, "you'll have a great success."

"I don't believe that," I asserted. "I think this is the kind of show that will suffer significantly if the wrong director is at the helm, and I'd like you to helm this production."

"I'm very flattered," was Martin's reply. "I'll let you know about my decision in a few days."

I thanked him, and we parted. I knew in my gut he would say no, and I was right. I also knew I had been careful not to oversell my show. I credit this with my years as a job placement counselor: There were some applicants who, when pushed too hard into accepting a job, inevitably refused or left the position prematurely. My limited experience in the theater had taught me this as well.

Martin *did* go on to direct *Oh, Kay!* at Goodspeed, co-produced by none other than Broadway's "Abominable Showman" David Merrick. In typical Merrick fashion, Martin was replaced by Dan Siretta (his choreographer) by the time it opened on Broadway.

With Martin out of the running, David Kernan was at an all-time low. He had secured a West End actor, Martin Smith, for Morris, and an American actress living in London, Susannah Fellows, for Sarah. But they were enquiring about a director, and prospects for the other two roles were following suit. No one was keen about doing an out-of-town tryout in Leatherhead without a first-rate director boasting West End credentials. I was beginning to wish I had done a better sales job with Martin Conner.

Rather than leave matters in David's hands, I decided to take on the quest of finding a director. My first thought was Jason Alexander. Why not? He was "hot," having just won a Tony Award for *Jerome Robbins Broadway*. Who cared if he had never directed a show before? I knew Jason was very capable and had "apprenticed" as an actor under gifted directors Hal Prince, Gene Saks, Jerry Robbins, A. J. Antoon, Jerry Zaks, and . . . Paul Lazarus! Unfortunately, when I mentioned his name to David Kernan, he said, "Who's he?" (So much for being "hot.") But David was intrigued that Jason had appeared in a special West End performance of the Kander and Ebb musical *The Rink* and thought he might have a British Equity card. He gave me the green light to pursue.

Unfortunately, Jason did *not* have a British Equity card, and I was beginning to realize he held little clout with London audiences, much as I considered Jason a born leader. My next thought was Barry Harmon. David had actually mentioned Barry when we were discussing American directors, having admired his work on *Romance/Romance*, a major Broadway credit with multiple Tony nominations.

I asked George's assistant Michael Traum for Barry's agent. He did one better by contacting his lawyer's assistant who provided Barry's number in the Hamptons!

Curiosity got the better of me, so I called Barry and had a good conversation. His questions were succinct and intelligent. We discussed changes I had made and how significant revisions could dramatically alter a piece. He wasn't as effusive or charming as Martin, but Barry expressed a desire to read the show and had no problems listening to crudely recorded tapes. I promised him the material when he returned that Wednesday. I also explained I was acting without David's prior knowledge.

Vivian Matalon poses with his 1980 Tony for Best Director of a Play (Morning's at Seven). Photofest

Monday morning, David called to triumphantly proclaim, "I think we have a director. I spoke with Vivian Matalon over the weekend, and he's interested in speaking with you. What's more, he's British, his residence is in New York, and *(insert drum roll)* he's Jewish!" On that last point I thought, who cares? I mean, if that suggests he has a sense of humor, great. But being Jewish was not the only criterion. I also was a bit disappointed because by this time I had decided in my mind that Barry Harmon was the director, and now David had stolen my thunder.

"I spoke to Barry Harmon this weekend. You know, the director of *Romance/Romance* you liked. He seems interested," I said.

"Good, love. Keep him warm . . . but call Vivian," David said emphatically.

Between 1980 and 1981, Vivian Matalon had three productions running on Broadway, an astonishing feat for a director. One of those productions, a 1980 revival of Paul Osborne's *Morning's at Seven*, earned him a Tony Award as Best Director. A previous failure when first produced in 1939 (lasting only forty-four performances despite having been directed by Josh Logan and designed by Jo Mielziner), the revival ran 564 performances and earned three Tony Awards. The cast, which included Maureen O'Sullivan, Theresa Wright, Nancy Marchand, Elizabeth Williams, Gary Merrill, Lois de Banzie, and David Rounds, was lightning in a bottle.

As Vivian would later tell me, "When you're a success directing a musical in the West End, they offer you a play. In the States if you're a success directing a play, they offer you a musical." The following season after *Morning's at Seven*, he directed *Brigadoon*, which was also a critical (if not commercial) success, earning three Tony nominations, including one for Martin Vidnovic as Best Actor in a Musical. Vivian loved to tell the story of how Martin would introduce him around town as his "dentist," for Martin credited Vivian with "pulling a performance out of me."

Formerly a successful West End and British film and television actor, Vivian had studied at the Neighborhood Playhouse in New York. Twenty-five years after we worked together, I taught song interpretation at the Playhouse, creating and directing their annual musical showcases for casts of thirty-two students. I would often pass Vivian's early framed photo on the wall of famous alumni realizing that most of my students had no idea who he was. However, they would undoubtedly be familiar with his roommate at the time: "Jimmy," better known as James Dean, had a propensity for lighting candles and incense around their apartment, jumping from candle to candle like a mischievous sprite.

But I was not mischievous by nature and did exactly as David Kernan had instructed. I phoned Vivian.

"*Mr. Matalon, hello. This is Douglas Cohen.*"

"*Oh, yes, Douglas. I just spoke to David. I'll tell you what . . . I'm eager to read your show. Can you get me a copy?*"

"*Sure. I'll have my agent messenger it to you.*" (No matter how often I've said it, I still love that phrase.)

Now David had instructed me that Vivian does not like listening to tapes until after he has read the script and approved, so not to offer a cassette. I was a little sensitive about my score since David related actress Maureen Lippman turned down the role of Flora/Alexandra/Victims based on the music. Also, David and Barbara are famous for calling me out of the blue and saying, "I think what this show needs is a ballad," or "We need a song we can use out of context, for example, Morris singing a song like 'Come Back to Me' to Kit," or (their favorite) "Maybe a song to satisfy the queens of England. How about one involving Flora and Sarah when they meet, like a real Kander and Ebb showstopper? We need some good numbers in the second half." (Are "Once More from the Top," "One of the Beautiful People," "Front Page News," and "I Have Noticed a Change in You" chicken liver?!)

Anyway(s)—Vivian later said we'd get along much better if I don't add the s—I decided it was wrong not to send the tape. What if Vivian liked the book but not the music? Better we should know while Barry Harmon was being kept warm. So I broached the subject, and Vivian suggested I include the cassette. I must admit I was surprised when he asked when it would arrive, as his building was without a doorman. Don't Tony Award winners have people in the lobby who collect their packages?

Tuesday came and so did a phone call from Vivian at 1:30, just as I was dashing to jury duty.

"Douglas, I've looked at the show and first let me say, I find you are immensely talented . . . truly I do," he began.

Uh, oh. If they begin by complimenting you, watch out. It can only mean a "but" is sure to follow. "But" he continued, "I do have some problems with the piece."

"Yes . . ."

"Well, there seems to be a dichotomy in style between the script and the score. The songs do not seem to spring naturally from the text, and the book does not reflect the emotionalism of the songs . . ."

I'm all for constructive criticism, but it sounded like Vivian wanted me to start from scratch . . . with one month before rehearsals were to begin, no less!

"I'm listening," I said rather brazenly. "I'm not necessarily agreeing, but I'm listening."

"Yes, of course. I have particular moments I'd like to cite—"

"Mr. Matalon—"

"Please, if you're to continue to call me that, I'll have to call you Mr. Cohen."

"I'm sorry. It's just David Kernan suggested I show respect."

"I sound old."

"Sorry, Vivian. I would love to talk. Forgive me for being abrupt, but I have to be at jury duty downtown in a half hour. Is there some way we could possibly meet?"

"Of course," he replied. "I don't think we should continue without first meeting. I tell you what. I have a very small apartment. Would it be possible to meet at your place?"

I was afraid that would end our collaboration before it had begun. "I don't think that would be a good idea. I live in a small apartment, and it's kind of messy. How about William Morris?"

"William Morris?" Vivian asked incredulously.

"They have a room with a piano. I could see if it's available."

"Listen, why don't you come here. I'll put Stephen"—his partner, acclaimed playwright and actor Stephen Temperley—"and the dogs in the bedroom so we can work."

At jury duty, I kept thinking about his comments. It seemed as if they were insurmountable problems, problems I might not agree with. I wasn't even sure a meeting was worth the time but kept saying, "Keep an open mind."

I got to his building at 6:45. East 14th Street, right near Stuyvesant Town. *Not exactly as chic a location as Barry Harmon's Central Park West address,* I noted in my journal . . .

I buzzed myself in and took the stairs to the second floor. A very friendly man opened the door. Vivian is short and solid and surprisingly nimble—like an aging leprechaun. In the background, two small dogs yapped.

"Douglas, please come in . . ."

The apartment was dark and, as one-bedrooms go, not flashy. It was tidy, however. There were lots of books and records neatly put away.

Then I met the dogs.

One of them seemed barely alive; the other looked stuffed as a result of a sizable scar on its back, probably having had discs removed. Vivian explained that they were seventeen and eighteen, which sounded ancient. They hobbled along the carpet, dragging their hind legs, shedding what little fur they had.

Vivian let them out on a small terrace. One of the privileges of living on the second floor was he has an honest-to-God patio. He has no view, or only a view of other buildings, but there is a little veranda. The dogs seemed to enjoy it as they urinated with glee. I didn't stay to watch their next move.

The phone rang; Vivian answered it. I asked him if he wanted privacy in the bedroom. He said it didn't matter. I asked him if he minded if I looked at the memorabilia which covered his walls.

"Go ahead, I've got nothing to hide," he responded.

He does have an impressive array of memorabilia. There was a Hirschfeld for Morning's at Seven *personally inscribed by Al Hirschfeld, posters containing Hume Cronyn and Jessica Tandy, Alec McCowen, Elaine Stritch, and one boasting Lee Remick in* Bus Stop. *Not too far from his desk in a less than prominent spot sat his Tony Award for Best Director of a Play (*Morning's at Seven). *At least Jack Hofsiss knew how to display his.*

Vivian's phone call began with "Oh, love, I'm all right. It just seems everything I've touched these past two years has died . . ."

With that, he left and closed the bedroom door behind him.

I looked down at the two feeble dogs and the posters decaying slightly with age. I knew he had directed The Tap Dance Kid *on Broadway, but that was five years ago. Maybe there was some truth in his last sentence.*

"Just talk to him and leave," I thought. "He's obviously not the one. Do it as a courtesy to David and make sure to get the materials to Barry."

Vivian's phone call was rather lengthy, and I became acutely aware there was no air conditioning, although one was in plain view. Instead, there were overhead ceiling fans circulating stale air. I was beginning to sweat, as it was a humid night. The dogs sniffed my clothes until I gently shooed them away. Finally, Vivian emerged from the bedroom. I had already decided if he offered me something to drink, I would decline, intent on a hasty retreat.

"Would you like something to drink?" he asked.

"No, thank you."

"Are you sure? It gets hot in here. I'd turn on the air conditioner except for the noise."

"No, thank you, I'm all right."

"I won't ask you again, so do let me know if you change your mind." Vivian sat down next to me on the couch.

"Let me say again," he began, "how talented your work is. I've read the show twice and listened to the tape and feel you have real talent. People sometimes lose sight of the compliments as the criticisms follow . . ."

I braced myself.

Vivian produced a legal-sized pad that seemed to be covered with meticulous notes. Martin Conner had only a few mental notes, so at least Vivian had already earned points.

"On this first note, we may have a major disagreement . . ."

Can you take points back?

"I don't think one actress should play all the character women," he continued. "Why did you specify that it be one actress?"

I explained that I wanted to show a relationship between the two men, a common denominator, and having the same actress play both their mothers reinforced it. I also explained that it was natural for the same actress who played Kit's mother to be playing his victims, as psychologically he was killing his mother. On this last point, he disagreed.

"I think it's much too overt. It's there—trust your audience."

I asked him what he'd prefer.

"Have one actress play Flora and Alexandra . . . and one actress play the victims."

This seemed strange to me.

"I can see maybe having one actress play Flora and then another actress playing Alexandra and Kit's victims. That tracks for me and connects Alexandra to the women who bear a certain physical resemblance."

Vivian brightened. We were exploring common ground.

He also explained to me that finding a West End actress who was credible as a Jewish mother was slim, and to have that same actress perform four other roles was an impossible assignment. By dividing the role in this way, we were opening the talent pool.

Vivian felt the first act (apart from that confounded opening) was in better shape than the second and asked me to give several scenes closer examination. He happily shared his notes with me to take home and study. They were valid points, and there was no denying that we were clicking. He had a wonderful sense of humor, and perhaps David was right—maybe the fact he was Jewish connected us on a deeper level. Vivian, though British, wasn't far removed from a member of my father's synagogue.

When Barry Harmon called to say he was unable to take on another project, I realized it was "bashert," destiny. I dove into Vivian's proposed rewrites, embellishing Alexandra Gill's ghostly Act Two rejection of her son's recent headline in *The New York Times*, which followed Kit's new ebullient reprise of "Front Page News":

KIT:
NOW THAT I'M FRONT PAGE NEWS,
ISN'T LIFE AMAZING?
A CORNUCOPIA JUST BRIMMING WITH SURPRISE.
NOW IT IS THE BAD BOY THEY CRAVE,
SEE IT DOESN'T PAY TO BEHAVE
WHEN THE NEW YORK TIMES WRITES A RAVE—
ALEXANDRA: ·
All lies.
KIT: My victims can attest—
ALEXANDRA: Darling, your victims are dead. Rule number one: never send your audience into rigor mortis. *(Kit is mortified.)* Poor Christopher. Whether you're a successful killer or an unsuccessful actor, you still can't get arrested in this town!

For our second meeting, we met at *my* apartment—yes, I was beginning to trust Vivian to that degree. Noticing a faux wall previously constructed to create another bedroom, Vivian glanced at our living room, devoid of natural light, and inquired, "Are you growing mushrooms, love?"

I proudly showed Vivian my latest changes. Not only was he happy with the rewrites but also howled with delight.

"That's genuinely witty, Douglas. Do you see where I'm going with all this?"

"Yes, Vivian. I do, and I like the direction the show is taking."

And with that, I had a director. David Kernan and Barbara were ecstatic. In fact, everyone seemed happy with the decision except for my lawyer, Elliot Brown. His voice dropped two octaves when I revealed my choice.

"Oh, Doug," Elliot moaned. "Not Vivian."

"Why do you say that, Elliot?" I asked. "I've met with him a couple times, and we're getting along famously. He's very bright and surprisingly funny—"

"I hope you're right." Then, without elaborating, he went on to ask, "When is the production? I plan to be in London in September, so let's meet up there, hopefully at your show."

It was a date. And although Elliot's reaction made me a little apprehensive, every show has its specific challenges. Vivian had been through some tough times—he admitted that to the person who phoned his apartment. But he had turned a corner, and so had I.

Less than two weeks later, I flew overseas to begin a lengthy out-of-town tryout. Vivian, due to a deathly fear of flying, boarded a barge (or "banana boat" to quote David Kernan), less costly than a luxury liner. Despite our different modes of transportation, we shared a common destination . . . London.

My father had always promised my family we would travel to London for his sabbatical, which sadly never happened. *Oliver!* was my favorite cast album as a child, and I desperately wanted to play the title role. I remember my dad saying Georgia Brown, the original Nancy, was Jewish, and we might meet her when we visited London. (I guess with Jews it's *two* degrees of separation.) The movie, starring Shani Wallis as Nancy and the inimitable Ron Moody as Fagin, literally gave this fifth grader something to live for: The same year it came out, my mother was hospitalized in Boston after falling through a sidewalk and had to undergo a spinal fusion. During her hospitalization, both my grandmothers died rather unexpectedly within a week of one another. But my folks promised me once my mother came home, we would see the film version of *Oliver!*, a promise they fulfilled.

And now I wasn't going to enter Dickens's London for a scant three hours—I was going to live there for three *months* as a *writer*.

9

"AMATEURS!"

The luggage my bosses had given me when I left M. Luca & Associates was beautifully extravagant but impractical. Made from walnut-colored leather, it was badly scuffed by the time two of the pieces arrived in London. Perhaps I should have seen it as an omen.

Much as I appreciated the parting gift, I had hoped for a bonus. My stipend in London was adequate but not particularly generous. I had to pay for my flat, my meals, transportation, and any miscellaneous items like seeing theater, which I planned to do. On my last day at work, I'd had a heart-to-heart with my bosses, and they generously agreed to keep me on the payroll: It was somehow more advantageous than handing me a lump sum, and perhaps it was wishful thinking on both our parts—they were leaving the door open. So I left for London feeling I had a safety net in the event I needed it.

My flat wasn't going to be ready until the first of August, so my wife's close friend from college, Denise Vingiello, graciously invited me to stay with her for two weeks. It would also make the transition easier, as I hadn't been separated from Cathy in many years, and Denise's company would ease the transition.

One of the first entries in my journal indicated conflicting emotions giving way to exhaustion and finally surrendering to euphoria.

7/17/1989

I have arrived!

I am writing from Denise's flat on Sinclair Road after having pulled my first all-nighter since college. It's hard to imagine that I made a frequent habit of this way back when. Either I was younger, or it helps to eat pizza and drink Coke at 4:00 a.m.!

Cathy went with me to the airport (British Airways at JFK). At least, I think she did. You see, due to my comatose state, I have very little recollection of what actually did occur this morning. I seem to remember putting some tough French toast in my mouth and then boarding a plane. Oh yes, then I remember sleeping . . . and awakening . . . and sleeping. (This process was repeated several times before we touched down.)

I felt very melancholy saying goodbye to Cathy. Usually, she wells up with tears and I stay rather unemotional (especially considering I was embarking on an exciting journey). But this time, it was difficult to say goodbye. I kept turning around even after we parted to catch a glimpse of her as she walked toward the exit. She did the same, which only made our goodbyes more excruciating. I think this experience taught me more than ever just how important she is to me. I truly felt married in the way that most people only experience after spending a lifetime together; somehow it didn't seem natural for her not to be beside me.

I really can't quite believe I'm here—it has yet to sink in. Rather, it feels like one of those Mission Impossible *episodes where they trick the person into believing he's someplace he isn't.*

Tomorrow, I meet at 9:00 a.m. with Vivian, Barbara, David, Dorris Carr (the third and final producer), and prospective Floras and Kits.

Break a leg and goodnight.

7/17/1989 11:15 p.m.

We had our first day of auditions, and my first day in London.

First, waking up this morning and walking to Showpeople's office, I was on such a high (my mouth in a perpetual grin) that it's a wonder people didn't mistake me for the village idiot. Everything I did felt like a new and exciting experience. I wanted to reach out and touch people and rejoice in their Britishness. I walked without fear or inhibitions. Rather, I felt like Oliver upon his own arrival in London: at any moment, I threatened to break into "Who will buy this wonderful morning?" The temperature was warm and brisk with just a nip in the air, like an early fall day. Every street looked more picturesque than the one before. I couldn't believe the natives seemed to take so much for granted. I wanted to throttle them and cry out, "Aren't you f*ing overjoyed to be living here?!"

I feel as though I belong here. In New York, I adapt to my surroundings, but here it feels natural. I want to shed my Americanism so desperately and enjoin Margaret Thatcher to proclaim, "My boy, you have proved yourself worthy. You are now officially British."

I must admit when I spotted an American tourist, I had this secret desire to go over and say, "Hello, brother. You are not alone: I, too, am American." With my ABC London atlas, this should be fairly obvious. In fact, I've done nothing to disguise my accent. It serves me well when I ask for directions or when the tube man asked for ninety pence, and I gave him ten pence. "Don't be cross," my accent seems to cry out. "I'm not trying to shaft you. I'm just ignorant of your customs."

I arrived at Showpeople's office hot and sweaty after having sprinted the last half mile (so much for a good first impression!) and met David Kernan. Although twelve years had passed since *Side by Side by Sondheim* debuted on Broadway, he was still the dapper, charming performer I remembered.

Vivian's impression of David had improved (in a previous conversation, he expressed a healthy amount of skepticism), but his assessment of co-producers Barbara Bonfigli and Dorris Carr remained the same: "Amateurs!" I couldn't blame him: For the auditions, they sent performers scenes without his approval and only arranged to have actors read monologues, hence there was no need for a reader (who was hired!). Vivian thought this was "idiocy" since you can't tell how an actor responds to another actor through monologues.

Of course, I took in Vivian's comments, and although I admit they gave me pause, here is something you need to know before we go any further: I believe anyone who wants to produce my work must be highly intelligent, professional, and beyond reproach. I mean, if they exhibit exceptional taste in wanting to present quality work, how can they be otherwise? If Bernie Madoff, while serving a life sentence, had called me to say he wanted to produce one of my musicals, I would have probably said, "Why don't we discuss this over meatloaf at your mess hall?" Obviously, I'm exaggerating, but it's my way of saying I listened to Vivian's opinions but wanted to deny their veracity.

During the auditions, I discovered Dorris was Barbara's *mother*! They didn't share the same last name or deny they were related, but it wasn't exactly advertised. They looked nothing alike—Dorris was diminutive with very delicate features, like Maureen O'Sullivan with a tight face lift. She was very kind if somewhat ditzy, at least on the surface: Having been under contract with Universal Studios while still in high school, she later studied at Stanford and hosted a midnight television show, *Dorris Carr's Club Four*, reportedly NBC's first version of *The Tonight Show*. Barbara was more stolid in manner but shared a creative side: She had done some musical underscoring and composing for film and theater. She too was very pleasant but didn't quite inherit her mother's charm. However, Barbara was much more intuitive and able to read a room. Certainly, she was able to read Vivian.

David Kernan had enjoyed a film and television career (including *That Was the Week that Was*, *The Avengers*, and *Upstairs, Downstairs*) and West End musicals, most notably *Side by Side by Sondheim*. The transfer to Broadway deservedly earned him a Tony nomination. However, he wasn't quite celebrated enough to command leading man status in prominent book musicals: Vivian revealed Sir Cameron Mackintosh had offered David a supporting role in his 1987 starry West End revival of *Follies*, although David aspired to play one of the two male leads. Now "co-starring" side by side with Dorris and Barbara, David and his cohorts were an interesting trio.

I thought there was going to be a minor fracas when Barbara Bonfigli, without Vivian's approval, announced in auditions that Sadie (the barfly) should *not* be British, and it was pointless to ask British actresses to read with a British dialect when they had rehearsed an American one. Vivian was quite perturbed, and his temper began to show (though I could see his point).

His direction of the performers auditioning was quite good. To *Game of Thrones'* Michael Heath, playing Kit (disguised as Ramone, the Arthur Murray dance instructor), he said, "Pretend people see the sun when you smile." He got Martin Smith and Susannah Fellows (David's choices for Morris and Sarah) to play the beginning of their first scene together a lot gruffer: "*They* don't know love is just around the corner." The results were genuinely excellent.

Shani Wallis was the first to audition. Far from being the glamorous, buxom Nancy of the film *Oliver!*, she had evolved into a character actress. I found her very endearing, although Vivian felt she was a bit "long-winded." She had never seen the script and didn't even know what the show was about. ("My agent said 'go,' so I'm here.") She was reluctant to attempt an instant Italian dialect, but an hour later when she returned, she was quite good as Carmella, possessing vitality and warmth. She was even surprisingly good as Flora (who was to be played by a separate actress), explaining she had converted to Judaism when she married her husband. (Vivian balked at her attempting such a feat: "Shani Wallis has never eaten Kosher food, let alone played a Jew.")

Ultimately, we didn't cast Shani. But I later wrote her a note of appreciation, and she wrote me a classy reply: "You are an extremely talented young man, and I for one would have given my eye teeth to play those juicy roles! It seems at present I'm to keep them in my jaw . . ."

As for the rest of the casting options:

For all my concerns about Martin Smith (I had previously heard him on an Alan Jay Lerner tribute album and thought his voice was limited), I seem to have underestimated him. I predict he will be a wonderful Morris: charming, sensitive, passionate. He looks perfect, although that's the trouble—he's a bit too good looking. But that should be our greatest problem!

Susannah is a dream . . . although a stronger actor than singer. It's not that she doesn't possess a good voice—it's just her "belt" is not as pleasing as her "mix." But she and Martin have genuine chemistry, and Vivian and I were eventually won over.

The next day, the Kits arrived.

We only saw four candidates, but two emerged as real possibilities: David Burt (the original Enjolras in Les Misérables*) and Simon Green, rising West End performer. Vivian favored David—he looks more the part and has the advantage of being the son of Pip Hinton, an actress who once worked with Vivian. But Simon, though youthful looking, is really a better choice. I prefer his voice and movement, and his angelic face can become chillingly demonic. David Kernan concurs.*

No major altercations, although at one point Dorris seemed more interested in fetching coffee than listening to the performer sing. Vivian mumbled, "Forget about the fucking coffee. Your job is not to serve coffee!" I don't think Dorris heard but Barbara may have. She wisely pretended not to.

Vivian was very pleased with my rewrites, although he suggested Alexandra reprise "What shall I sing for you?" (Kit's plaintive lullaby in Act One) at the end of the show. Not a bad idea; in fact, I like it.

I went to see my first West End production this trip: Nöel Coward's The Vortex. It was a directorial tour de force—very theatrical and engrossing. This same director had been offered No Way to Treat a Lady but turned it down saying, "I hate musicals."

Go figure!

On July 20, Vivian invited me to Leatherhead with our new choreographer, Lindsay Dolan. I almost declined, as I thought "I'll see enough of the theater in the coming weeks." Plus, I was eager to return to the West End. But something told me this should take priority—and a good thing, too.

Leatherhead is in the county of Surrey, twenty-one miles southwest of London, about fifty minutes by rail, give or take. The countryside was lovely if a tad monotonous, and the town itself was unexceptional. In all fairness, I didn't get to really explore much of Leatherhead apart from the inside of the theater. My routine was to arrive at the quaint train station and walk about a half a mile to the Thorndike Theatre. I did eat at a few of the restaurants and pubs, but nothing made a lasting impression: I was too busy witnessing a real-life production of Noises Off!

As a way of introducing our "cast of characters," like Noah's ark, we had duplicate names associated with our modest production: Vivian Matalon, our director, and Vivienne Martin (cast as our Alexandra, Mrs. Sullivan, Sadie, and Carmella); Martin Smith (Morris) and Martin, the technical director; David Kernan (co-producer) and David Burt (Kit); Barbara Bonfigli (co-producer) and Barbara Young (performing the role of Flora).

Vivian, Lindsay, and I arrived at Leatherhead late, having missed an earlier train. At around 2:00, we were brought upstairs to the green room to meet the team: Martin, the technical director, was an amiable, heavyset man; Gordon, the business manager, rotund with whiskers, looked like a diminished Santa Claus; and Roger, the artistic director, had a shockingly unkempt appearance and wild mane more befitting a killer (and not one I'd like to spend two hours with onstage). Chris, our set designer, had already arrived and looked a bit vexed, but I was to find out later that was among his limited repertory of expressions.

Soon after we sat down to chat, several hard facts were revealed: The theater had only planned on one day of tech rehearsal, factoring in that we'd have our final dress rehearsal the afternoon of our opening night. They also reported we couldn't use the stage or set until two days prior, as their summer season would still be in progress!

Rehearsal space in the theater was limited to one room significantly smaller than the stage and "semi-promised" to a youth theater group. The only other available space, literally "down the road," was a single room: There would be no way to teach music to part of the cast while others were doing blocking. They even suggested we rehearse in London, which was prohibitively expensive and defeated the purpose of a regional try-out in Leatherhead. There were also no provisions in their schedule for an orchestra call, and we were told their lighting designer on staff was going to be taking a two-week holiday and returning close to our last week of rehearsals!

Vivian showed signs of apoplexy: I literally thought he would foam at the mouth. To his credit, he tried to be very civilized about it all, but his "darlings" and "loves" were multiplying like rabbits, a sure indication that a strong undercurrent was brewing. (I noticed that the British often sublimate their anger in terms of endearment.) Roger, the artistic director, offered little comfort: He kept repeating he had allotted us more rehearsal time than any other show, and it was possible to work under these conditions.

"We do reasonably good work here, I think you'll be proud of our product: Gordon is a good manager, Martin is a good T.D., I am a reasonably good artistic director and director. *Stepping Out* was first performed here, had a success on the West End, and went on to New York where it is now enjoying regional success . . ."

This is all Vivian had to hear. He hated, detested, loathed that play! Whenever Vivian tried to speak ("Love, I understand your position. I too was an artistic director—"), Roger would interrupt by saying, "Please, I would like to finish my sentence," then would go on at great length, at which point Vivian would interject, "Love, that sentence was more like a paragraph."

It was also revealed that Leatherhead had crosses to bear since they felt they had not been properly consulted on certain artistic decisions. Roger referred to "the dreaded Barbara" (our co-producer) and expressed disappointment that David Kernan had misled them in terms of the extra cast member and additional costs. Vivian just nodded and tried to interject a "love" here and a "darling" there. I later told Roger that I'd be happy to listen to any suggestions he might have and emphasized I had total faith in Vivian.

"I can see you are all very professional," Roger said, thanking me for recognizing his existence, no doubt.

From there, we went to see the theater. It was certainly adequate in terms of size, although it had limited wing space. What it lacked in charm, it made up for in intimacy: The audience looked down onto the stage, so even with 550 chairs, there wasn't a bad seat in the house.

This was really the only good news of the day.

Even our meeting with their resident designer proved fruitless since he claimed Barbara, our co-producer, had failed to tell him to bring his portfolio and, like everyone else there, he had failed to read the play.

Vivian, Lindsay, and I trudged back to the station, plotting how we would reveal these "minor" inconveniences to Showpeople. On our scenic walk we passed a sign bearing the words "Rail" and below it, "Crematorium." I wondered if it was prophetic.

12:10 a.m. 7/21/1989

Earlier today, Vivian and I had a terrific time in Chichester. We took a train 1.5 hours into the country to see his production of The Heiress. *Except for some underwhelming acting in the first two scenes (and some static blocking), it was a fine production. We went backstage to see Alec McCowen, who was an excellent Dr. Sloper. He is one of the kindest people I've ever met and was very complimentary of my score to* No Way to Treat a Lady. *Alec told us he was opening a new show in the West End in September, and they were making him learn how to word process: It takes place in newspaper offices, and they are striving for authenticity. I kidded him that they always say an actor should have something to fall*

back on. He told Vivian when we first met that he knew I was in the audi-
ence as he heard a great burst of laughter following one of his lines and
(from Vivian's description) suspected it was me! It seems my laugh is now
famous here.

Well, that's all for now. Tomorrow is callbacks, so I need my rest.

Our final day of casting yielded our Kit—David Burt. I was
excited by his genuine presence, mercurial nature, and powerful
voice. Occasionally, the sound settled in the back of his throat, but
I was optimistic we could break him of the habit.

David Burt was our unanimous choice, apart from David Kernan. This troubled me since David Kernan and I were usually in
agreement. He clearly favored Simon Green, a major talent but,
to quote his surname, a bit "green." Simon had an innocence that
was very touching, but he hadn't yet developed into the performer
around which everything revolves. It was almost a shame both
Simon and David couldn't perform the role together: As a duo, they
were capable of capturing Kit's complexities.

Vivian gave me a first glimpse of how the set worked. It was
much more in keeping with the way I had envisioned the staging:
various set pieces came in and out, a room transformed into a different locale with the slight alteration of a door frame. And I was
finally gifted with a raised platform for Kit's loft complete with a
large skylight which, at the end of the play, became perpendicular
to the stage. The icing on the cake was a pair of red, neon lips suspended above the action, precisely timed to light up following each
murder!

I stepped in dog crap on my way to auditions. I was beginning to learn that London was full of contradictions: Everything
was immaculate, but dogs were rarely curbed. Everyone was so
civilized *except* behind a steering wheel. Although the lifestyle and
pace were much easier, it was nearly impossible to find a cold glass
of water . . . or any cold beverage for that matter. The summer was
unseasonably warm, and ice cubes were more precious than gold. I
walked around in a state of perpetual thirst.

11:40 p.m. 7/24/1989

Just returned from a performance of Aspects of Love. *I found myself*
drifting in and out, appreciating how Sondheim handled similar material
in A Little Night Music *with far greater skill and subtlety. However,*

Andrew Lloyd Webber has written some very attractive melodies: He's a modern day "pied piper," enticing his children to listen to his song as he leads them down the garden path. Our instincts tell us to resist, but the music is so potent that it's nearly impossible to turn a deaf ear.

I CAN'T WAIT FOR REHEARSALS TO START! Here I am in paradise, attending theatre two or three times a week, exploring pubs, museums, Hampton Court, Stonehenge for God's sake . . . yet I feel in limbo. I think I'm also homesick; I desperately want to fit in. When I found out today that Lindsay (our choreographer) worked with Jason Alexander on The Rink *concert in London, I positively lit up: Suddenly, my previous life existed. That's what's tough here—it's bad enough when you're making all new friends and hardly know a soul, but when your new friends have no means of knowing your loved ones, you feel isolated, like a person without a past. At least with Denise, I can talk about Cathy, but everyone else here doesn't care that I left a wife in the States. Good God, it sounds like some bloody war saga!*

Which brings me to another point: I'm beginning to think in English phrases, even if I haven't adopted the accent. And I'm not ready to let go of my Americanism. Even though I believe by and large our country is f*cked up, I am an American, and I have a sense of pride about that. I can't say New York can hold a candle to London, but Maine and Cape Cod can compete with the English countryside, and there are things about New York City that I miss—like ice cubes! But all kidding aside, the various cultures in New York are refreshing, especially the Jews. That's what's missing! There are no Jews here, or they're English Jews, which aren't the genuine article. At least if I had a corned beef sandwich at a deli counter while listening to some alte kaker, I wouldn't feel so far away from home.

At this time, I moved out of Denise's flat. I was sorry to go but also realized it was time to be on my own, especially as we were approaching rehearsals. Showpeople found me a nice, three-story walk-up flat near the Fulham/Chelsea stop on the tube in Chelsea. (I kept thinking of Sally Bowles in *Cabaret*: "I used to have a girl-friend known as Elsie with whom I shared four sordid rooms in Chelsea . . .") I really liked my flat: It was quite spacious and had a separate bedroom with a comforter—no need to make my bed when a comforter masked any signs of disarray. It also boasted a living room, small bathroom, tiny kitchen, and a washer and dryer stacked on top of one another like bunkbeds. It was everything I needed and very homey. But it emphasized that I no longer had the company of a friend from the States.

8/1/1989 11:30 p.m.

The first of August, and I'm still plagued with homesickness.

It bothers me that I'm not enjoying this freedom as much as I should. But I grow restless when I'm idle for too long. I long for direction and purpose. Otherwise, without the interaction or mental activity, I grow listless.

I bought a Sarah Brightman cassette ("The Songs that Got Away") to cheer me up and keep me company. Without a television or radio, the flat can get lonely.

Tomorrow, I'm meeting with Vivian to show him my new song, "So Much in Common," to be sung by Flora and Sarah on the occasion of their first meeting . . . in lieu of "Mother Likes Sarah." David Kernan was insistent that I write a number for the two women in a Kander and Ebb style. Vivian, who usually doesn't submit to pressure, asked me to have it ready just in case but not to breathe a word to David or Barbara. Well, somehow, they found out because Barbara referenced it when we met to go over my recent amendments the other day. I don't know how they unveiled our secret except I called David Kernan last Friday to ask him about practice rooms. Maybe my phone is bugged. (I wouldn't put it past them!)

Much as I was reluctant to write a song to replace "Mother Likes Sarah" (a standout at the Hudson Guild, albeit a solo for Morris), I loved writing "So Much in Common." Having improvised the verse in Denise's flat, I now needed a piano to compose the chorus. I rented a practice room in the heart of London for an hour. I remember praying inspiration would strike with a lyric that began, "We've so much in common," but nothing did. Then with five minutes left on the clock, I started experimenting, and "we've so much common" became "oh, we have so much—so much in common." That small but significant change sparked a tune, and I hit record quickly on the tape recorder. Since this attractive melody was in the same vein as a Kander and Ebb/Jerry Herman song, I knew my producers would be pleased. I gathered my possessions just in time to turn the room over to the next tenant.

The lyrics in my new flat flowed effortlessly. I couldn't wait to perform it for Vivian when it was complete. Like a dutiful child, I was also eager to prove to Showpeople that my stipend was justified.

I have had a fine relationship with Showpeople so far, although I'm sure any day now the bloom will leave the rose. I got to meet their respective significant others at the Blues in the Night *taping for the BBC last Saturday. David's partner, Basil, is very nice, as is Barbara's Jennifer. (When Vivian learned of our introductions, he said, "Poor boy, you're surrounded by dykes and poofs!")*

David Kernan told me Saturday night that David Burt was showing signs of uncertainty upon reading the show and hearing the tape and asked his agent (who is also David Kernan's) to read/listen and give her impressions. I started to feel my ego deflating. I mean, here's a great tour de force role, so why is the guy too thick to realize it? Was it the arrangements? Why are the Brits so tough on my music yet they genuflect over Blood Brothers?! *Am I not writing the sort of music they go for in London? Can't David Burt appreciate a seamless book?*

I learned the next day that he accepted after his agent explained that, despite not being given a big ballad, it was a very "integrated theatrical piece" and the songs were effective within the context of the show. This did little to alleviate my worries, though David Kernan encouraged me to discuss potential orchestration changes with our music director, hereby known as Kate Young, MD (I know, she sounds like a television series!) Seconds later, I was on the phone with Kate, and we're meeting Friday. Barbara requested a meeting with me as well.

What I began to discover was Vivian, while appearing open and accessible, would express his feelings before you came to the first comma. When he and Barbara Bonfigli arrived at my flat to discuss my latest rewrites, she had barely begun when Vivian jumped right in saying, "I must interrupt, honey. I must say what you're doing is dangerous. It doesn't allow us to discover things in rehearsal. I really can't approve these notes before we have a chance to work with the scene."

Now, he was perfectly justified, but his tone was condescending and quickly silenced her. While I was not legally bound to accept Barbara's suggestions, we should have been given the opportunity to hear them and then decide which to take seriously. Certain cuts prior to the rehearsal process can be helpful, and I was amazed Barbara had come up with some apt eliminations. But what Vivian did was to disrespectfully thwart a producer. In many ways, I felt there was an invisible alarm system that surrounded him, and if you stepped one or two inches in the wrong direction, there wasn't a warning light but a veritable siren!

David Kernan requested I play an active part in the musical rehearsals, but to be safe, I first consulted with Vivian. He wasn't as enthusiastic about the idea and asked me to keep a low profile so there was no confusing who was boss. Fair enough. But then the next morning on the phone he casually mentioned, "By the way, I hope you haven't got anything planned for the first few days because after the show is completely blocked, I'm turning the cast over to you for music." (Could David Kernan have spoken to Vivian in the interim?)

Barbara drove me to Leatherhead the following Thursday in her snazzy convertible. She reminded me that Allah (or to whomever she prayed) would decide if we should get there in one piece. Considering her disregard for the speed limit, a higher power surely must have played a starring role!

When we arrived, Gordon ushered us in where all the principals behind the scenes were assembled minus Roger (the artistic director), who we were told was—surprise—"on holiday." Chris, our set designer, had a three-dimensional model complete with lights to suggest some lighting effects.

Barbara asked a question, which Vivian treated with his customary disdain, punctuated with a "honey." (Everyone else was "love," but Barbara was always "honey." Somehow "love" didn't sound sexist, but "honey" reeked of misogyny.)

Things suddenly got tense when Martin, the technical director, mentioned that he couldn't get us into the theater until that final Monday, possibly in the early afternoon. Considering we were to open on a *Tuesday night*, this was of little comfort to Vivian. A matter of contention from our last meeting two weeks before, it was supposed to have been ironed out by Roger, David Kernan, and Barbara. David, who arrived looking quite dapper having just attended a funeral (in a suede jacket, no less!) was displeased concessions had not been made.

We then turned our attention to Gordon, the Thorndike's business manager, to see if we could possibly buy more time by treating our original opening night, Tuesday, as a dress rehearsal and not selling tickets. He informed us that was not possible, as the brochures had gone out, and the box office had already begun to accept ticket requests. Barbara asked if the ticket holders could be notified by phone if necessary. Gordon said that was not possible, and he didn't want to instruct "the ladies in the box office" about a change of schedule, as they would be "inconvenienced."

When I heard that word, I bristled. Weren't *we* being "inconvenienced" by being given insufficient time to tech and rehearse our show onstage? I asked Gordon what would happen if they simply canceled the performance only to add another performance for these ticketholders at a later date.

Before Gordon could answer, Vivian interjected, "Doug, you don't understand these people but being an artistic director, I do. These are not the same people who attend performances at The Hudson Guild." I said I *did* understand but wondered what would happen if an actor fell sick? Wouldn't they have to cancel the performance? "No," Vivian replied for Gordon, "they just have someone stand with a script and read."

"Well," I countered, "when they had to postpone the first previews of *Legs Diamond* by a few weeks, the Mark Hellinger Theatre was able to cope."

Looking back, I can't believe I used *Legs Diamond*, one of the most notorious Broadway flops, as an example. Certainly, that did not bode well for our little show.

"Douglas, love," Vivian continued, "Trust me, I know from experience. These people are a different breed altogether. It would be chaos if they were told that the performance had been canceled—"

"But Vivian, Gordon isn't saying the *patrons* won't accept a change in performance. He's saying he doesn't want his box office *staff* to be 'inconvenienced.' If they've only sold a small number of seats, why can't they just explain to their patrons—"

"No, love," Vivian continued; the uses of "love" were growing in intensity. "We can't just come in here like we're renting their space and ask them to change their spots!"

I suddenly realized I wasn't arguing a point with Gordon but with my own director. I felt like Paul Newman, the prosecuting attorney in *The Verdict*, confronting Milo O'Shea, the judge: "Your Honor, with all due respect: if you're going to try my case for me, I wish you wouldn't lose it." I ceased fire, but added, "I don't want them to change their spots, but I *do* know what kind of audience patronizes their theatre."

I must have said it with some authority for Vivian later apologized to me and said that when I mentioned the Mark Hellinger Theatre, Gordon's hair "stood on end."

As I noted in my journal, *Frankly, it would be difficult to tell if Gordon had a sudden coronary and died. The man does not project a personality.*

What's infuriating is that until a week ago, Gordon had never read the script, yet he assigned a budget to each major area. This means that our costumes were originally allotted only fifteen hundred pounds! David and Barbara got Gordon to consent to twenty-five hundred pounds, but that doesn't approach the amount of money needed to do a professional job. Gordon would not allow any more money to be spent on the production, lest it affect "the Global budget." ("Global" was to become a big catch phrase that day.) Gordon had also told David Kernan that wigs would be an additional part of the budget, but Thursday he said they were part of the costumes, which left even less for Tim, our costume designer.

Every time Gordon opened his mouth to answer David Kernan's questions, he insisted that the lines between what one spends on costumes, sets, or props can blur, but "globally the budget stands firm." Gordon had also neglected to figure sound into the budget, and now we are told that is to come from the set *budget! I really think they believe they are producing another* Stepping Out: *one set and two costume changes. They probably asked the performers to bring their own tap shoes!*

Some problems were resolved. Martin, the technical director, upon hearing my altercation with Gordon and Vivian, decided that if he could hire extra workers and use split shifts, we might be able to start our first tech Sunday night at 7:00, instead of Monday at 2:00 p.m., a tremendous savings of time. Vivian added that if we had our first performance Tuesday night, he could make a pleasant little pre-curtain speech explaining that the audience is really privileged to see a final dress rehearsal.

Vivian and I felt the gray-haired ladies would be enamored!

However, I was far from "enamored" with the brochure announcing the autumn/winter schedule. In fact, I haven't seen a more ludicrous illustration to accompany a show in my lifetime! It features a coffin (yes, you read that right) with the lid slightly ajar and musical notes issuing forth from where a body presumably lies. Don't ask me what music it is: If the

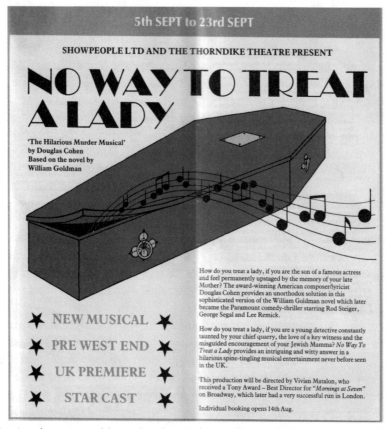

Don't judge a musical by its brochure: The Thorndike Theatre announces the UK premiere of No Way to Treat a Lady. Author's collection

Thorndike Theatre didn't bother to read my show, they certainly wouldn't strive for authenticity in the music represented. I'm only thankful the person who designed the brochure is not designing our musical!

What strikes me as I review these notes from over thirty years ago—besides the nearly insurmountable challenges we faced—is how Anglicized I'm beginning to sound. It feels as if Vivian and company had a profound impact on how I expressed myself, like I was submitting to Stockholm syndrome. And in a way, I was losing much of my identity as an American. Yet I was resistant to assimilating for fear I would not stand firm on the issues. And the next few weeks were going to test my stamina and sanity.

10

"YESHIVA STUDENT" IN CHISWICK CHURCH

On the eve of our first rehearsal, I went to the Lyric Theatre and bought a ticket for the final performance of *Steel Magnolias* starring the great Rosemary Harris. Vanessa Redgrave suddenly appeared in the lobby wearing a striking white turban and no makeup. She was starring next door in *A Madhouse in Goa* by Martin Sherman and was displaying brochures for her show!

I approached her with a mixture of awe and trepidation.

"Excuse me, Miss Redgrave, but I just wanted to tell you how deeply your performances have affected me."

She was gracious, her eyes generated by some candle-watt power. I asked her what she was doing at the Lyric, and she mentioned her leaflets. I added, "Isn't there someone else who could make the rounds?" and she looked at me quizzically. *Of course,* I thought to myself, *This is a woman who won an Oscar for playing Julia, a doomed heroine who dared to smuggle Jews out of Nazi Germany. She purportedly funded a documentary on the Palestine Liberation Organization by selling her home. Why shouldn't she step next door to distribute a few fliers?*

I then remembered William Goldman's advice to me: "Doug, you have to be your own cocksucker." Maybe that's what Vanessa Redgrave was doing by watching her own back and indulging in a little self-promotion. It was comforting to see we had "so much in common."

Later that night as I climbed into bed and pulled the comforter under my chin, I ruminated over our impending first rehearsal, just hours away. Three weeks earlier, we had our first day of auditions. Then all this time had elapsed while I wandered around the countryside and most of London, intermittently performing rewrites, mostly to serve as a reminder of why I was there.

I was anxious. I didn't expect the piece or the actors to be letter perfect at our first read-through . . . but I wanted our cast to be good, and above all, I wanted my work to be good. By putting my life in the States on hold and traveling all that distance, it seemed only fair that I be granted a good show.

8/5/1989

Our first day of rehearsal did not start auspiciously.

It was called for 11:00 a.m. in Chiswick, London: Due to the lack of rehearsal space at the Thorndike, our producers secured a sizable room in a church in Turnham Green, an hour from the theater. This morning, I got up in plenty of time, meditated, ate, showered, and allowed for an additional half hour for vocal warm-ups, as I would be singing the entire score for the read-through. I guess my chords were rusty, and a half hour didn't suffice . . . so it soon became forty minutes, then fifty minutes, then finally I realized I'd be late, so I tore myself away. I just missed the tube to Earl's Court by thirty seconds and expected another train any minute. This was not to be. Twenty minutes went by and still no train. All the terrific benefits that I derived from meditating evaporated. Finally, the blasted train came, and I got to Earl's Court where I then waited another five minutes for the connecting train . . . before embarking on an interminable ride of five stops before my stop at Turnham Green. It was 10:52, so I ran. (Why do I always end up meeting people in a sweat?)

Dashing through the town, my eyes desperately roamed the countryside for a church.

I asked two denizens who pointed to one I had mistakenly passed. I retraced my steps and ran inside. All I saw was the inside of a church: Of course, there was Jesus and the Virgin Mary, but no sign of our cast. And though producers and directors often act like God, I doubted if they would assume such a likeness. (Too "on the nose.") I saw a woman kneeling in prayer. I didn't want to disturb her, but I was desperate for directions. I went over and politely asked her where I could find rehearsal rooms. She shifted her eyes from Jesus and told me she would take me there. People who pray in church, however, don't just leave right away, despite my great sense of urgency. She kneeled or curtsied, then crossed herself. Then she walked a few feet, passing another statue of Jesus and had to repeat the bowing and crossing all over again. At the door, she stopped to dab herself with holy water.

Finally, she took me outside and pointed to another building where David Kernan was standing, sighing with relief. I ran over to him as he patted me on my sweaty shirt and led me into the huge rehearsal hall where everyone was assembled in anticipation of the reading. David announced, "I found him!" and I lamely explained that I had been to the wrong church and had already been "baptized and confirmed." This brought some laughter, but then I began to perspire profusely and started fanning myself with a letter from home.

Vivian asked me if I was ready to sing. I made a feeble gesture, then went over to the piano to join Kate Young, MD. I started off with Kit's brief opening stanza of "Five More Minutes," for which I accompanied myself before turning the piano over to Kate. My mistake! She sounded as if she had attended the Wrong Note Rag Conservatory! I guess she was mostly sightreading. When we finally got to "Killer on the Line," I thought David and Barbara might tear up my contract. It was humiliating. And then every ten minutes, I'd have to explain to Kate that the music had changed, or we couldn't find the music, resulting in interminable pauses filled with only my nervous laugh. By the end of the reading, I was croaking out the tunes. The low point came when I sat down to play the new song ("So Much in Common") and forgot how it went!

After my ordeal, Vivian dismissed everyone except the stage management and the cast. He had a lovely speech prepared articulating how excited he was about the piece and how fortunate he felt as our director. He also said it had been written by "a terrifically gifted young man . . . and he is *very* young," and went on to say that "there are themes, but we shouldn't concern ourselves with what they are. Actors should not perform themes but characters and should not be obsessed with reality but rather truth." He warned against camp, which he felt we could easily play if we weren't careful. But he did emphasize how the piece must be entertaining or the murders would be unwatchable. It was a speech so beautifully presented that a great sense of calm washed over me. I thought back to when Jack Hofsiss first started rehearsals. He didn't say much about the show, but his gift for gab put us at ease. Vivian had a similar gift, but his speech was substantive. And the differences didn't end there.

All my previous feelings of combativeness with Vivian ended that first day. I could see instantly that he was every inch the industrious worker he claimed to be. Now he was in control, and I felt we were in the most capable hands. All those weeks Vivian must have been "waiting in the wings" in nervous anticipation, eager to contribute.

Since that first day of rehearsal, Vivian and I demonstrated nothing but the greatest of mutual respect. I could barely wait to finish individual music sessions with the cast before witnessing him in action.

It's difficult to capture the way Vivian worked, but I'll attempt two examples.

He instructed David Burt (Kit) that despite Kit's humiliating "audition" at the top of the show, when he sings "Five more minutes to places, tell those butterflies that they'd best be gone, only five more minutes—I'm on," it must *not* be done with venom, or he'll telegraph to the audience he has murder on his mind. Rather, Kit's anger disappears as he faces the dressing room mirror and prepares for his "entrance." The child in him takes over: the delight in performing, the anticipation of an opening night in all its splendor, psychologically priming himself. It's all performed with great joy, so the audience is held off-balance, unsure of how to grasp the situation.

Later, when Martin and Susannah ran their "So Far, So Good" song and scene, Vivian observed that whenever they performed too sensitively or preciously, the scene lost energy and charm. He astutely observed that it's winning when grown-ups exhibit some of the insecurities and infatuations associated with teenagers. When Morris asks for orange juice in lieu of coffee, Vivian directed Martin to stare into Susannah's eyes, as if he's just confessed his deepest, darkest secret. Here are two people on the verge of making a first, tentative step toward a relationship.

Vivian and I were so often in sync that sometimes I didn't even need to say a word—he could read my face perfectly. If I looked somewhat vexed, complete with a furrowed brow, Vivian christened it my "yeshiva" look. (A yeshiva student is devoted to studying the Jewish Talmud, the body of Jewish civil and ceremonial law.) It's ironic since I was brought up a Reform Jew, which compared to a yeshiva student is akin to saying I'm a gentile.

Whenever I would get that look, Vivian would excuse us from rehearsal and walk five paces outside of the nearest exit door, which he labeled his "office." He always wanted to approve any comments I had about the acting and/or writing *before* the actors had a chance to hear. In this way, the note would always come from Vivian, so there was no disputing who was in charge.

On August 17, everything was going swimmingly until I started putting two and two together. When Martin Smith left rehearsals early, I asked, "What's the matter? Don't you like us anymore?" He merely responded, "This is something that was set up before I got involved with this show." Two days later when I heard the word "callback," I enquired, "Oh, is this a commercial?" Martin replied, "Vivian's going to talk with you later."

Immediately, I began to panic. I was so aware of all those times my parents kept bad news from me. Whenever I was away from them for more than a week or even a weekend (summer camp, a school trip, college), I would enjoy an ebullient homecoming followed almost immediately with the inevitable "talk" which began with, "We didn't want to upset you, *but . . .*," and then they'd proceed to inform me of 1) the death of a beloved relative, 2) the death of a beloved family pet, 3) distressing news about the health of a beloved relative or family pet, or 4) any other distressing news that they felt would interfere with my welfare. In the last category, my parents waited until I came home from camp before disclosing Ted Kennedy had plunged his car off the bridge at Chappaquiddick. I'm not sure if they thought the report would have impacted a crucial game of capture the flag, but it got so bad that I dreaded going home. Now, thousands of miles away, people were doing the exact same thing, covertly sheltering me from an approaching storm. I wondered if my parents were somehow involved.

I told Martin I couldn't wait for Vivian to tell me. He put his arm around me, led me outside, and said, "You have me for Leatherhead." I asked, "Do we have you for the West End?" And he repeated, "You have me for Leatherhead." Then he went on to reveal he would most likely be cast as the Phantom as soon as Sir Andrew Lloyd Webber gave his consent; Martin's final audition was scheduled for that night. I was sure he'd get the role (he was 99 percent certain), and all I could think about was how much I wanted to cry: I felt so entirely helpless—here was a wonderful performer slipping from our grasp simply because Showpeople didn't have the commitment of a West End Theatre. I foolishly resented them, as well as Messrs. Mackintosh and Lloyd Webber for plundering our cast.

Martin explained how he had no assurance *Lady* would go to the West End, and now he would make a thousand pounds a week playing the Phantom of the Opera. Who could blame him, although I believed it would be better to originate a role instead of hiding behind a stifling mask for a year. I felt betrayed, jealous, sad, suddenly aware that this "party" in London (or Leatherhead or Turnham Green) would soon end for me in a few weeks, and the future was a frightening prospect.

I told Martin I felt helpless giving him Jewish guilt, as he wasn't Jewish. He gave me a playful slap and said, "Behave yourself." I left to copy music where I came close to breaking down. When I returned to rehearsal, he had bought a piece of cheesecake for me. (Song cue: "Cheesecake, he bought me cheesecake, from Marks & Spencer, imagine that?") It was a thoughtful gesture, but I'd rather have had the assurance he'd remain in the role.

Vivian called me upstairs a few hours later and told me the very same news. I feigned ignorance to protect Martin. (My early acting chops were being put to good use.) Vivian reminded me that no actor is indispensable, it would be more catastrophic to lose David Burt, and having seen only Martin audition for the role, there was the possibility of better candidates. He emphasized the show was the star, and even he was dispensable. On that last point, I disagreed.

Perhaps as a distraction or maybe out of necessity, Vivian asked me to consider writing a new song for Morris after he and Kit have their first real communication, and Kit confesses to being a "bad boy." This was to replace a mini reprise of "Five More Minutes." (Yes, I had stubbornly reinstated that song as an opening number, defying the lessons learned at the Hudson Guild.) Vivian felt the moment Morris receives the "call to adventure" should be more substantive and illustrate the possibilities presenting themselves. I went to work right away on a song called "Never Again," which essentially dealt with Morris saying, "I'm no longer taking a back seat to the other guys." The music and lyrics were very generic (like a poor imitation of a Frank Wildhorn song), and the more I worked on it, the less I liked it. I played it for Vivian, and although he was very polite, I could tell he didn't like it either. We talked about the moment, and Vivian perceptively noted that I'd never written about why Morris became a cop and what he really hopes to achieve. For some reason a William Goldman line from the novel kept echoing in my mind: "Goliath from the neck down." It's Flora's term of "endearment" which riles Moe. Vivian also felt the line resonated. I told him I wanted to give the moment another try. He gave me his blessing and left around 7:00 p.m.

By 9:00 p.m., I had completed the song and was so proud that I didn't want to wait until morning to play it for Vivian. I tried calling him to ask if I could come over that night . . . only his line was busy. Undaunted, I took the subway to Earl's Court and walked to the flat he was subletting from Alec McCowen. It was 10:15 p.m. when I pressed the intercom button, and Vivian's voice sounded surprised and not particularly overjoyed. However, he buzzed me up, opening the door while noting, "Well, you must be pretty enthusiastic about the number to have raced over." Suddenly, I realized maybe this wasn't such a good idea, but at 10:15 it was too late to apologize and head home. I played Vivian the song, and he was quite moved and asked me to play it again and then a third time. He made a lyric suggestion (a splendid one), but otherwise he found the song just right. I didn't know if it worked within the context of the show, but I did know I'd written a damn good song.

Looking back on my experience in London, this moment stands out as perhaps the apotheosis of my three months. Amid Alec McCowen's Queen Anne furnishings and generous theater memorabilia, I performed on his modest spinet, my voice gliding over the opening phrase:

GOLIATH FROM THE NECK DOWN—
ALL BRAWN, SURE, AND NO BRAIN.
BUT COULD I BE A HERO
IF I'M ABLE TO CATCH CAIN?

GOLIATH FROM THE NECK DOWN
BUT I'LL PROVE THAT I'M SMART:
A GIANT WITH A FRAGILE HEART.

HISTORY SAYS GOLIATH LOST
WHEN HE STEPPED INTO THE RING.
HE GOT A ROCK BETWEEN THE EYES
WHILE DAVID WAS MADE A KING . . .

GOLIATH FROM THE NECK DOWN!
IS THAT ALL I'LL EVER HEAR?
IF I UNLOCK WHAT'S INSIDE ME
WILL A DAVID APPEAR?

The next day, when I played the song for David Kernan and Barbara Bonfigli, they were complimentary, but David wondered, "Is this a song Sinatra is likely to record?" However, that previous night with an audience of one, I felt I had answered Joseph Campbell's "call to adventure." It was also when I felt closest to Vivian, as if I had just shared some intimate secret, forging a common bond. No matter what would eventually transpire, that moment was pure and lyrical and ours.

8/19/1989

Well, we did lose Martin; he didn't even have to see Lloyd Webber. I remember at 5:30 Thursday, Martin, Vivian, and Susannah were working on "Sarah's Touch" and the subsequent scene. During the break, when I asked Martin what time he had to be at Lloyd Webber's, he replied "I don't have to go now." "The part is yours?" I asked, dying a little death inside. "Yes," he responded. Then after we said our perfunctory "congrats" and "thank you," he added "I'm going to go out and buy a convertible."

That line reverberated in my ears all that night and the next morning. Up until this time, I had tried not to judge Martin, but suddenly I started to question his values. Didn't the four performers at the Hudson Guild work their asses off for three months (with no commercial producers in the wings) for $150 per week? Why? Because they believed in the show and knew what it could mean to their careers and their growth as performers. Martin as the Phantom will be the third or fourth actor to play the role in England, so he'll be seen mostly by tourists who won't

remember him except that they saw A.L.W.'s Phantom of the Opera.
*He'll be imprisoned for a year, having to arrive at the theater at least two
hours ahead of time for that hideous makeup, and he'll only be onstage for
less than forty-five minutes (and most of the time his face will be covered
by that friggin' mask). Plus, he's performed Che in* Evita *for Hal Prince
and Lloyd Webber, so it's not as if he's suddenly been invited into their
"inner circle." The more I thought about it, the more I began to resent
Martin and his decision.*

    *The next morning at 10:00, I was scheduled to teach him "Goliath
from the Neck Down." I went in practically baring my teeth. I decided I
wouldn't say a word about* Phantom *or the people he must have called
with the news. All I said was, "How are you?" and Martin replied, "A
little hung over." So, I said, "Oh, were you out celebrating?" And he
told me he had taken his vocal teacher out, a man who recently went
through open heart surgery, and Martin felt winning the role was a dual
victory. I asked him if he had called his parents, and he said, "Not unless
I can call heaven." He explained they were both dead—his mother had
died in her fifties a few years ago of cancer, his father had died of heart
failure ten years ago at sixty-two. He also told me a little bit about his
childhood in Glasgow, Scotland. Growing up in a working-class family,
they had very little. But like other working-class families, they put a high
premium on music, and there was always a piano in their home. He had
discovered his pianist gifts when he was three (Martin was very accomplished), and at sixteen set out to be a performer. He never attended any
school after that. His mother died when he was on a soap opera, knowing
at last he was financially secure. He also mentioned going to California
for a brief time last February and discovering that his French male lover
of more than a year had been having an affair behind his back. Sure
enough, the night Martin found out about* Phantom, *he called his ex
to rub it in.*

    *I began to understand Martin and his decision. The car and the inte-
rior decorating (he plans to give his flat a face lift) may be trappings, but
for someone who has never fully experienced these luxuries, they're important. Since Martin doesn't have a diploma to point to on his wall, the role
of the Phantom is almost a substitute sheepskin—he's "graduated" to the
big time. After spending half his life in the profession, it must be something of a milestone. And finally, it all comes down to ego: In* No Way
to Treat a Lady, *he would have a wonderful role but not one with Kit's*

Susannah Fellows as Sarah with Martin Smith as Detective Brummell. Thorndike Theatre, Leatherhead, September 1989, directed by Vivian Matalon. Frank Page

"flash." In Phantom, *he's the titular character and center stage when he's on, and this is where Martin needs to be right now—for his ex-lover, for future lovers, for his friends, for his voice teacher, etc. What I think is sad is that a lot of these things will quickly evaporate, and Martin, who seems to be someone who thrives on a challenge, will be left with a somewhat routine job . . . for an entire year. Not only is he saying "No" to* Lady *but also future productions of* Sunday in the Park with George *and* Into the Woods. *He will be a fine replacement, but he won't be available to originate roles.*

Frankly, I was now concerned for the rest of the cast. Susannah had already told Vivian that she'd been offered the Kate Nelligan role in *Spoils of War* and was tempted to take it: She wanted to do something non-musical and was upset at losing Martin. She worried about our finding a suitable replacement (which was ironic since the only person who had even been discussed was her current partner, Teddy Kempner, a wonderful West End performer who later became her husband; to be fair, Teddy was physically the antithesis of Martin and more closely resembled the schleppy gumshoes of previous productions).

David Kernan came by later, and addressing him in person helped me to understand his position. He explained that even if Showpeople were to raise all the money, London theater owners were tasked with numerous shows waiting to come in and few theaters available. It sounded eerily like Broadway.

So we were forced to play the waiting game. Considering September 10 was only two and a half weeks away, this was not an eternity. David emphasized that he hoped Susannah and the rest of the cast would realize what we had was special and worth their commitment. He also scheduled eight different "Morris" candidates to audition.

Meanwhile, the "killer surprise ending" still proved to be elusive:

Vivian had some sensational suggestions regarding the final scene. He staged everything up to where Morris says, "Screw the case." Then he suggested that Morris eventually should say to Kit, "You're a lousy actor," and go head-to-head with him as Morris assumes the role of a "director" to gain the upper hand. Ironically, it's drawing upon elements found in the opening "audition" where Kit is also at the mercy of a director.

Well, I wrote the scene in five minutes and came up with a wickedly funny line of which I'm very proud. After Morris begins to exit to locate Sarah tied up in the next room, Kit cries out in desperation, "Morris, please don't go," mirroring his plea to his mother in "I've Been a Bad Boy." Morris turns around and utters, "Don't call us, we'll call you." Isn't that a killer line? (Please say yes!)

Toward the end of the day, we all had a meeting with the Leatherhead production team. Everyone met us at Chiswick including our producers Barbara and David, and Roger, the artistic director, back from "holiday." I was feeling faint—there was little ventilation in the room and five people were smoking—and was desperately hungry. I excused myself, went into the kitchen, and ravaged the last digestive biscuit plus the cheesecake Martin had gifted me.

When I returned, I walked into what seemed to be the Six Day War, or at least the Falklands skirmish! Vivian was publicly attacking Leatherhead for never having attended our first reading or bothering to call Vivian to ask how things were progressing, or even stopping by for a Saturday rehearsal. "I ran a theater for many years, and I would never treat a director in this shabby manner," Vivian protested. "Either you treat me as a member of your team, or we can say our goodbyes." Martin, the technical director, took great umbrage with this argument, until Vivian pointed out, "Martin, love, I'm not talking to you. You might as well not be here. I'm so happy with you, I'd marry you."

Finally, Gordon (business manager) spoke up. "I think Vivian's referring to me, Martin, and I feel I have been remiss." He then added, "I would like to publicly apologize for my lack of involvement. It is not typical of the way we conduct business at Leatherhead."

It was a great triumph for Vivian.

The more I worked with him, the more I believed his reputation for being "difficult" wasn't warranted. Rather, Vivian struck me as a consummate professional who always did his homework and expected others to maintain the same professional standards. When they disappointed him, he was justifiably angered. From what Vivian related, this happened during *The Tap Dance Kid* on Broadway and was happening with Leatherhead and our current producing team. Vivian had a modicum of respect for David Kernan, who he believed would be better served if he weren't partnering with "those two rich ladies."

While I was writing the new final scene, Vivian came in and started chatting. Referring to his defiant stance in the Leatherhead meeting, he said it didn't take courage but rather a "moral duty": He was provoked, and this was his only response. He mentioned that he once went through a traumatic experience as a child of fifteen when he attended military school in Jamaica. A heavy child, Vivian was perpetually taunted in drills by his teacher, Mr. Donlevy. One day, Vivian decided he wouldn't take any more abuse and feigned forgetting to report to practice until Donlevy personally came to fetch him. Later, on the field, when the other students took a step forward, Vivian took a step backward and vice versa. This continued for a while until Donlevy screamed at Vivian and ordered him to bend over for a public beating.

The way Vivian related it, he had an out-of-body experience as he observed himself striking Donlevy twice over the shoulder with his rifle, crying out, "For years I have done nothing but follow orders and you continued to hurt me and ridicule me simply because I'm fat! Well, not this time!" Donlevy was stunned. Vivian was taken into custody and the headmaster, a decent man, threatened him with expulsion unless Donlevy was permitted to beat him. Vivian responded, "Sir, I disobeyed orders and should be beaten . . . by anyone *but* Mr. Donlevy." Eventually, the school had to submit to Vivian's wishes, or he threatened to expose their sadistic ways, apparently in violation of protocol.

That story revealed more about Vivian than anything else I was privileged to observe. At the time, I noted, *Vivian is a fair person who listens to reason and is willing to accept the consequences of his actions . . . but he will not submit to the Donlevys of the world.*

Tuesday, 8/22/1989 9:15 p.m.

Oh, I am steaming! If there's one thing I dislike, it's a lackadaisical attitude toward work.

I hadn't realized it but when Vivian invited David Kernan to Saturday's run-through, David replied, "Does it have to be Saturday? Monday is a bank holiday, you know," meaning, "I really would rather go away for the weekend." This is his f-ing show we're talking about! The one he and Barbara are "dying to see," the one they reminded us they put their own money into, as if to say, "so we must care." How dare he intimate that the run-through isn't paramount. It's an insult to Vivian and me. Here we are busting our asses, and they can't afford to give up a Saturday. My God, I haven't been home before 10:30, 11:00 every night. I see theatre only on Saturday night. I don't own a television or a radio. I've rewritten scenes so many times I've stopped counting, in addition to writing three new numbers and a new reprise in the last three weeks.

One of those new songs, "Lunch with Sarah" replaced "A Killer on the Line" and would ultimately become one of my favorite songs in the show. A musical scene, it dramatizes how Morris's romance with Sarah erodes as he doggedly pursues contact with Kit. Beginning as a breezy jazz waltz, it soon morphs into a child-like, sing-songy bridge which turns slightly maniacal when Morris realizes he may have lost Kit's support:

CALL PLEASE
CALL ME ON THE LINE
TELL ME YOU'RE NOT MAD
AND I'LL KNOW EVERYTHING IS FINE.
IF YOU CALL *NOW*
WHY THE LONG DELAY?
MOMENTS PASS AND MINUTES FLY
IT'S NOW ONE WHOLE DAY!
AND THERE'S *NO WORD!*
I'M ABOUT TO DROP.
COULD IT BE YOU'RE SOUNDING OFF
TO SOME *OTHER* COP?!!

Luckily for the performer, the song is obsessive without becoming strenuous. (Apologies to Peter Slutsker for all the previous heavy lifting!)

I also wrote a reprise of "So Far, So Good" for Sarah after Moe prematurely leaves her candlelit dinner . . . but not before she cajoles an invitation to have brunch with his mother. I was particularly pleased with the bridge:

ALL RIGHT, ENOUGH!
WHY DWELL ON WHAT WENT WRONG?
I'VE HIT SOME STUMBLING BLOCKS,
NOW CLOSE THE BOX, PANDORA.

SOON ANY DAY
FAY WRAY WILL MEET KING KONG
WHEN SARAH STONE IS INTRODUCED TO FLORA!

As for the brilliant "killer" ending that Vivian and I concocted a week earlier, my journal refutes prior feelings of optimism:

Please disregard previous scribblings in this diary proclaiming we came upon the perfect finish—it ain't working. Vivian had sheltered me from rehearsals of the final scene so I would see it "in toto." Well, what I saw missed the mark (David Burt was "over the top"), but more importantly, the scene was not accomplishing what I had hoped. Somehow, Morris adopting the lingo of a stage director and playing critic to Kit's acting didn't ring true. And Kit seemed as manic as ever, forever "acting." There was a single, honest moment, however: when Morris ridicules Kit and says, "What? You care for me?" Kit's response, a quiet "yes," was moving and seemed genuine, reflecting the soul of the man.

After this debacle, it was 6:00 p.m. and Vivian, Lindsay, and I went upstairs to discuss what went wrong. Vivian said, "It's a shame because we're so close to a good show. If we could just solve the last scene."

For me, this echoed Moss Hart's great conundrum in *Act One*—how to solve act three in *Once in a Lifetime*.

I explained to Vivian that this has been my greatest challenge for the last four years, and I was exasperated. We all agreed that what was inherently wrong with the scene was Morris, having a distinct edge by possessing the only weapon, looked positively callous engaging in psychological banter with Kit instead of searching for Sarah. His repeating "Where's Sarah?" seemed idiotic considering Kit's loft is not constructed like the Hampton Court maze: There are only so many doors—if Moe is truly interested, he should find her.

It dawned on me that what was so effective about Carleton (Kit in disguise) and Sarah's previous scene was at one point they are both talking about the same person, Morris, but Sarah has no idea Carleton's "friend" is her lover. The audience shares her horror as she comes to this gradual realization. Why couldn't the Kit/Morris scene operate in a similar vein with Kit as Carleton shooting the breeze while Sarah is presumably in the loo. Carleton, in his attempts to unburden his soul to Morris, talks about his "friend" (aptly named "Kit") who desires affection from another person. Slowly but surely, Morris realizes Carleton *is* Kit, and Morris is the person Kit cares deeply about. In essence, it is a confession of love delivered obtusely. And it is one of the few times the true Kit emerges—someone with basic human needs who unfortunately doesn't know how to channel them productively. Morris, realizing he is face to face with the Strangler, doesn't panic, as Kit subtly lets Morris know he was unable to kill Sarah.

Writing the scene was a real challenge, but two hours later I was done. It was so dramatically different from any ending I'd attempted that I was concerned: There was no big confrontation, no "Oh, my God! What have you done with her, you bastard?!" It was almost faintly reminiscent of *To Kill a Mockingbird*'s final scene when Boo Radley is revealed as someone who is more a victim than a villain, capable of tenderness and compassion. Atticus Finch's "Mr. Radley, thank you for my children," is not unlike Morris's "Thank you, Kit," after Kit indicates where he's hidden Sarah. There was something oddly dignified about this conclusion as well. After Vivian worked on it with the actors, he invited me to look at it. I wept (well, I teared actually). Sensing my work on the ending was finally over, I was relieved and more than a little sad.

Tuesday, 8/29/1989

The big news is we finally did a run-through for David and Barbara. The first half of the show (sixty-nine minutes) seemed to fly by. "Safer in My Arms" had improved considerably: I didn't attribute this to rehearsal as much as interference from Vivian and me—Lindsay took my sugges-tion and cut a section out of Carmella's portion of the tango. Not only did this mean that Vivienne Martin had less to remember, but it also helped her over a psychological hurdle. She was enlivened and began perform-ing the number with great gusto. It's amazing how important a person's expressions are in a dance number: When the face registers enjoyment, it's almost secondary what their feet are doing.

The second half of the show, which we've always maintained was the easier act, did not fare as well. The actors, feeling confident that the worst was behind them, began to coast a bit, and we lost energy and momentum. This was especially apparent in the last scene, which was most unfortunate as we were keenly aware of Showpeople's scrutiny. David Burt forgot most of Vivian's direction, and the result was long-winded, anti-climactic, and aimless.

After Vivian gave his notes to the cast, he, Lindsay, and I met with David Kernan and Barbara Bonfigli in a small conference room at the Thorndike. They began by saying how pleased they were with the show, then went on to mostly harp on two issues: "Once More from the Top" and the final scene. With the former, I was in total agreement, although there was a difference of opinion as to what was wrong. David felt the number was too busy and not tight in its execution, like "One" in *A Chorus Line*. He felt the movements did not suggest a "show biz" number and the choreography couldn't decide on its objective—a perfectly valid summation of its problems.

Then it was Barbara's turn. "I felt David Burt looked faggy," she began.

The room was so silent you could hear a pin drop. "What do you mean, darling?" Vivian queried.

"You know, he seemed very gay," Barbara responded.

"What is that supposed to mean?" Vivian asked incredulously. "When I hear that word 'gay,' I take it to mean one is happy."

Barbara began to grope for the appropriate words.

"David seemed very coy," she explained.

Vivian pretended not to understand. "By coy, darling, do you mean *effeminate*?"

It was as if we were playing Password, and Vivian had just won a crucial round.

"Yes!" Barbara exclaimed. "David Burt seemed *effeminate*."

Now it was Lindsay's turn. "I don't understand, Barbara. He only has a few hand gestures."

"Oh, come on, he didn't stop moving," Barbara elaborated. "I decided that he must be dressing up in women's clothes as he's performing the number."

Once again, the room fell silent.

"Where did you see that?" Lindsay sputtered.

"It looked like at one point he was getting into a dress for the drag scene," she said somewhat defensively.

David Kernan tried to soften the blow, but the damage had been done: Lindsay's eyes glazed over and Vivian's reflected daggers.

Vivian said his interpretation of the moment was, "When all else fails, Kit decides 'I'm a successful legit actor—now I'll conquer musicals.'"

I explained that I felt Kit was playing make believe, as he did as a child, and a Fred Astaire–type number allowed him to truly escape into the world of fantasy, demonstrating he's losing his grasp on reality.

No matter how each of us interpreted the song, David and Barbara were unhappy and insisted that the staging be re-imagined. Since I too was not a fan of the choreography, I secretly breathed a sigh of relief.

Then they began to discuss the last scene. With this, they were both in agreement and expressed themselves in similar terms: it was anti-climactic, talky, undramatic, implausible. We tried to defend the scene by saying it was under-rehearsed, but this didn't quell their fears. Both David and Barbara craved a film noir–type ending where Detective and Killer square off until it ends in bloodshed. Barbara detested any hints that Kit was secretly "gay"—she felt it was gratuitous and not a true explanation of his motives and feelings. On this second point, I was partially in agreement: Before Morris surfaced on the scene, Kit's killing spree was ignited by his obsession with stardom and competition with his mother. Vivian explained the present scene had plenty of tension when performed correctly. They disagreed and felt that once Morris realizes he is face to face with a killer, he would pounce on Kit. I agreed to give them a more "suspenseful" ending, which meant rewriting it for the forty-eighth time!

I was tempted to call William Goldman as a sounding board, but we were in two separate continents with two distinct time zones. Besides, hadn't Bill and I already arrived at a solution which I was now abandoning due to pressure from my producers? Hadn't he given me advice to stand my ground and watch my back? I realized it was too late to reinstate the earlier version of the show with rapiers, and without a collaborator, I had to solve this alone. It was not a comforting thought.

The next day, I attended band call. The new arrangements by Jason Carr were exciting, especially "Lunch with Sarah," which is probably my favorite arrangement in the show. Kate revealed an orchestration of "Goliath," which was quite effective while remaining faithful to my original piano arrangement. (Let me explain that I'm using "quite" in the American sense meaning "very or rather," not the English definition of the word meaning "just okay." It's like their word "brilliant," which they overuse until it no longer signifies brilliance. For example, someone will say, "I think rather than meeting friends, I'm going to stay home, go over my lines, and wash my hair," to which their roommate replies, "Brilliant!")

Barbara Bonfigli came by to discuss the last scene. I showed her a new rough draft which she basically liked but felt I should "get to the point quicker."

When I showed my new scene to Vivian that night, he had already written his own version. I wish he wouldn't do this as it puts me in a difficult position if I don't like it. I'm convinced he's a frustrated writer, and alas, his scene emphasized Vivian's "frustrations" more than his talent.

I realized the only way I could get a new scene to Barbara and David without injuring Vivian's feelings was to selectively use three of his lines and add them to mine. That night when I wrote up the scene, I sensed it didn't look hot on paper. "Oh well," I thought, "maybe it will look better in the morning."

It didn't. The scene seemed forced and rushed, so I wrote a longer version hoping it would be an improvement. Only slightly. When we had a rehearsal that morning, Vivian explained to David and Martin that this would be the last time we would tinker with the scene before opening. They sat and read both new scenes, and it was immediately apparent that they were inferior to the scene they had previously rehearsed. We decided to reinstate this scene (even though Showpeople would object), albeit with a few changes which mostly eliminated any strong feelings Kit has for Morris.

The next day, we had another run-through, and this time the second act held its momentum. David and Barbara were much happier with "Once More from the Top." (It was interesting that aside from the deletion of a few measures of music and some obvious moves and gestures, nothing had radically changed since Tuesday's run-through!) The last scene they still detested, especially when Morris "thanks" Kit for telling him where he can find Sarah.

Barbara's suggestion of having Morris dash off to find Sarah— only to re-enter to find Kit with a loaded gun aimed at Morris— struck me as wrong. Morris would never leave Kit unless he knew Kit was incapable of killing again, like a tiger who's been defanged and declawed.

By this time, Vivian was sick and tired of Showpeople's suggestions. He explained that I had written two scenes, both of which "stank." He also explained that he would not subject the cast to more changes, even though I agreed with Barbara and David over the present ending.

My final suggestion was to have Morris draw a gun when Kit talks of not meaning to be "bad." Kit, however, is strangely relieved when Morris aims his weapon—it means he has succeeded in revealing himself to Morris and will soon say goodbye to his miserable existence. When Kit admits he did not "succeed" in killing Sarah, Morris puts away the gun, realizing Kit is no longer a threat to anyone. It is a small, simple gesture which creates suspense and answers questions.

You would have thought this would please Barbara, but she went right on to criticize Kit's penultimate line. When I offered to rewrite it, I thought Vivian would combust!

"NO! NO! NO! I won't allow it!" he bellowed, gesticulating in a very authoritative manner.

"Vivian, it's only one line," I pointed out.

"NO! I tell you! I will not do it to the cast, I will not do it to the show, you'll have to get a different director. You must not fuck with good material!"

David Kernan wisely agreed with Vivian. (What could he say?) I more or less accepted it, although I felt he was being unreasonable. But I wanted to deescalate the situation before we approached a situation comparable to his confrontation with Mr. Donlevy back in military school.

And this time there was no telling who would be the recipient of Vivian's wrath.

11

"FORGET IT, JAKE. IT'S LEATHERHEAD."

Even though the show had vastly improved, there were still staging elements that bothered me. One was the scene where Flora meets Sarah, and they sing "So Much in Common." Originally, Lindsay had ended it with Morris and Sarah clapping in time to the music while Flora performed a little dance. Why couldn't they just duplicate the ending of "Mother Likes Sarah" at the Hudson Guild with Sarah and Flora doing a peck on the cheek and Morris looking on in disbelief?

Every time I watched the number, I would think, "Why didn't I insist on my original ending? How could I allow this to happen?" But I concluded that this is what collaboration is all about: looking at the big picture and learning to live with the smaller irritants. Up until our first day at Leatherhead, I was panicked about "Safer in my Arms" and "Once More from the Top," numbers whose failure to deliver spelled disaster for the show. Things like the ending to "So Much in Common" took a lesser priority, though they felt important. It's kind of like having a child who has a drug problem *and* a messy room: You can live with the messy room, but the drugs are another story! Whenever I saw these embarrassing moments, I'd repeat to myself, "Forget it, Jake. It's Leatherhead."

Sunday 9/10/1989 2:30 p.m.

Cathy arrives in just seven hours (and yes, I'm doing laundry).

Far from the home I love: Waiting at the Leatherhead train station, September 1989. Photo by Cathy Kiliper

What a week! I'm almost afraid to write about it knowing I'll have to dredge up painful memories and tamper with freshly healed wounds.

I'd better begin with opening night, or shall I say our very first night, September 5. We finished our dress rehearsal only two hours before the curtain went up. It was insanity to expect a good performance from the cast that night, and yet the evening went relatively smoothly . . . to a point. Technically, there were glitches, but it was wonderful to hear an audience's response. I had half-worried that the humor of the piece would not be universal and successfully "cross the pond," but thank God that was not the case. The audience reacted in all the right places, although the Morris/Sarah scenes didn't percolate. I semi-attributed this to a somewhat bland performance by Martin. His scenes with Susannah had been directed with great subtlety. Unfortunately, subtlety wasn't reading onstage, and the dim lighting in the park scene didn't help. Also, so much of the show has been blocked upstage, which on the Thorndike stage seemed miles away from the audience. I think there is a definite danger in rehearsing in small rehearsal rooms where everything seems closer than it will appear onstage.

The surprise of the evening, which by now should come as no surprise, was how much the audience responded to Kit. Whenever David was onstage, the show once again shifted into high gear. His scenes with Vivienne Martin were terrific, but starting with the first act finale, his energy began to wane. In Act Two, he gave an erratic performance. The strain of the past week must have proved too much for him in his final scene with Morris—and he went totally blank. Hilary, our stage manager, fed him lines while Martin Smith indicated important words. It was no use: David just shook his head sadly and said, almost inaudibly, "I'm sorry." What's ironic is this is exactly the point when the character of Kit unravels. Once again, life imitates art . . . or at least, good theater!

Flaws and all, I felt it was a victorious first night. At intermission, I ran into Dorris Carr, who had returned after a month's absence. She was positively kvelling (if Dorris still remembers how to "kvell" . . . but she definitely was "glowing"). She treated me to a drink and couldn't stop saying how well she thought the first act had gone. Barbara Bonfigli too seemed pleased. Later, Dorris ran into Vivian and told him she thought he was "brilliant." (Again, that word is used far too often here. However, since Dorris is American, I think it should be interpreted as a strong compliment.)

After the show, there was a party at the second-level bar. David Kernan was there handing out bottles of champagne. As he handed me a bottle, I said, "Well, you should be pleased." To which he replied, "There were great problems in Act One where it seemed unfocused." I said, "David, relax, you have a good show," although I knew my words of comfort would have little effect on him.

Barbara and Dorris drove Martin Smith and me home. Martin relived his horror in the last scene as he realized David Burt had "lost it." I could tell Martin was not happy with the audience's response to his performance, as he noted, "Kit really is the flashy role." I said they were both great roles, but he remained unconvinced.

In truth, they are *both* meaty parts, but having an exceptionally handsome, strapping leading actor play the role didn't help. Morris is forever aware that he is not good enough for Sarah—reinforced by Kit, who questions if Sarah would be attracted to Morris *if not for the case.* A precursor to Detective Columbo, Morris needs to be a bit schleppy. Martin capably filled many requirements for the role, but a schleppy character actor he was not.

After we dropped off Martin, Dorris and Barbara started chatting over inane things like Susannah's laugh and David Burt not understanding the lyrics, "Now you see there is this priest/and his mother is deceased/so he spends his time in search of dear old mum." Barbara believed those three lines held the key to the show's success. Were it only that simple.

When Barbara dropped me off, she kissed me and congratulated me on a job "well done."

After meeting with Showpeople at their offices the following morning, however, it would become clear Barbara must have been referring to her prime rib. When I arrived at 12:05, Vivian was already there, and everyone seemed to be in good spirits. Then we sat down at their round table and David started the ball rolling with "Dorris has some depressing news for you." (Why did I feel a sense of foreboding?)

"I have a few close friends who are very wealthy, and we were depending on them to contribute heavily to the show. But based on what I saw last night, I am not prepared to invite them," Dorris said. "Now, I know that speaking my mind doesn't make me popular, but I have to say how I feel."

Vivian looked as if he had been run over by a double-decker bus.

"Dorris," he began, almost breathlessly, "last night you told me I was 'brilliant,' but today you are saying you're not prepared to invite people to see my work. What happened between last night and this morning?!"

"You're right, Vivian, you *are* 'brilliant.' I meant what I said. But I have been away these past four weeks so I think I can give an unbiased view on the show, and it isn't at a point where we can invite investors."

At this point, I interceded. "Maybe if you could tell us what areas of the show you were displeased with."

Now David took the reins. "The show last night lost its black comedy. It lost its edge. It wasn't the show I read eight months ago."

"If you're saying it's not camp," Vivian began, "you're right. The show is about romance: the romance between Moe and Sarah, the romance—though not a sexual one—between Moe and Kit, and the romance between Kit and Alexandra. If you want a *Rocky Horror Picture Show*, which it seems you do, I will be perfectly willing to leave, and you can get someone else to direct."

Again, I intervened. "David, how can you say the show is not the musical you optioned when I followed almost every one of your instructions to the letter?"

"I know," David replied. "But somehow with the focus of the show and the way it's been directed, it has lost that edge."

"Give us specifics," I said, a certain "edge" creeping into my voice.

"All right," he said. "You *cannot* have Alexandra, this lady in heaven, embracing Kit while he dies in her arms. It is laughable and condoning murder!" His voice was becoming rather highly pitched and growing in decibels. "The romance of the show between Morris and Sarah is killing the murder aspects. We're losing the thread of the story. I hate the schmaltz at the end of 'So Much in Common.' All that Morris kissing Flora and putting his arm around her is purely sentimental. We don't need to be told he loves her—we see them sparring all the time. We know it's a love/hate relationship."

Now I was beginning to understand why *Steel Magnolias* and Neil Simon plays shuttered quickly in the West End. In the eyes of the British, the least amount of sentiment was sentimentality.

"David," I injected, "it seems last night's audience didn't think 'So Much in Common' died." (It had been a great success, perhaps getting the most laughs and applause.)

"Think how much more tremendous the response would have been," was his reply. "Too many scenes are way upstage. Martin and Susannah are doing television acting, not theater acting. Their scenes go on forever and it's not reading. People aren't projecting properly."

To be fair to David, the style of acting for Morris and Sarah was too naturalistic. It was a little jarring when compared to the more theatrical performances from Kit, his victims, and the two mothers. And Martin and Susannah were also relying too much on their body mics.

It may seem strange we were receiving these notes so late in the game, but this is often what happens when you experience a show with an audience as opposed to attending rehearsals and run-throughs in an intimate rehearsal space. Plus, due to the fact we had such limited time in the theater, that first performance was a revelation. David's notes also reinforced a point William Goldman makes repeatedly in his book *Adventures in the Screen Trade*: "Nobody knows anything." In other words, no one can predict a vehicle's ultimate success until the rubber meets the road, especially with so many variables in the balance.

"I know I asked for a ballad in Act One for Morris," David continued, "but now I realize I was wrong and want 'Goliath' cut."

This time, Vivian interrupted.

"Excuse me," he began, "but that is not a song which can be cut. It reflects the soul of the man, and if we lose it, we lose the soul of the show. I am prepared to make cuts in dialogue—the first act is running long—but I am not amenable to cutting 'Goliath,' nor will I change the ending or direct a show which I feel you want as camp. I am outraged at Dorris for saying what she said at the beginning. I am insulted and no matter what is said to mollify me, the damage has been done. Either let me do my job correctly or fire me. I really am so upset; I can't sit here anymore. I am physically and emotionally drained, and I think it's best that I leave."

"May I say something?" I asked.

"Certainly," David replied.

"Thank you. As you know, I am often in agreement with you, David, more than you realize. I agree that last night wasn't perfect, but I also know what we provided was good, solid entertainment. That's why I find Dorris's comment so offensive," I added. "If there were things you felt needed improvement, Vivian and I would have been more than happy to hear them if they were given constructively. But when you say the show has 'no focus,' I don't know what to do. Many times, I find you don't say what's really on your minds, but rather use scare tactics to motivate us—"

"Douglas," David interrupted, "do you think we do this on purpose? The show has problems. For Christ's sake, it's important to us that it succeed. We put eighteen thousand pounds of our own money into this!"

"David," I said, feeling my blood rising like Old Faithful at Yellowstone, "I have devoted the last five years of my life investing in this show, so please don't talk to me about commitment or passion. At times I've shut my family and friends out of my life at the expense of getting this show right. You people are lucky—you have a good product. You weren't there for the major growing pains at the Hudson Guild and in Florida. And if you are all so committed to the piece, how come you and Barbara declined to come to the first run-through when it was scheduled on a Saturday of a long weekend, preferring to go away?"

Barbara chimed in, "I didn't realize it was definitely set for that Saturday."

Now it was Vivian's turn. "Don't give me that, love. I spoke to you over the phone, and you asked if it could be pushed up to Friday . . ."

I looked at David Kernan, who had remained silent. "David," I asked, "did *you* understand the run-through to be on a Saturday?"

"Yes," he quietly responded.

Recriminations followed, ultimately leading to a truce and a plan of attack. Soon we all had our scripts open and were going through the text line by line with Dorris and Barbara saying which should go and which should remain, all based on one performance. By the time we got to Morris and Sarah's first date in Central Park, Barbara asked for an explanation of a directorial decision. Vivian could no longer contain himself.

"Look, I'm going. I cannot take this editing by committee," Vivian protested. "I am very tired, and Dorris's words have truly upset me . . ."

"I'm so sorry, Vivian. Really, I am. It was not my intention. It was a poor choice of words," Dorris acknowledged.

"I think the choice was deliberate, but no matter. I have to rest and clear my head. And when I have, we will speak again," Vivian said, rising from his seat.

"Do you want me to leave, too?" I asked.

"Do as you like," he said.

And with that, Vivian left the building.

I only hung around for another hour, as I was quickly fading, and this line-by-line editing was getting to me as well. I said we could continue our discussion the next day.

That night, I saw the show, and of course, I hated it. Every flaw Showpeople had pointed out weighed on my mind. The audience hardly laughed, and it was only 50 percent full. Of course, this was also the night the critics were invited! Vivian was too emotionally exhausted to attend, so Annie, our public relations director, asked me if I would object to being interviewed "live" in his stead later that night at the BBC radio station with cast member Susannah Fellows. Would I object? Twist my arm!

I also met the press at intermission. Most of them consisted of young kids, hardly twenty-two years of age. They complimented me on "a good first half." One young woman requested a brief interview with me where she proceeded to ask me if I had ever worked for Sir Andrew Lloyd Webber(!).

Surprisingly, later at the BBC interview, I was able to mask the stress of the day and even managed an unintentionally funny line: When Brian, the interviewer, asked if Dame Sybil Thorndike still asked people to take their seats," I said, "Oh, I believe she's deceased," not realizing he was referring to a recording.

The next day, Vivian asked if he could come over to my flat to talk before going to Showpeople's offices. He arrived around 11:15 and said he was considerably more rested but also thinking clearly, and yesterday's remarks were "unconscionable." He was not willing to submit to such treatment again, nor was he willing to hear their suggestions: I could be the go-between, if necessary, but that was my own choice. Showpeople could continue to speak with me, and Vivian and I would ultimately decide what would stay, go, or change.

Never having been the product of a divorce, I didn't relish the idea of being the go-between, although I should have been used to it by now: When my parents and sister were in conflict, I was the human "buffer." In fact, Debby's trips home were often predicated on whether I would be visiting my folks during that time.

Vivian and I went to Showpeople's offices where he made the same speech, albeit standing. (He wouldn't even sit in their chair for fear it would distract him from his mission.)

"It is only my respect for Douglas and my love of the show that have kept me from quitting," he added. He realized if Showpeople could not work with his terms, he would have to be fired (which was preferable to quitting and forfeiting a percentage if there were a West End transfer).

Then Vivian abruptly exited.

David Kernan started letting off steam vowing he would "fire Vivian and put him on the next boat!" Barbara tried to placate him. I think her Buddhist practices enabled her to maintain an equilibrium we could all have used. She had a photo of a female spiritual leader that followed her wherever she went (car, office, etc.). Four weeks earlier when I had first commented to Barbara that it was a shame we were losing Martin Smith to *Phantom*, she said, "It's not in the design of life." When I once told Vivian how Barbara believed our show was in good hands due to her deity, he said, "It must be a very lonely God if it's only concerned with a production at Leatherhead!" From then on, we referred to Barbara's deity as "the God of regional theaters."

After Vivian fled, I dutifully took down Showpeople's additional suggestions. They sent me away in a cab to Vivian's new flat near Kensington. When I got there, I opened my notebook and began to describe the changes we had just agreed on. He looked at me with a mixture of astonishment and revulsion, as if I were turning into the titular character in *The Fly*. At the end of the list, he just sadly shook his head and said, "Oh, Doug, they have gotten to you. They've really gotten to you."

Most personal attacks I can deal with, but when a person suggests that I no longer have a mind of my own, I get slightly crazed and could feel my blood pressure rising and my jaw tightening.

"I can be accused of many things, Vivian, but one thing I'm not is a pushover. I am a very determined person. Do you think I would submit to their requests if I didn't feel strongly about them myself?"

"All I know," Vivian began, "is that yesterday you said you wouldn't touch 'Goliath,' but now you want it cut; you didn't think there was anything wrong with the 'Safer in My Arms' tango and now you are favoring a horrible idea of Carmella getting a heart attack, which is pure camp; and you're willing to rethink the ending after you told me yesterday you felt it was working. How else am I supposed to feel about your recent change of heart?"

Throughout the last two months, Vivian had been my mainstay, my comrade-in-arms. Sure, we'd had our ups and downs, but at the end of the day, he was my ally. Now he doubted my allegiance, and I seriously began to doubt his.

"I hate it when people suggest I don't have a mind of my own!" (I was now almost shouting.) "I can see this is getting us nowhere," I said rising from my seat. "I have to leave if you insist on being totally inflexible!"

"That's the way I am, Doug. I will not submit to the advice of amateurs; I will not fuck up something good and turn it into camp. I can't do it even though I know the consequences, and quite frankly, I need the money."

This last revelation took me by surprise. I sensed that Vivian might listen to reason.

"Vivian," I began, "why can't people work *together*? Why do you assume they are the enemy?"

"Because I have no respect for them," he said. "I don't blame you for submitting. You are particularly vulnerable right now: You're worried about your show's future, you're alone in a strange country. They know this and are using it to their advantage . . ."

I felt numb, as if I had just been chloroformed and was going under.

"I've called a rehearsal today at five to give notes on last night's performance, but I don't know if you want me to continue as director," Vivian queried.

"No, go," I said, not sure if I was forming the words voluntarily or involuntarily.

"I'd better hurry if I'm going to make it," Vivian said.

"I'll go with you," I agreed, thankful that I had showered that morning but sorry I had neglected to shave, eat, or dress for a performance.

The train ride to Leatherhead was a blur. We barely spoke. I don't even remember how we got to the theater; all I know is we were carried by some vehicle.

That night, Vivian and I sat together and watched the show. It was a good, responsive audience and a fine performance. I forgot my worries, and for the first time, relaxed. At the end, Vivian turned to me and asked if I had liked what I'd seen and if I wanted him to continue as director. I answered affirmatively to both questions.

The two of us met the next day and went through the script to implement judicious cuts, mostly impacting Morris and Sarah. We also changed the ending of Act One, placing a "button" immediately after Kit, appearing in a hat and trench coat, says, "Detective Brummell. Detective Morris Brummell." Originally, we had Kit lifting his hands in the act of killing, followed by Morris discovering his coat and hat at the scene of the crime. (All three previous productions had begun with this ending, and all eventually reverted to Kit delivering his final line before simply stepping through a door in disguise as "Detective Morris Brummell.")

We talked about cutting "Goliath"—I still loved the song but felt it slowed down the action and undermined Kit's ballad following close on its heels, "What Shall I Sing for You?" Two back-to-back ballads are not advisable, but Vivian and I had hoped "Goliath" would prove the exception to the rule. However, now I realized it was a "darling" that had to be dispatched. Vivian was less resistant this time but still not entirely convinced. We both decided to wait and see.

My wife arrived the next day. I picked her up from Heathrow, and we rode in the back of a nearly empty tube together. It had been two months since I'd left New York, and it was suddenly both comforting and discomforting reuniting. I felt at times like I was looking at a mail-order bride; whoever said absence makes the heart grow fonder probably wasn't working on a musical out of town. I had been so laser-focused on *Lady* that the most important "lady" felt like an afterthought. Although we had talked on the phone several times a week, it was strange having Cathy suddenly descend in the middle of a war zone . . . like a major character being introduced into some epic story while the final chapters were in sight.

Cathy, being an exceptional human being, knew how to navigate through these travails. But now that we were sharing the flat, I realized it wasn't roomy enough to comfortably accommodate my life as a writer and husband: I felt guilty if I wasn't paying Cathy enough of my admittedly divided attention. She was always magnanimous about it, although I'm sure she didn't fly six hours only to watch me go off to work. We tried to incorporate a little R&R into our itinerary, deciding a day trip to Brighton might help me gain perspective and serve as a romantic interlude.

That Monday, I received word that Susannah Fellows had a bad cold and was unable to perform that night. Faced with no understudies, David Kernan did what is normally considered verboten—he canceled the performance. What made matters worse was Susannah was not well enough to attend the 2:00 p.m. rehearsal the next day when all the cuts and changes were implemented. In fact, I had to play Sarah, and modestly speaking, fulfilled my assignment. However, this did little to mask the cast and Vivian's distress over Susannah's absence.

What was particularly depressing about our canceling Monday was the number of people we turned away: It would have been a full house largely due to word of mouth—and our BBC interview! Also, a potential investor was to have been in the audience and had to fly back to the States the next day, so he never saw the show. David Kernan said he might have given five units (or roughly twenty thousand dollars). I consoled myself with thoughts of giving 2.5 units of my own to help defray the loss. Then Cathy dropped a bombshell: My former employers' weekly checks—my bonus money—had stopped a month ago! Here I assumed I was earning an income only to discover the reservoir had long since dried up. Needless to say, I abandoned the thought of putting money into *Lady*.

Tuesday night, I took Cathy to see her first performance of the UK premiere of *No Way to Treat a Lady*. Susannah was well enough to perform that night and an hour earlier had gone through the cuts with Vivian, continually challenging him as she felt there was little left of the Sarah/Morris relationship. Perhaps due to her lingering cold (Susannah usually gave a spirited and inspired performance), she spoke quietly during her dialogue that night, and her scenes with Martin suffered. An amendment to the previous ending went in for the first time. It seemed to work well, although I wasn't thrilled with Vivian's direction. After finally giving Kit the approbation he craves, Alexandra sings "Time to go now/so take one final bow." Kit nods his head, acknowledging his time is up. He rises, taking one last look at his dominion and exits upstage. A shot is fired. The light on Alexandra begins to fade as she utters, "Bravo, at last a performance."

At this point, I wanted Morris and Sarah to rush on, responding to Kit's shot, then have Morris investigate the wings and confirm Kit is dead. Instead, Vivian had them wait a few beats before entering, deciding they had already seen Kit die offstage. So, in they come, looking somewhat catatonic. (A major dip in energy!) Morris goes to the phone and now actually completes the call to his associate. ("Bronski, you'll never guess where I'm calling from. You ready?") He looks at Sarah and says into the phone, "I'll call you back. It can wait five minutes." Music swells as he walks toward Sarah and the curtain falls. It seemed like an appropriate finish.

Barbara and Dorris were two rows behind us, entertaining a man who appeared to have a lot of money. He also seemed indifferent to the show. In contrast, Cathy sat next to a young man who asked which theater in the West End we were occupying (he just assumed the show was moving to a larger venue . . . shades of the Hudson Guild production). He was quite a theater aficionado and had come to Leatherhead because he had already "seen everything in the West End." P.S.: He loved the show. Why can't people like that have the money to finance?

Later that night when I went backstage to congratulate the cast, I walked down a dark hallway when a man passed me. I looked at his long, oval face and immediately knew his identity. "Excuse me, but aren't you Ron Moody?" The Academy Award–nominated star of *Oliver!* smiled and asked, "Whom do I have the pleasure of addressing?" It was like Oliver being introduced to Fagin!

I explained I was the author and asked him what brought him to Leatherhead. "I'm a good friend of Vivienne Martin," was his reply.

"Oh, she's wonderful. I hope you enjoyed her performance and the show."

"Yes, yes, I did. It's a good show . . . a very good show. It could use a little more . . . magic in the production. Do you know what I mean?"

"I think so, yes."

"A little more color, more pizzazz."

He wished me good luck, and I told him again what a thrill it was to finally meet a childhood idol. He smiled warmly and disappeared into the shadowy corridor. Even though my father never made good on his promise that we'd travel to London and meet Georgia Brown, I had met both Shani Wallis and Ron Moody, the two movie leads from my beloved *Oliver!*

The following night, Cathy and I got home around 12:45 a.m. after seeing a hugely disappointing West End play, *Exclusive*, by best-selling author Jeffrey Archer starring Alec McCowen and Paul Scofield. (Alec, as usual, was splendid and our backstage visit with him afterwards proved to be the high point of the evening.) I opened the door to let us up to the flat, and there on the stairs was an envelope addressed to me from Showpeople labeled, "By Hand." I opened it on the stairs with trembling hands. A lengthy two-page letter was addressed to Vivian with a cc: to me and a personal note from Barbara:

Dear Doug,

It has been a very difficult fortnight for all of us, most especially you. I am sure you know that in our minds the show's the thing and personalities cannot predominate. We think you are tremendously talented and that the changes we believe will make this a West End show are ones you can accomplish brilliantly. Every person we have taken to the show has said it needs edge, more laughs, more black humor if it is to really stand out.

This is and has been our unanimous opinion also. We hope you are of like mind.

Yours, Barbara

The letter that followed quite unraveled me. Looking at it now, it doesn't have the impact of a first, second, and third reading. But keep in mind it was 1 a.m., and I had endured a tough couple of weeks. Also, although some of Showpeople's demands were quite reasonable (cutting "Once More from the Top" due to the poor staging or trying to clean up the Carmella ending), they were also quite unreasonable considering our choreographer was a hundred miles away in Manchester, Vivienne Martin was slow to learn steps, and Martin Smith found it nearly impossible to rehearse due to his *Phantom* obligations. Their proposed "killer" ending I found repulsive and tasteless: Kit draws a lipstick kiss on his own forehead and swivels his chair to face upstage, followed by a gunshot—we see his arms and head jerk back. By adding, "we insist on the following changes," it left absolutely nothing open to discussion.

I kept reading and re-reading the letter, saying to Cathy, "They've ruined my sleep" (very Macbeth, I know!). I even dialed Barbara and left a message on her machine saying, "I will be up for most of the night. I can no longer sleep; this letter has totally taken the wind out of my sails." I then decided I was going to write Showpeople and express myself, rather than weather another meeting. I wrote a highly cathartic if excessively long letter and turned out the lights at 5:00 a.m.

In the morning, Barbara rang around 9:00. Cathy played the role of my personal assistant and politely but succinctly explained I was indisposed and would respond by *letter* to their letter. Then Vivian called with news he had spoken to his agent, Peter Murphy: They were trying to arrange a showdown with Showpeople at 3:00 at the Curtis Brown Agency. Vivian had been totally upset but now felt better knowing our agents would intercede.

I had to condense the previous night's tome into an opening statement. (I felt like I was appearing before a Senate subcommittee.) Cathy and I quickly decided what was choice material, and I abridged it to a three-and-a-half-minute speech. At 2:30, I was fortunate to grab a cab and arrived at Curtis Brown offices with one minute to spare. I was ushered into Peter Murphy's office (a far cry from the cold, intimidating William Morris offices in New York), and there was Vivian waiting. He seemed in good spirits. A minute later a woman notified us that David Kernan had arrived, and Barbara and Dorris followed shortly. Vivian and I went to an oval room to await the enemy. They had all dressed for the occasion—Dorris looked as if she were ready for the Ascot Gavotte. I was distant to all three but rose from my chair as Dorris took a seat.

Peter was clearly the moderator, and Barbara began that she hoped the letter would be interpreted as an encouraging sign: If they didn't have faith in our work, they would no longer wish to improve the show. Vivian kept silent as Peter was speaking on his behalf, although Vivian did address their insistence that these changes be met. In their defense, Showpeople felt justified in taking a stance due to Vivian's "intransigence," and this was a last resort to get him to make changes. (Fair enough.)

I read my opening statement, having rehearsed the speech carefully in the taxi coming over. After I was finished, I asked Showpeople if we were all in agreement as to the kind of show I was writing (i.e., "focus," "edge," "humor"). David wasn't sure. He felt we had an imbalance of Sarah/Moe scenes, so I went scene by scene through the show, explaining how with the latest cuts, we were down to the bare minimum. They seemed to agree and were further placated when I told them Vivian and I had agreed to cut "Goliath."

Things got a bit heated when Vivian pointed out the impracticality of trying to alter the ending to a dance number when our choreographer had moved on to his next assignment. David protested: "Oh, come on, Vivian! This is what doing musicals is all about. Every show goes through changes," intimating that Vivian's reluctance stemmed from his "intransigent" nature.

Aside from some initial tense moments, the meeting went relatively smoothly—each side seemed to receive some satisfaction. Near the end, Vivian excused himself because he did not favor our going through the letter step by step. Peter left to encourage him to return, and David said in exasperation, "You see what we're up against? I don't know why we don't fire him!" Barbara politely told him to keep still.

The next week was a productive one. After implementing some of the changes Showpeople insisted on, Cathy and I were free to leave for Paris the next day, September 20, my birthday. Before I left, there was some discussion of filming a performance, which Vivian quickly pre-empted. Showpeople, as a peace offering and way of celebrating both my birthday and Cathy's (we were born ten days apart), treated us to a convivial dinner at a restaurant near Sloane Square. They also invited Vivian, who was still fuming and refusing to accept their "charity."

At some point, I brought up the show and said I didn't know if it was right to talk shop. Dorris graciously began to discuss its uncertain future, noting it was difficult for them to work with a director "who hates us so much." (David added, "He treats us as if we were three ding-a-lings.") They were quick to praise me, and David said he had only favorable things to say about my professionalism and talent. The bottom line, however, was that Vivian had condemned nearly all their ideas, and their "prospective investors"—though clearly impressed with much of what they saw—had not come up with the money or commitment Showpeople was expecting. As a last resort, they had invited people who book tours with the hopes it might a have a life on the road, albeit with a different director and soap opera stars. I was sure that should this occur, it would bear little resemblance to the show I had written and more closely resemble the artistic rendering in the Thorndike Theatre brochure: a singing coffin suggesting a Ray Cooney *Run for Your Wife* farce, or Jack the Ripper meets *Arsenic and Old Lace.*

There was one thing I could control, however: the button on a musical number. As anyone who has worked with me knows, I'm a stickler for buttons. I loved "Lunch with Sarah," but the applause was never quite as generous as I expected. In hindsight, it was probably because it's ultimately a musical scene illustrating the deterioration of a relationship. But to my mind at the time, the problem was the button: There was a timpani roll that led to a rather muted final downbeat. I believed I had a solution.

I asked Vivian if he would allow an extra downbeat at the end of the number for additional punch. Vivian said it was fine, but to make sure to tell Kate Young, our music director. I spoke to Kate before the show, and she said she would speak with Brian, our percussionist. Cathy and I took our seats and witnessed a truly exciting show. The cast was really performing well, especially Martin, who had never projected such passion (although he still seemed to be marking—holding back to save his voice—in Act Two's "Sarah's Touch"). His "Lunch with Sarah" was genuinely compelling, however, and although the extra button—an added "boom" on the kettle drum—didn't make a significant difference, it at least signaled to the audience when they should applaud.

Elliot Brown's friend, Munroe Pofcher, a mergers and acquisitions advisor to American and European publishing companies, attended that night. Clearly, he was well-heeled and had previously invested in *Phantom of the Opera*. By the end of the evening, Munroe was asking me what our plans were for the show and inquiring about the capitalization. At one point, Dorris Carr walked by, signaling an opportunity for an introduction. When Munroe's companion, a business associate coincidentally named Kit, stated how much she liked the show, Dorris queried almost incredulously, "You did? Did you *really* like it?" I could now understand why Showpeople's affluent friends would have nothing to do with the property: David, Barbara, and Dorris were so insecure about the piece that one would have to be oblivious not to notice.

I bid Munroe and Kit goodnight and walked backstage to congratulate the cast, feeling as if there was a light at the end of the tunnel . . . with a little help from Munroe Pofcher. ("Have an eggroll, Mr. Pofcher!") While I was waiting with Cathy outside the men's dressing rooms, I saw Kate and congratulated her on a fine show. She smiled sheepishly and said, "Oh, I got chewed out by Martin. He was furious with the end of 'Lunch with Sarah.'"

I thought she was joking. "Didn't he see you yet?" she asked. I shook my head no. "It was really my fault," Kate continued. "I should have told him about the final downbeat."

At that point, I heard Martin's booming voice firing away at Vivian in the corridor next door. I nervously opened the door. Martin saw me and started to verbally assault me with the fury of a madman.

"How dare you change a song without notifying me!!" he screamed. "I am an artist! Don't you ever do that again! Who do you think you are? What possible right—"

"Martin," I interrupted. "I'm sorry."

"Apologies aren't good enough."

"Honestly, I don't know why you're so upset. The extra downbeat occurred after your final note—"

"How can you fuckin' change a song without telling me?! Don't you think I had a right to know? Do you know what it's like to be up there with fuckin' egg on your face?!"

"Martin, that's really an exaggeration. The blackout had already occurred. You were in the dark—"

He didn't want to hear this. It only made him more maniacal.

"NEVER, EVER do that again! Do you understand?! Never do that to an *artist*!!"

By this time, I had had it with this "artist" crap. As much as I felt Martin was justified in complaining, this vicious attack was unwarranted. With my back literally up against an exit door and his intimidating muscular arms flailing this way and that, I felt like a trapped animal. My only recourse was through words.

"I'll remember to let you know the next time, if you remember to sing out on 'Sarah's Touch.'" As soon as those words left my mouth, I wanted to press rewind. Martin's face matched my horrified expression. For a split second there was silence. Vivian softly murmured, "Oh, no, Doug." Then Martin announced, "Fine, you don't like 'Sarah's Touch'? Good. From now on, YOU are playing MORRIS!" And with that, he stormed out of the theater, slamming the door behind him.

I started fumbling with the door to go after him. "Don't, Douglas," Vivian said. "Let him go." I wasn't about to: In the morning, Cathy and I were scheduled to leave for Paris, my first real vacation after two arduous months. "I don't want to play Morris!" I sputtered to Vivian as I opened the door and ran out into the night after Martin, hoping I could persuade him to stay for the final week.

Suddenly I had an overwhelming case of déjà vu. When I was ten years old, I made my musical comedy debut at Camp Hadar in Clinton, Connecticut, playing Randolph, Kim MacAfee's brother, in *Bye Bye Birdie*. The director accidentally left my name off the cast list in the program but listed every cast member, including my sister as the "sad girl." I was deeply upset by the oversight and took refuge in my bunk. The director, a young woman prohibited from entering a male bunk, was forced to apologize through an open cabin window. I remember answering back, "If I'm not important enough to be in your program, then I guess I'm not important enough to be in your show." This kind of juvenile behavior—well, I was ten—was now haunting me with Martin, only now I was getting a taste of my own medicine.

I caught up with him a hundred feet outside the theater. I called out his name, but he wouldn't stop.

"Leave me alone, Douglas! You're playing Morris 'cause I ain't."

"At least let me apologize," I implored.

"I have to catch my train!" he bellowed.

Then I did something that later, in retrospect, could have led to violence. I grabbed his arm.

"Please stop!" I begged. "I am sorry, Martin. It was a horrible, stupid thing that I said. I wish I could take it back—"

"Do you realize how you've hurt me?" he cried out. "I can't sing that song again now without thinking of what you said."

"Of course, you can," I said. "See my comment for what it was—a stupid, irrational statement said in self-defense. Surely, you've said things before that you've later regretted?" I asked.

"No," was his response. "For the last few years, I have never regretted my actions."

I wanted to yell "Bullshit!" but thought Martin would not find that word consoling.

"Well, Martin, consider yourself lucky. I unfortunately have regretted saying things in the past, and this is such a time."

"Do you think I enjoy playing this thankless role?" he sputtered. "Barbara Bonfigli's always bringing people backstage to see David Burt, but never me! And everyone thinks I'm marking because I'm not able to rehearse *Phantom* AND do this part! Don't think I don't know what they're all saying about me! And Vivian is driving me up a fuckin' wall with his stupid notes. Well, you know why tonight worked for you? Because I decided to hell with his direction: I'm doing this show *my* way! Jesus, Doug, and then on top of everything you tell me you can't hear 'Sarah's Touch' when I'm singing as loudly as I can. How do you think it makes me feel?"

"Martin, all I can say is you must be doing a damn good job when the only critical thing I could say is that you were singing quietly on your ballad."

He then broke into a run. "I have to make my train!" he said. "Go back to your wife."

Since he still didn't say he would finish out the run as Morris, I sprinted after him. There was something bizarrely comic about it all: Here was an author running after an actor who was running after a train! Martin was soon winded as we approached the tracks, although surprisingly I had plenty in reserve (but then I hadn't just performed for the last two hours).

"Martin," I began, "I wouldn't run down here, abandoning my wife, if I didn't feel a great sense of remorse for what I said. I am sorry, Martin. I reacted out of anger and stupidity. Please accept my apology."

"Douglas," Martin confessed, "you should know singing is mostly in your head, not in your throat. If you don't believe in yourself, it won't come out."

"Martin, you are a marvelous Morris: totally charming, funny, touching, and explosive." (Well, that last adjective certainly could not be overstated.)

"You picked a hell of a time to tell me," he murmured.

"Well, what can I say? I've got lousy timing."

A small smile crossed his lips. I took this as an encouraging sign.

"All right," he conceded. "I'll do the show."

"Thank you, Martin. I appreciate it."

And with that, I trudged back up the hill to find Cathy.

Remembering this painful incident, I'm struck by a few things. One is Martin's comment about Vivian and his "stupid notes." I remember telling Vivienne Martin how much I was enjoying her Sadie scene. Instead of saying thank you, she practically broke down telling me how excruciating it was receiving notes from Vivian every night, indicating precisely when to execute every single gesture and inflection, including exactly when to shake her posterior. She felt as if she was an indentured servant. The sad thing is, Vivian Matalon was so gifted and knew how to direct actors. But he didn't know when to let our cast ultimately do their job.

It reminds me of my favorite passage from John Guare's *Six Degrees of Separation*, when a leading male character recalls attending parent-teacher meetings at his children's school: "I remembered asking my kids' second-grade teacher: 'Why are all your students geniuses? Look at the first grade—blotches of green and black. The third grade—camouflage. But your grade, the second grade,

Matisses, every one. . . . What is your secret?' 'I don't have any secret. I just know when to take their drawings away from them.'"

And that was perhaps Vivian's greatest offense: he couldn't quite grasp when to let go of his art. He wanted to justify his role as director, but he started to undo all the beautiful work until we were back to "blotches of green and black." I also worried in my heart of hearts if I too was guilty of the very same thing.

I realized I was critical of Martin's "Sarah's Touch" because I knew on a subconscious level it wasn't good enough. I should have abandoned it altogether after Ed Kleban criticized it in BMI. Instead, I rewrote the lyric, polishing it until it positively gleamed with craft. But it's like polishing a turd—at the end of the day, it's still a turd.

That night's most poignant lesson was that the source of Martin's angst wasn't the additional downbeat in "Lunch with Sarah": He was going through major doubts about his vocal capabilities. To be performing a show regionally while rehearsing the title role in the West End's most celebrated musical must have taken the stamina of a Goliath. Sadly, Martin would leave the role of the Phantom after two months. Perhaps I shouldn't hypothesize, but he tragically succumbed to AIDS five years later, so maybe his health had begun to deteriorate in subtle ways. Or it's possible there were vocal issues performing the role eight times a week. Either way, I'm relieved he returned to *No Way to Treat a Lady* to finish the run. Martin was an exceptionally accomplished performer and songwriter, having penned at least five musicals. I have no doubt he would have continued to enjoy a thriving career, and it's a genuine tragedy that AIDS cruelly deprived us of his gifts and the pleasure of his company.

Cathy and I left the next morning for Paris, and it was everything I'd always hoped it would be. I actually forgot about the show, but four days later it came roaring back, like an injured animal taking a last stand before succumbing to its wounds.

Cathy and I decided to see the final Saturday night performance in Leatherhead. There was a matinee that day, and we were able to catch an earlier train so we could leisurely eat dinner nearby before attending the evening performance. We quietly walked into the house close to the end of Act Two and stood in the back. There was a sizable and responsive audience, always a good sign. When my eyes became accustomed to the dark, I noticed there was also a video camera on a tripod near the center of the last row operated by a cameraman. I looked at Cathy and whispered, "I guess they got approval to film it."

Minutes later, the door behind us opened and in crept Vivian. He too had come early to attend the last performance and greeted us warmly. I gestured that there was a camera to our left and smiled as if to say, "Shh, our voices might be picked up." When he saw it, he went ballistic.

"NO, NO! What are you doing? Who gave you permission?!" he demanded of the videographer in a very loud stage whisper that could be heard across several rows. It was like a car accident—I wanted to turn away and run, but something compelled me to stay. It looked as if Vivian was preparing to rip the camera from the tripod if not for the young operator standing between them.

"This must stop! I did not give permission!" The young man reluctantly agreed and hit the off button. Vivian, watching the light go out, brusquely fled to the lobby. Cathy and I followed close behind.

"Did you know about this, Doug?!"

"Of course not. I just assumed when I saw the camera that you had given *your* permission."

"I did nothing of the kind!" he retorted. "This is the mark of Showpeople! I expressly said I would not consent to their filming, and they do this behind my back!"

I knew the proverbial shit had hit the fan. This was to be our last performance in Leatherhead, and it was going to be a bumpy night.

Vivian later pressed charges through his agent, while Cathy and I flew back to the States the next day.

Two days later, I got a frantic phone call from David Kernan.

"Douglas, I'm in need of your assistance. As you may know, Vivian has confiscated the only film we have of a performance in Leatherhead." (Well, it was nine-tenths of a performance since Vivian had discovered the subterfuge during the last scene.) "It's vital that we get it back. There are investors who were unable to see your show in Leatherhead, but they want to see the video. This is our last chance to raise money."

"What do you want me to do, David?" I asked.

"You're the only one Vivian listens to. Please convince him not to destroy the film. He's setting sail by boat tomorrow and has vowed to throw it overboard into the Thames."

"Vivian has always followed his own dictates, David. I don't think my words will have much effect."

"Please," David implored. "He's only in London one more night. Here's his number. Try to dissuade him."

If three months with Vivian had taught me anything, I knew once he made up his mind, it was fruitless to employ reason.

I dialed the number. Vivian answered. He was cordial but he also knew why I was calling.

"Let me guess, you were just speaking with David."

"Yes, Vivian. He told me about the film."

"It's no use, love. I will toss it overboard tomorrow."

"But it doesn't need to end like this. That film—that's everything. Without that film, we have nothing to show for all our hard work."

"First, Doug, have you seen this film? No? Well, I have, and so has my agent. It's crude, poorly shot with one camera by a young man who clearly doesn't understand theater. There is nothing here that would impress a potential investor. They are grasping at straws."

He had a point.

"Trust me, it's better that no one sees this film."

Resigned, I said, "Well, I guess now they won't be able to transfer our show."

"Doug, they never were able to produce our show in the West End. I know we all worked very hard and what a grave disappointment this must be for you. But they are amateurs. Did David tell you what he said to me? 'Vivian, I hope you get on the first banana boat for the States. You are desperately in need of therapy.' To which I replied, 'David, the only thing that equals your mediocre talent is the paucity of your ideas.' I was very pleased with that one."

"Yes, Vivian," I said, clearly deflated. "Well, safe travels."

"Thank you, Doug. My love to Cathy."

And with that, we hung up. The next day, Vivian traveled by barge, while the only tangible proof of the UK premiere of *No Way to Treat a Lady* traveled to the bottom of the sea.

12

MICHAEL CORLEONE ATTEMPTS DRAG

I returned to New York City unemployed, lacking prospects for a West End production and grieving over the death of my last grandparent, Nathan E. Cohen, affectionaly known as Zadie. My parents had recently seen him at my first cousin's wedding, which I was supposed to attend, but Cathy and I opted to spend four days in Paris. I sent my grandfather a postcard, which sadly arrived the day after he passed.

We all stood in the pouring rain without benefit of a canopy as they lowered his plain pine coffin into the ground. There was only a simple Jewish star on the box. The men all took turns shoveling dirt onto the coffin. I almost felt as if I were transported back to his homeland, Russia. He had come to this country when he was twelve, had only a sixth-grade education, and went to work right away in a tube factory, which he later owned and operated with his younger brothers. He was exceptionally well-read and surprisingly liberal, subscribing to *Mother Jones*. In his later years, he became a bookbinder, dedicating himself to mostly altruistic, pro bono acts, which led to his being gifted with a cherished relic from a convent in Lowell.

At his headstone's unveiling a year later, a woman at the cemetery introduced herself to me as "a friend of your grandfather's" at the independent living residency. "He used to speak of you all the time," she said, pressing her hand into mine. "He told me all about your working in Europe."

My eyes welled with tears. Was I grieving over Zadie or the still painful disappointment from England?

I shifted my focus from Christopher "Kit" Gill to Christopher Columbus. Jay Harnick and Barbara Pasternack of TheatreWorks/USA had commissioned Tom Toce, Jonathan Bolt, and me to write a musical based on the famous explorer in time for the quincentennial of Columbus's arrival in the Americas. Tom and I had previously collaborated on *A Charles Dickens Christmas* for TheaterWorks, and *Columbus* guaranteed us major bookings from 1991 to 1993. Our director was David Armstrong who later assumed the position of producing artistic director of The 5th Avenue Theatre: His tenure ushered in a new era for pre-Broadway tryouts beginning with the mega smash, *Hairspray*.

In addition to being a freelance director/choreographer, David was the artistic director of the Cohoes Music Hall. A landmark theater first erected in 1874, it had once hosted such stage attractions as Buffalo Bill Cody and P. T. Barnum's Tom Thumb. Of special note was twelve-year-old Eva Tanguay, who went on to enjoy great success a decade later with her racy performing style, earning her the moniker, The "I Don't Care" Girl (based on a song she popularized). Her ghost is believed to haunt the theater, and based on personal experience, I'm now a believer.

David had an opening in his season and needed a small musical. He read *No Way to Treat a Lady*, listened to the score, and offered me an opportunity to continue working on the show in this former textile town near Albany.

To give you a sense of the bleakness that awaited us in Cohoes, when William Kennedy's Pulitzer Prize–winning novel, *Ironweed*, was filmed with Jack Nicholson and Meryl Streep, many of the scenes rooted in the Great Depression were shot on the city's streets. No need to create a facsimile on some back lot!

The Godfather III had been released the previous year. As much as I relished the chance to revisit *No Way to Treat a Lady*, a part of me felt like Michael Corleone: "Just when I thought I was out . . . they PULL me back in!"

David challenged me to once again re-examine and reinvent the opening of the show, proposing that the curtain rise on Alexandra Gill, now not merely a celebrated dramatic actress but a musical comedy star. She is performing her signature song, "Once More from the Top," in a Broadway show while her son, Christopher/"Kit," watches from the wings. Suddenly, her spotlight is extinguished, and we see Kit auditioning as a priest in a musical version of *Going My Way* (the film that earned Bing Crosby an Oscar). Kit launches into a priestly monologue before incurring the wrath of an unseen temperamental director who unwittingly ignites Kit's killing spree.

It was an intriguing framing device, so once again I decided to travel by rail, leaving Manhattan every week for a few "idyllic" days in Cohoes. David occasionally consulted a psychic who encouraged him to cast a Broadway star in the role of Alexandra/Flora/victims, believing a box office draw could save his theater from hard times. (It seemed *Ironweed* cast a long shadow.)

Tony winners Helen Gallagher, Dorothy Loudon, and Broadway's Joan Copeland were courted but wisely did not wish to spend the next seven weeks in the "Spindle City." Chita Rivera was very intrigued. As part of the seduction, I sent her flowers on her birthday. Chita personally called to thank me and said how much she responded to the project. Her agent, the great Biff Liff of William Morris, emphasized, "Chita would love to be considered *when your show comes to New York*."

Not exactly the response David and I were hoping for.

We eventually cast Barbara Irwin, a delightful performer who had some strong theater credits including originating the role of Lily St. Regis in *Annie*. A week before our rehearsals began, however, Barbara added another important Broadway credit to her resume when she accepted Arthur Laurents's offer to portray Tessie Tura in his Broadway revival of *Gypsy* starring Tyne Daly. To sweeten the deal, producers Fran and Barry Weissler had guaranteed Barbara special billing and her own dressing room. In Cohoes, she'd have been lucky to have her own bedroom.

Even without a celebrated actress for the character woman, we had assembled an excellent cast: Adam Grupper (who had performed the role of Morris at Florida Studio Theatre), Kathy Morath, and Ray Wills. They knew important names had been bandied about and were eager to see who would show up on the first day of rehearsal.

Darlene Popovic.

Chances are you haven't heard of Darlene, but she's an actress from the San Francisco Bay area. She had played the role when TheatreWorks in Palo Alto produced my musical the year before and proved to be a versatile, funny, endearing performer. But she wasn't going to get any butts in seats or entice New York commercial producers to make the trek up to Cohoes.

"It's okay," I told myself. "We're still working on the show. Good to have a haven where I'm free to make changes without the peering eyes of industry."

Rehearsals began on an up note. The cast was strong, and everyone responded favorably to the new opening with Alexandra Gill belting out "Once More From the Top." It appropriately signaled we were in a musical.

On the first day, David addressed the room and said he saw every show as "something perfect, and it is up to us to find the clues the writer has given us."

I may have left a few clues, but we didn't achieve perfection. In fact, we eventually ran out of time to tech the show, so the first preview became the final dress rehearsal. I sat in the back of the theater, anxious to see how the new opening unfolded. Thankfully, it seemed to perfectly set the tone for the tongue-in-cheek evening which was to follow. It was hard to tell if the rest of the show worked, as technically there were major rough spots (although I loved Tom Sturges's slightly askew set). Most of the changes from London were effective, but the script still could have used some judicious pruning. Not wanting to replicate the problematic ending at Leatherhead, we reinstated the song "A Close Call," featuring Kit and Morris dueling.

The night before the first preview, I went to bed on the early side, hoping to get much-needed rest. My father had insisted I take a Hammacher Schlemmer smoke alarm to the rustic apartment I shared with three other theater personnel, bordering a Ukrainian cemetery. At 1:30 a.m., the alarm went off apparently for no reason. It awakened me, my three other occupants, and probably the dead. I couldn't get it to stop, no matter how much I tampered with the product. In frustration, I shoved it back in its box, wrapped a wool blanket around it to muffle the sound, and buried it deep in a bottom dresser drawer. Somewhere between 5:00 and 9:00 a.m., the infernal beeper died.

The next morning while eating breakfast, I witnessed a little dog attempting to mount a huge lab in the Ukrainian cemetery. The smaller dog kept missing its mark by a good foot. Finally, the huge lab got fed up and ran away. I wondered if this was a bad omen.

The run garnered mixed reviews. All the critics but one came on the same night, which ran twenty-five minutes long due to technical challenges—and, admittedly, some overwriting. The last critic came to a performance halfway through the run and gave us a rave. By then, the piece had found its footing and audiences were responding in kind. Business was good, the cast was performing well, and I was beginning to feel cautiously optimistic. I left for New York, promising to attend the last weekend of the run.

Three weeks later, I returned with Cathy for the final five-show weekend: a Friday night performance, two on Saturday followed by two final Sunday performances. Cathy and I planned to leave Sunday morning and were enjoying the Saturday matinee when I started thinking about Eva Tanguay. An old-timer at the theater had predicted her ghost might have a field day with *No Way to Treat a Lady*, as she was rumored to have kept an illegitimate son hidden away to perpetuate her youthful reputation. I decided there was no truth to this ghost story.

It was late in the second act when Sadie (Darlene) offers Kit (Ray in drag) a drink: "Honey, you look like you could use a visit from the spirit world." They soon launch into the song "Still," and Darlene was directed to rush toward the door when Ray dramatically removes his wig. It was always a tricky bit of staging, as Darlene had previously kicked off a high heel, leaving her with one shoe on, one shoe off. She ran for the door, only this time, she slipped on her stocking foot and began to fall backward as if in slow motion. Ray tried to help her by grabbing her arm to break the fall, but inadvertently, his impulsive gesture pulled ligaments in her rib cage. I could hear Darlene whispering, "Let go! Let go!" but Ray held on, finally letting go as she collapsed onstage. The audience, unsure of what had happened, applauded after the blackout.

In a newspaper article I later discovered online, the ghost of Eva Tanguay was rumored to hang out just off stage left, exactly near where the accident occurred.

Darlene had one final song before the curtain: the trio "I Have Noticed a Change in You." Looking catatonic and gasping for air, she was excruciating to watch, and suddenly the trio became a duet with a heavy breather. I turned to my wife and said, "I have a feeling this is the end of the run." My prediction gathered traction when Darlene didn't appear at the curtain call. I went backstage to check on her condition only to be told the company manager had already whisked her off to a hospital. With only two hours before the next performance, the remaining three cast members convened in the green room and began to eat dinner. No one seemed to know the extent of her injuries or even which hospital was treating her. Without an understudy, we wondered if there was an intern who could assume the role. I half-jokingly volunteered my services to David Armstrong. He smiled faintly and later disappeared. We heard he went to the hospital, but which hospital? When would he return? And would Darlene be with him? With a nearly sold-out house, would the show go on?

We were sanguine when I called a local hospital and found out Darlene had been released. They couldn't comment on her condition but at least offered that "She'll be okay." However, David called soon after, leaving word the evening performance was canceled.

Kathy Morath, my Cathy, and I went back to Ray and Adam's apartment feeling totally helpless. Instead of responding to the laughter and applause of 350 patrons, the five of us huddled together in their depressing living room, conjecturing about what went wrong and wondering if the two remaining Sunday performances would resume. Cathy and I went back to our hotel at midnight and promptly fell asleep.

The next morning, as we were checking out around noon, the phone rang at the front desk. A clerk answered.

"Doug Cohen? You're in luck, he's right here," she said into the receiver. "Mr. Cohen, I'm transferring the call," indicating a house phone across from the desk.

I picked up the phone with eager anticipation. "Hello?"

"Doug, it's David. You'd better get over to the theater soon. You may be going on for Darlene."

My heart was racing. This was like a Christopher Durang parody of *42nd Street*—"You may be going out there an obscure author, but you're coming back an obscure actor!"

When I got to the theater, David explained the situation: Darlene was in pain and didn't want to perform. There were two nearly full houses (many people from the previous night had opted to return). The theater couldn't afford to cancel these last shows, as they were already struggling. Would I consent to perform the role holding a script? David would introduce me to the audience and explain the situation. I wasn't about to fool anyone, especially with a beard. He and I decided we'd select only certain elements of Darlene's wardrobe so it wouldn't be a drag act.

"What about her major tango with Kit?" I asked.

David had already found a solution.

"You'll sing from offstage while I dance the role of Carmella."

In other words, David would be my Dream Laurie in *Oklahoma!*

With less than an hour to go through the paces, I didn't have time to be nervous. Besides, I had seen the show about eight times plus rehearsals, so I knew the lay of the land. I also knew the lion's share of the songs and lines, but I was grateful to have a script in hand.

Cathy wished me luck and went out into the house. She had a video camera I had brought with me from New York hoping to take some footage of the cast backstage. The battery was only half charged, so Cathy would have to choose judiciously.

David and I decided I would wear my regular clothes but convey Alexandra with a sparkly red robe that Darlene donned (minus the turban!). It reminded me of something Leading Player would wear in *Pippin*. I used a ratty cardigan sweater and glasses for Mrs. Sullivan, a pink bathrobe for Flora, and a boa for Carmella. It was like deconstructing each role and retaining the essence of the character. When it came to Sadie, the barfly, we weren't sure how to proceed. If I didn't wear the wig and dress and Kit came on in drag, would it look strange? We decided to play it by ear (or fear).

The audience assembled. David, as promised, came out and explained about Darlene's accident. The good news—she's recovering. The not-so-good news—she can't perform. A few disappointed "ohs" could be heard. I suddenly realized it was a blessing we didn't attract a Tony-winning Broadway performer: "In the role usually played by Chita Rivera . . ."

David introduced me to some tepid applause and laughter. He explained that I had no rehearsal, but, hey, isn't it historic to see the creator play the role? Most people seemed to be on board, but just in case anyone wished to leave, they could get a full refund or see the box office at intermission. No one left . . . yet.

David thanked them, thanked me, and we scurried off into the wings. Our music director George Kramer hit the downbeat, and I came out as Alexandra with the red sequin robe. It reminded me of a funny, oft-repeated anecdote in the BMI Musical Theatre Workshop. In the 1970s, Lehman Engel was critiquing a song when the somewhat defensive writer assured him the song will work: "I forgot to mention the actress is wearing a green sequin dress." Occasionally whenever a song fell flat in class, a writer would say, "Yeah, but wait till you see the green sequin dress."

I was wearing a red sequin robe—probably closer to *Joseph and His Amazing Technicolor Dreamcoat*. But that robe must have had some magical powers for the show got off to a strong start: Not only was I miraculously able to finesse Darlene's musical keys but I also remembered the musical staging. It was truly an out-of-body experience as I transformed into the other four women. Every time I got off track, the other cast members would lovingly guide me. I didn't get Darlene's laughs, but I didn't exactly suck either.

My wife took her place in the house right balcony. She said a man sat down near her ten minutes into the show, having missed the curtain speech. He was thoroughly confused watching a hirsute Flora Brummell! By the time Sadie appeared in Act Two, that bearded performer now donned a dress and long Dolly Parton tresses.

I got through the matinee with a decent, legitimate performance. David told me only two people at intermission requested their money back. The performance that night was much more assured—no one asked for a refund.

At 10:30 p.m., Cathy and I wearily walked out with the cast to the parking lot to board our rental car. After exchanging congratulatory hugs and saying our goodbyes, Adam Grupper turned to me and asked, "What are you working on now?"

It was a question fraught with subtext. Adam is indeed one of the good guys. It wasn't exactly Sydney Pollack entreating Dustin Hoffman to seek therapy in *Tootsie*, but in a subtle way Adam was encouraging me to move on.

"I have a reading of *God's Hands* with Goodspeed, and I've started working on a new musical, *The Gig*."

"Good," Adam said. "Safe travels."

"You as well, Adam. See you in the city."

A few weeks later, I ran into Jack Hofsiss at a Broadway play and related both the near fatal stabbing of Kate Cornell and my stepping into the shoes of the injured Darlene Popovic. In his inimitable way, Jack laughed and, alluding to the most accident-prone of Shakespeare's plays, proclaimed, "Oh my God, it's the Macbeth of musicals!"

13

I NEED A LIFE

The reading of *God's Hands* with Goodspeed Opera House didn't result in a production, despite Artistic Director Sue Frost's enthusiasm. Michael Price, Goodspeed's menschy executive director, wished me and the project godspeed. Fortunately, Robert Kelley, producing artistic director of TheatreWorks in Palo Alto, produced and co-directed a first-rate production. Faintly autobiographical, it focused on a child prodigy pianist and his rabbi father. In hindsight, I was probably too young to be drawing on my youth without the benefit of more time and perspective. However, I no longer felt young: When I had met with Frank Gilroy to ask permission to musicalize his movie *The Gig*, he wondered why a thirty-one-year-old was interested in exploring the lives of middle-aged men. The truth was *No Way to Treat a Lady* and recent events had aged me.

There were some bright spots, however. Following an idyllic reading at the Eugene O'Neill Theater Center in the summer of 1993, *The Gig* won a 1994 Richard Rodgers Development Grant which led to staged readings at Manhattan Theatre Club at City Center Stage 2. Halfway through rehearsals, I went uptown to receive the award at the American Academy of Arts and Letters. Jonathan Larson, recipient of a Richard Rodgers Studio Production Grant for *Rent*, attended as well. During the cocktail party, Stephen Sondheim made a surprise appearance, admitting to Jonathan and me, "Only for you guys would I get dressed up to come here."

*Stephen Sondheim with two of his disciples: Jonathan Larson and the author.
American Academy of Arts and Letters, 1994.* Photo by Dorothy Alexander

*From the looks of it, Stephen Sondheim is sharing his predilection for killer musicals
with a captive audience (including Cathy Kiliper and her husband).*
Photo by Dorothy Alexander

There is a candid photo of the three of us together which I treasure and find very intriguing. Sondheim is deservedly in the center, as well as the center of our universe. Jonathan, however, was to soon ascend with *Rent* (although it tragically coincided with his death). Smiling diffidently in the photo, I'm staking out the middle ground.

When Jonathan and I took our assigned places on the stage with other honored recipients, we flanked Sondheim's teacher and mentor (dating back to Williams College), the esteemed composer Milton Babbitt. I wish I could remember more of our conversation, but we asked him which was his favorite Sondheim score. If memory serves, he answered *Sweeney Todd*. I then asked Jonathan to describe *Rent*. When he related it was a rock opera based on *La Boheme*, I remember thinking, "It will either be brilliant or a misfire." Well, you know the rest.

Michael Kerker, who assumed the title of director of musical theater at ASCAP after Bernice Cohen sadly passed away, was a wonderful champion of my work. He asked if he could feature my songs at the Cabaret Convention at Town Hall in 1992 as part of the Songwriters Showcase. He chose two co-written with Tom Toce: "The Wrong Man" (a witty send up of romance gone south using Hitchcock titles, performed by Mary Cleere Haran) and "Shalom, Santa" (also known as "My mother is a lapsed Catholic and my father is a cultural Jew"), which I performed. Both numbers went well, particularly "Shalom, Santa," and outside the stage door, I was greeted enthusiastically by two very smartly dressed women. They were a mother and daughter, not unlike Dorris and Barbara of Showpeople, who went by the names of Mimi Levine and Randie Levine-Miller. They proudly exclaimed they had seen *No Way to Treat a Lady* two times at the Hudson Guild and "even paid retail!" Randie, the daughter and the chattier of the two, ran her own public relations firm and wanted to know all about the show, why it hadn't been picked up for a commercial transfer, what went wrong in the United Kingdom, what went right, and did I have clippings, aspirations, prospects? We exchanged cards, promising to explore the conversation at greater length.

Randie lived only four blocks from me with her older, more sedentary husband, Ted. He was an investment banker but seemed to tolerate Randie's passions, and *No Way to Treat a Lady* was chief among them. The more material I showed her, the more she was intrigued by the possibilities of a commercial run. She was upfront about the fact she didn't have a lot of money and lacked producing credits, but she would gladly shepherd the show with the hopes of attracting someone qualified. Lawyers were contacted and an option was exercised, giving Randie an opportunity to produce my musical.

Through fortitude, networking, and unbridled chutzpah, Randie schmoozed nascent producer David Stone and lead producer Michael Frazier, the latter still basking in glory from another *Lady*: Lena Horne's one woman show, *The Lady and Her Music*. Michael and David wanted to view the archival video of *No Way to Treat a Lady* housed at the New York Public Library for the Performing Arts at Lincoln Center. They asked if I would accompany them, so we watched the footage together, weathering polite reprimands from the librarian for laughing too loudly at June Gable's antics.

Michael Frazier ultimately decided he didn't want to work with Randie, but David offered to co-produce. They met for lunch, and Randie later confided that although she predicted David was on the brink of a huge career, they weren't quite aligned. Sadly, David moved on, fulfilling Randie's prophecy by eventually being a lead producer on *Wicked*, *Next to Normal*, and *Kimberly Akimbo*.

Randie entertained other prospects before finally deciding on Robert V. Straus. Bob had graduated from a seasoned Broadway stage manager to a seasoned Broadway general manager with producing aspirations. He knew everyone, even if he, too, was navigating new territory. I liked Bob, although I felt there was a certain bluntness that was alternately refreshing and disconcerting. His wife, Marguerite, was lovely, however, and his associate, Mike Rafael, was young, hungry, and eager to make his mark. So even though I felt David Stone was the better prospect, I respected and accepted Randie's decision.

During my first meeting with Bob, he pitched Lonny Price as director. They had worked together on the Broadway musical *Rags*, and Bob didn't have to do a hard sell: I knew Lonny and had great respect for him as an actor and more recently a director, having seen his acclaimed Off Broadway production of *The Rothschilds* the previous season. He was also a television director on *One Life to Live*.

Lonny attended the next meeting. He was very complimentary of *Lady* but agreed with Bob that the opening and ending needed work. Lonny is the kind of person who instantly and effortlessly becomes the smartest guy in the room. His pedigree is exceptional, having first worked in Hal Prince's office and later starring in the historic, ill-fated world premiere of Sondheim, Furth, and Prince's *Merrily We Roll Along*. He's prudent and doesn't suffer fools gladly, but then you bring your A game to any meeting you have with Lonny.

I felt for the first time that I had met a director who totally had the right sensibility for *No Way to Treat a Lady*. Lonny could have played Moe Brummell, but being a Broadway baby, he also understood Kit Gill. Possessing Hal Prince's gift for theatricality and conceptualizing, Lonny is also very strong communicating with actors, having forged a distinguished thespian career.

Lonny understood the style of the piece, the high wire act of acknowledging both the light and dark aspects in equal proportion. He knew it wasn't quite camp but a theatrically heightened style, and our backer's auditions cast reflected that. For the role of Kit, he chose Bob Stillman who, like Stephen Bogardus, was a leading man not afraid to show vulnerability, projecting authenticity even when employing artifice. Never quite disappearing into Kit's characters, he remained the little boy lost, eager to graduate into manhood.

Carole Shelley, hired to play the mothers and victims, avoided a stereotypical Jewish mother while favoring Flora's tartness. Interestingly, Carole won a Tony as Best Actress starring in Jack Hofsiss's original Broadway production of *The Elephant Man*.

If there was a trait Lonny was attracted to in actors (besides talent), it was intelligence. The smarter the actor, the more intuitive, and the more intuitive, the quicker they were able to grasp his direction and staging. Lonny didn't give line readings, but you could often read on his face and in his posture what he was after.

Lonny challenged me to write an opening number that, unlike "Five More Minutes," would truly function to unite Moe and Kit. Meanwhile, Geoffrey Sherman, producer of the Hudson Guild run, invited me to write a new opening for the Portland Repertory Theatre production he was directing, lamenting that the cast of four only performed one song together, the Act Two opener "Front Page

News." I got the inspired idea of expanding "Five More Minutes" to include Sarah and Flora, as these excerpts reveal.

KIT:
FIVE MORE MINUTES OF STRUGGLING
NOW I'M DUE FOR MY LUCKY BREAK
SOON THE WORLD WILL AWAKEN TO MY NAME
ONLY FIVE MORE MINUTES TILL FAME!
Sarah was introduced trying to hail a cab.
SARAH:
FIVE MORE MINUTES OF FOLLY
A SKIN-DEEP LIFE IN A SKIN-TIGHT DRESS
WHERE'S MY WHITE KNIGHT AND WHY THE LONG DELAY?
IS HE FIVE MORE MINUTES AWAY?
It continued along in this fashion until all four principals sang,
MORRIS:
CAN'T YOU SEE THAT I'M NEAR THE BREAKING POINT
KIT:
THE STARTING POINT
SARAH:
OH, WHAT'S THE POINT?
FLORA:
MY NEEDLEPOINT!

By now, you get the point: I was dutifully trying to check all the boxes. I was also making characters too self-aware and bringing them together in an artificial way. But at the point of creation— or even several days later—I was glowing with achievement. I proudly played the song for Lonny. He listened intently (which is what Lonny does). Finally, he spoke:

"It's a perfectly decent BMI song."

"Okay . . ."

"You did everything correctly, but it's not the opening number we need."

By referencing BMI, Lonny had his pulse on something that often occurred in the Musical Theater Workshop. Many times, I would witness songs landing with my peers only to elicit a very different response in front of a paying audience. Where peers might marvel at a piece's invention and craft, audiences might find it too flashy and dramatically inert. Apparently, this rewrite of "Five More Minutes" fell in the latter category. (I later flew cross country to see the Portland production only to have it confirmed.)

Lonny encouraged me to leave "Five More Minutes" in the trunk. (Trunk tunes are equivalent to the misfit toys in the *Rudolph the Red Nosed Reindeer* animated special. They have a certain value and appeal but are constantly searching for a home.) He wanted me to not only focus on Morris Brummell's dysfunctional life at home but also his thwarted ambitions at the office. Deep down, the show was about two ambitious men who develop a symbiotic relationship as they help each other to achieve their respective goals.

I mulled it over and landed on a title that applied to both our protagonist and antagonist: "I Need a Life."

I also came up with a vamp, which led to a catchy tune. It was dense, meaning there were lots of notes and potential syllables. But it also could enhance the storytelling.

MORRIS:
I NEED TO SILENCE THAT ALARM,
I WANT A MINUTE MORE TO DREAM—
WHY AM I FEELING LIKE A SALMON
AS IT TRIES TO SWIM UPSTREAM?
OH, THIS DREAM, IT WAS THE BEST:
SHE WAS BEAUTIFUL AND SMART.
THE ALARM WENT OFF
BEFORE SHE BROKE MY HEART . . .

At that point, I shifted the new song's action to Morris at his job, but Lonny encouraged me to keep it contained to his apartment, elaborating on his morning ritual. We briefly meet Morris's mother, Flora, who is reading of her older son's medical achievements in *The New York Times*, infuriating Morris:

I NEED THE SECRET OF SUCCESS,
I NEED TO FIND ANOTHER SHIRT,
I NEED TO FLY THE NEST BEFORE A CERTAIN SOMEBODY GETS HURT!
FEELING TRAPPED RIGHT HERE AT HOME,
FEELING TRAPPED AT WHERE I WORK.
PUSHING PAPERS TURNS A COP INTO A CLERK!

WON'T SOMEONE ANSWER ALL MY PRAYERS DUE
SPEED . . .
'CAUSE I NEED A LIFE!

Lonny approved, but like an astute director and resourceful
actor, he wanted it to be a little messier. He started to riff about "I
need a shoe, a shine, a shrink . . ." So I added those references and
a couple of my own. Soon Morris was off on a tirade:

'CAUSE I NEED A SHAVE, I NEED A SHOE,
I NEED A SHINE, I NEED A SHIRT,
I NEED A SHRINK, I NEED—
FLORA: *(Offstage)* MORRIS!
MORRIS: A LIFE!

Kit, too, needs a life. He wants to improve his station: As an
unemployed actor, he's being unfavorably compared to his late
mother, the legendary stage actress, Alexandra Gill—which also
rates a cursory mention in *The New York Times*:

I NEED A ROLE THAT'S TAILOR-MADE,
A CHANCE TO SHOW MY RANGE.
I WANT TO FOOL THEM ALL EACH TIME I MAKE
A BRILLIANT COSTUME CHANGE.

DOORS THAT OPEN WHEN I KNOCK,
EYES THAT LOOK UP WHEN I SPEAK.
GET AN AGENT: ONE WHO WON'T PLAY HIDE 'N SEEK!
I PRAY THAT TODAY'S PERFORMANCE MUST SUCCEED
BUT FIRST I NEED . . .
A LIFE!

Lonny and I discussed how this organically leads to Kit referencing "I'll give a performance that will get me in *The New York
Times*. THE NEW YORK TIMES!" Opening the paper, he turns to the
obituaries: "Nelson, Robertson, Sullivan. *(With a thick Irish brogue):*
Patrick Sullivan . . ." So now we haven't just unified these two men
but also established *The New York Times* as a yardstick measuring
their success. And Kit has even used the paper to identify his first
victim—Mrs. Alice Sullivan, Patrick Sullivan's widow.

The song celebrates the men's similarities and differences as
they strive toward reinvention:

MORRIS:
I NEED TO PACK MY .38
KIT:
WHO NEEDS ANOTHER 8X10?
MORRIS AND KIT:
MAYBE TODAY WILL BE THE DAY
I TURN THE PAGE AND START AGAIN!
IN NO TIME I'LL BE IN PRINT FOR ALL TO READ
BUT FIRST I NEED . . .
A LIFE!!

Lonny and I were very excited with the results. It was remarkable how our sensibilities meshed, and already I was projecting ahead to additional rewrites and future projects. He encouraged me to track the song throughout the show, particularly using it as a reprise within "I Have Noticed a Change in You," the eleven o'clock number. (To the lay person, this is usually the penultimate or last number where the main character, having arrived at some great realization and/or decision, puts everything on the line.) This song was built around Morris hearing the voices of Kit, Sarah, and Flora as they encircle him. But Lonny encouraged Morris to silence those voices with a forceful "STOP!" I didn't realize until later there is a similar device used in *Company* before Bobby sings "Being Alive." But Lonny knew how to borrow from masters. And it worked. It worked beautifully.

FLORA:
I WILL ALWAYS BE THERE FOR YOU.
SARAH, FLORA, AND KIT:
DON'T YOU KNOW HOW I CARE FOR YOU?
KIT AND FLORA:
MORRIS
SARAH:
I HAVE NOTICED A CHANGE IN YOU
SARAH AND FLORA:
MORRIS—
KIT:
COULD IT BE THERE'S A CHANGE IN YOU?
KIT AND SARAH:
MORRIS—

FLORA:
OH, THE CHANGES I'VE—
MORRIS:
STOP!!!!!
I NEED SOME QUIET IN MY LIFE,
A CHANCE TO BE ALONE.
I NEED TO KNOW THE VOICE THAT I AM HEARING
IS MY OWN . . .

We proudly invited Bob Straus, Randie, and Mike Rafael to my apartment to unveil both songs. I made a demo on my four-track mixer, and during a very muggy summer day, we assembled in my living room with the air conditioner going full blast. I pressed play and watched their faces out of the corner of my eye. It felt eerily like *Merrily We Roll Along*'s Franklin Shepard and Charlie Kringas (the role Lonny originated on Broadway) performing Sondheim's classic "Good Thing Going" as we awaited their verdict. Thankfully, our audience was clearly enthusiastic, and Sisyphus finally succeeded in getting the boulder up the hill.

I thought back to my teachers at BMI encouraging us to write our opening number last, as you first need to know what your show is about. Little did I realize that my opening number would materialize eight years after I began writing *No Way to Treat a Lady*!

Inspired by this sudden burst of creativity, I decided I wanted to write a new song for Kit as the priest: "It's a Very Funny Thing" wasn't "funny" and didn't sound at all Irish. I wrote a song which accomplished both, entitled "A Heartbeat Away." With a lilting melody that might have found sanctuary in *Brigadoon* or *Finian's Rainbow*, it gave the audience a chance to laugh at Kit's mordant and morbid sense of humor. It's the kind of song Showpeople would have loved for its nod to black comedy:

THERE, THERE, MY CHILD.
NO USE IN CRYING:
TEARS ARE FOR DRYING,
BE HAPPY, AMEN.
HE HAS PASSED ON—
TIME TO BE STRONG NOW.
IT WON'T BE LONG NOW
TILL YOU MEET AGAIN.

FOR YOU'RE ONLY A HEARTBEAT AWAY, M' DEAR,
YOU'RE ONLY A HEARTBEAT AWAY.
BEYOND HEAVEN'S DOOR
THERE IS ROOM FOR ONE MORE
FOR YOU'RE ONLY A HEARTBEAT AWAY . . .

In the meantime, a production of *No Way to Treat a Lady* was being planned at the Theatre Club of The Palm Beaches in Manalapan, Florida, thanks to a patron, Wileen Coyne, a dear family friend who contacted Louis Tyrrell, their artistic director. It was nearly impossible to say no to a prestigious theater and an opportunity for further exposure and exploration, not to mention much-needed income.

Bob Straus wasn't as enthusiastic but welcomed the opportunity to see what other changes were necessary. Bob, Randie, and Lonny flew down for the dress rehearsal and opening. This version, directed by J. Barry Lewis with music direction by Michael Lavine, still retained the old Hudson Guild ending with the sword fight, but the production was exciting to watch, and the cast was very strong, especially James Judy as Kit and John Brady as Moe. Barbara Tirrell was terrifically authentic as the mothers and victims, and Ellen Zachos delivered a memorable "One of the Beautiful People" to all the beautiful people who attended. Chief among them was Lois Pope, former Broadway performer and widow of Generoso Pope, Jr., who had created the *National Enquirer*. The sale of the paper after his death enabled her to become The Theatre Club of the Palm Beaches's chief benefactor.

She must have been pleased *No Way to Treat a Lady* was a smash hit. Every review was a rave, and Jack Zink, the major critic in Miami and a stringer for *Variety*, encouraged people to get their tickets right away, "as this one should go clean." (The entire run sold out in less than forty-eight hours.) Lest I feel too cocky, however, Bob Straus made sure I wasn't invited to his meeting with Randie, Lonny, and Lois Pope to discuss her potential involvement in a New York commercial run. He suspected my presence might prevent Lois from being completely candid about the material. Lonny later related it wouldn't have mattered: Among her requirements were cameo appearances by Morris's older brother, Dr. Franklin Brummell, and his wife, expanding the cast from four to six. That idea alone made her future participation a non-starter.

no way to treat a lady

Randie Levine-Miller & Robert V. Straus
In association with Jack Thomas
invite you to

A Backers' Audition of

NO WAY TO TREAT A LADY

A Musical Thriller

Written by Douglas J. Cohen
Directed by Lonny Price

With
Tovah Feldshuh, Jason Graae
Kay McClelland & Bob Stillman

Monday, March 7th, 1994
or
Thursday, March 10th

5:30PM SHARP

The Friars Club
57 East 55th Street

RSVP!: 398 2977

One of several backer's auditions Lonny Price directed in 1994 featuring an impressive cast. Author's collection

The Manalapan success galvanized us and gave our team a set of rave reviews that could help with financing. In the meantime, Lonny directed several backer's auditions with a rotating cast that included Bob Stillman, Carole Shelley, Adam Grupper, Kay McClelland, and eventually Jason Graae and multiple Tony nominee Tovah Feldshuh. Tim Weil, Jonathan Larson's music director on the world premiere of *Rent*, was our MD. I'd known Tim for a few years—we had lived a block away from one another. He and Lonny frenetically enhanced an arrangement of "Once More from the Top," which remains in the score today. I tend to look at musicals as a very expansive, collaborative quilt where some of the panels are created by talented artists laboring together. A line or an inspired bit of business here, part of an arrangement there—it all positively contributes to the total effect.

Lonny and I were only partially privy to how the fundraising was going. Mike Rafael would drop hints like "this last one was successful" or "we're nearly there." In the meantime, one of Bob Straus's co-producers on Off Broadway's *The Food Chain*, Randall L. Wreghitt, became enamored with *No Way to Treat a Lady*, as did Jack Thomas, the Shuberts's director of group sales. Jack originally saw a reading at the Berkshire Theatre Festival, and now he and Randall were signing on as associate producers, which helped to take some of the burden off Bob and Randie.

Lonny was directing *Sally Marr . . . and her Escorts*, a play he was developing with Joan Rivers starring as Lenny Bruce's mom. It had been Joan's passion project for several years, and they finally opened on Broadway in May 1994. Joan was nominated for a Tony, but the play unfortunately shuttered after fifty performances and twenty-seven previews. I remember congratulating Lonny on Joan's nomination, but clearly it did little to mollify his disappointment. However, I believed he would now channel his energy into *No Way to Treat a Lady*. Sadly, I misjudged.

On Friday, June 10, we were scheduled to meet at my apartment to discuss rewriting the final scene, the Moe/Sarah reconciliation. Lonny arrived at 10:00 a.m., asked for a glass of water, and parked himself in our La-Z-Boy chair. The air conditioner was making an awful racket, but I could hear every word:

"Listen, I've got some unpleasant news—"

He had my complete attention.

"It looks like I'm not going to be able to direct your show."

"Oh, my God . . ." I whispered.

"I'm really sorry, Doug, but—"

"Does Bob Straus know?" I interjected.

"I told Bob and Mike Rafael last night."

"*Why*, Lonny?"

"There's a new producer on *One Life to Live*. I went to her and explained I'll need to take some time off to direct *Lady*. They weren't thrilled with the show I did for them last month, so I waited until I did a show for them last week, which went better. The producer told me I could do the musical, but she couldn't guarantee there would be a job waiting for me when I return . . ."

He went on to describe his disillusionment with theater, how his projects never made any money, how Joan Rivers couldn't fill five hundred seats at the (Helen) Hayes Theater (he waived his 4 percent royalty to help shore up the finances of *Sally Marr*), and now he had a mortgaged co-op.

Having had years of experience selling people on job opportunities, I knew there was an outside chance I could convince Lonny that *Lady* was different: a significant commercial project that was going to handsomely reward him. I even offered Lonny part of my share as a librettist if he stayed on. He was very touched but said no. That's how I knew he meant business.

He started talking about the sad state of theater, pointing out that no one took risks, and musicals were a dying art form except for revivals. I confided that I too didn't know why I persisted. Lonny told me how much he admired my work on *Lady* and *The Gig* ("Manhattan Theatre Club would be foolish not to fully produce it"), and soon I was crying. I wasn't sure if this was a result of his news or my sensing *The Gig* wouldn't get picked up by Manhattan Theatre Club or because I was seriously considering chucking the whole thing. But I was wiping away tears telling Lonny I felt robbed of going the distance with him on an actual production: Lonny possessed Vivian's acumen and Jack's sense of style along with a show biz savviness all his own.

To help me through this crisis, he suggested Walter Bobbie as a replacement. I asked Lonny if there were any other reasons—aside from conflicts with his soap opera—that elicited his decision . . . like losing faith in our producers. He said it wasn't an issue but added, "Mike Rafael is your ace in the hole. He's a tireless worker and bright."

But Mike didn't foresee Lonny's untimely exit. In fact, he and Bob were aghast but careful not to let it affect their spirits, at least in my presence.

"Wow," I began my phone call shortly after Lonny left my apartment. "When Lonny said he was coming over to discuss the ending, I didn't know he meant 'the end.'"

However, I related we had parted with warm, bittersweet, amicable feelings. Indeed, Lonny left saying he wished we could work together on something in the future. Unfortunately, that has never materialized.

Bob, Mike, and I made up a list of directors that fateful Friday. Gerald Gutierrez (the Tony winner celebrated for *The Most Happy Fella* and *The Heiress* Broadway revivals), Rob Marshall (prior to directing the film version of *Chicago* and co-directing *Cabaret* on Broadway), Vicky Bussert (who had directed *The Gig* in concert at Manhattan Theatre Club), Graciela Danielle (*Once on this Island*), and Gene Saks (*Broadway Bound*) were my suggestions. Bob nixed Vicky ("No New York credits") and Gene Saks ("Too old!"). He and Mike had heard great things about Walter Bobbie from Jay Binder, a major casting director and friend. They also suggested Robert Jess Roth, *my* "Rob." How ironic that in 1987 Rob had been one of four directors under consideration but not viewed by others as a serious candidate. Now that he was a Tony nominee with a long-running mega hit, *Beauty and the Beast*, the ground rules had changed.

Graciela Danielle was not available but said lovely things about Rob Marshall (who left soon after for England to choreograph *She Loves Me*). The indispensable George Lane arranged for a meeting with Gerald "Gerry" Gutierrez, his client, although George revealed Gerry wasn't thrilled to learn he wasn't under exclusive consideration. (According to George, he said, "I beat cancer, so what do I need this for?!")

But meeting Gerry was sheer delight. After comparing the long William Morris corridors to airplane aisles, Gerry sat with me in a conference room and talked for two hours. We shared a healthy respect for Court TV and a morbid fascination with the Menendez Brothers trial.

On some issues, however, Gerry and I were on less common ground. He wasn't comfortable having the show begin with Kit as a frustrated actor—he wanted him to first appear as a psychotic priest. That represented a real step backward for me, which would probably necessitate losing "I Need a Life." He also favored delaying Alexandra's appearance until the very last scene—he felt her earlier presence telegraphed too much to the audience. Maybe so, but was that necessarily a detriment? He also didn't care much for "One of the Beautiful People," even with the last stanza, which many felt contained some of my best writing:

I'LL SAY GOODBYE,
GOODBYE TO THE BEAUTIFUL PEOPLE!
GOODBYE TO THE CHARGE CARD AT GUCCI,
GOODBYE TO THE ROOM WITH A VIEW.
I'LL SAY GOODBYE TO HAMPTON VACATIONS
AND NATIONS OF BEAUTIFUL PEOPLE . . .
AND SAY HELLO TO BEAUTIFUL YOU.

Gerry responded, "Can't Sarah have her Hampton vacations *and* her Jew?" He also felt the first Sarah/Moe scene wasn't interesting enough. On that last point, I agreed.

That weekend we found out that Rob Marshall really liked the show (Mike Rafael reported that he found the material "rich") but wasn't going to return from England until August. Since this would be his New York City directorial debut, he felt there wasn't enough time to prepare for rehearsals on August 20.

You see, time was of the essence because Mike Rafael had delivered a real coup—he'd arranged to have the American Place Theatre rent us their space! Lacking the finances to support their own season, they were talking to outside commercial producers, and Mike had skillfully seduced their artistic director into choosing *Lady*.

But that was before Lonny quit. Now we needed a director fast or the American Place Theatre was moving on. I told Bob Straus et al. that I wanted Gerry to direct, and the offer went out. The following day George Lane indicated Gerry was ambivalent about the project, having watched the movie. I called Gerry, who at the outset seemed dubious, but as we talked his enthusiasm grew. By the end, I thought there was a fighting chance he'd sign on. However, he stipulated, "I need until tomorrow to think about it." When I said "sure," he lovingly chided me, "Go to hell." I countered with "See you there," as we both laughed and set down the phones. Real Kit Gill/Moe Brummell stuff.

I called Bob Straus and told him we had a fifty/fifty chance Gerry would say yes. In the meantime, our possible candidates were dwindling in number. Walter Bobbie passed, citing his inability to find a consistent style to fuse it all together. A few years later, he struck gold with a musical revival focused on two publicity-obsessed killers wedded to a burlesque style: the City Center Encores mounting of *Chicago*.

Rob Roth sadly had to pass due to his Disney commitments (which was ironic since Rob would have thrown his mother off Space Mountain a couple years earlier for the opportunity). Agent Brett Adams faxed Bob Straus saying he heard we were looking and hoped we'd consider his client, Susan Schulman. His letter went on to list all the "lighter" musicals Susan had been involved with, as opposed to *The Secret Garden, Merrily We Roll Along*, and *Sweeney Todd*. (Pretty dark stuff, but then we are talking about a serial killer musical.)

Thursday came and went. George Lane reported that Gerry asked that John Lee Beatty, the celebrated set designer, receive a script and tape. We saw that as a positive sign and imagined a scenario where they were meeting later to discuss the show's design. I refrained from calling Gerry, hoping it would give him the opportunity to call me—except he never did. So the best I could do was speak to George who reported that Gerry said he'd be game if there were an out-of-town tryout, thereby taking the onus off of opening first in New York. George inquired as to how many weeks of previews we had, hoping that a liberal preview period would give Gerry more latitude. Mike Rafael faxed George an entire schedule.

That night, Gerry still hadn't called.

The next day, Mike, Jack Thomas, Randie, and I toured the American Place Theatre (which would be renamed The Laura Pels Theatre in 2000 following its acquisition by Roundabout Theatre Company). I wrote in my journal: *It's not glamorous like the Minetta*

Lane or the West Side Arts or the Promenade, but you can't beat the location: West 46th Street just east of Broadway! Susannah Halston, the artistic director, was lovely but bluntly said to Mike, "Give me an answer by tomorrow" . . . or else. Mike told her we were having contractual issues with George Lane and Gerry, which would be within the realm of possibility if Gerry would only say yes! Susannah threatened to call from her vacation to find out the verdict.

There was still no verdict by noon the following day. With no word from Gerry, Mike instructed me to make "the first move." Gerry was on the phone with London but called me back soon after.

"Hamlet," he said, as I picked up the phone, "This is Gertrude."

"To be or not to be, Gerry? *That* is the question."

"I still don't know what to tell you," he responded.

Not a healthy sign.

"You must think I'm playing Diva," he continued, "but I can't make up my mind, and I'm usually not like this."

I explained to him how the theater might slip through our hands if we didn't find out that day. Gerry said George hadn't fully articulated the need for an immediate response. He was still vacillating for reasons dealing with rewrites and other issues apart from the show.

"I just feel it may not be the right decision at this time," he concluded.

I decided for him. With a heavy heart, I told Gerry we had to move on but reserved the right to call him should we postpone the production. I referenced other projects I'd love to explore together. Gerry reiterated how impressed he was with my talents in turning "a thoroughly preposterous idea for a musical" into something he greatly admired.

I phoned Mike and said, "Let's see what Susan Schulman and Rob Marshall say."

I was saddened because we still didn't have a director and might lose our theater at any minute. But I was also relieved because I had sensed Gerry and I were not always on the same page. I was open to rewrites—as I had demonstrated with Jack, Rob Roth, Vivian, and Lonny—and I know I would have done somersaults to please Gerry. But it might have been at the risk of sabotaging my own project.

To make matters worse, one of our key associate producers, Randall Wreghitt, had been approached to put money into another new musical coming in the fall, *Das Barbecu*. If *Lady* were postponed, he might shift some of his investment to *Das Barbecu*. Suddenly everything was hanging in the balance.

Meanwhile, I was urged to attend *Lady* EPAs (Eligible Performer Auditions for Actors Equity candidates) with our casting director, Mark Simon, since there was no director or associate director in the room. Many of the actors asked me to send Lonny their regards, mistakenly believing he was still with the show. But then no one had disabused them of that detail.

Ultimately, we lost the American Place Theatre. Rob and Susan had other projects to pursue (Rob was recruited by Blake Edwards to choreograph and assist with *Victor/Victoria* on Broadway; Susan ironically directed a musical about another serial killer, Jack the Ripper, for Playwrights Horizons). We met with David Saint (I had seen a production he helmed of *Billy Bishop Goes to War* starring Roger Bart and Jonathan Larson at the American Stage Company, which I very much admired) and André Ernotte (*Goblin Market* and many other Off Broadway shows). David was bright, impressive, and loved the material. André was innovative and inspiring, one of the kindest people I've ever met. Both were eventually nixed by Bob and his investors. And we were back to where we started . . .

But not for long. Mike Rafael contacted me with some promising news: He was assisting a repertory company, Favored Nations, comprised of Broadway actors "dedicated to developing and performing new musicals and plays." *Rent*'s New York Theatre Workshop had donated space for an inaugural program featuring Audra McDonald, Susan Egan, Burke Moses, Sally Mayes, and Jonathan Freeman. Selections from new musicals included two songs from *No Way to Treat a Lady*, "I Need a Life" and "So Far, So Good," performed by members Brian Stokes Mitchell, Marin Mazzie, and Jason Graae. It was so successful that Mike discussed doing a full reading with Bob Straus's and Randie Levine Miller's blessings, as they still held the option.

Since Stokes, Marin, and Jason had been perfectly cast in the selections from *Lady*, I was disappointed to learn Marin and Jason had found work out of town and were no longer available. Their replacements, Karen Ziemba and Robert Michael Baker, were equally impressive, but I was soon to discover that the ineffable thing known as "chemistry" was missing. For the mothers and victims, Barbara Tirrell, who had scored a significant success in Florida, agreed to reprise her roles.

With the company of Favored Nations donating their time, you couldn't enforce a regular rehearsal schedule. Gabriel Barre, a highly skilled and inventive director and actor, was helming the event. He decided to fully stage the reading, thinking he would have the time and resources. Like all of us connected with this reading, he sadly misjudged.

In fact, there were only two days scheduled where the entire cast would be present for a big chunk of time—the final two days, which included the day of the actual readings at 3:00 p.m. and 7:00 p.m. When I attended on the penultimate day, I was concerned: The actors were still mastering the score, and the staging wasn't complete. Gabe assured me we had enough time: What we didn't finish that day would be completed the day of the reading. We had, after all, a full five hours before the first presentation.

Then we learned that Robert Michael Baker had to meet his ex-wife in court in Connecticut . . . on the morning of the reading! Cast as Morris, he was in 80 percent of the show. I began to panic, but Gabe said Michael's case was first on the docket, allowing him to return by 11:00 a.m. Mike Rafael sat in the house that day, nibbling on his nails. He had done an amazing job sending out invitations (we were also prominently listed in *Daily Variety*), and more industry people were expected to attend than had visited the Hudson Guild during the entire run. Around noon, Robert finally returned, exceedingly apologetic. We had only two hours to rehearse with the full cast, and the second act still hadn't been completely staged. Gabe did what he could, but we were operating on a wing and a prayer.

I did a lot of praying that day but to no avail. Most of the heavy hitters attended the first presentation, which was essentially a dress rehearsal—and a misfire. The evening performance, however, was greatly improved, although far less industry attended. Gabe had given excellent notes in the interim, the cast found their groove, and Brian Stokes Mitchell was particularly impressive, giving a

"What Shall I Sing for You?" Brian Stokes Mitchell, center, a memorable "Kit" Gill, rises like a phoenix at 54 Below, flanked by the author and his frequent collaborator, Cheryl L. Davis. Photo courtesy of Cheryl L. Davis

magnetic performance. But as I've witnessed with so many of my fellow writers, the presentation that counted failed to ignite. And with it, our future plans for a New York production withered as well. It seemed like the final nail in that cheesy coffin depicted in Leatherhead's brochure.

However, while Bob Straus and Randie held the option, one last director emerged who had received a very good *New York Times* review for a prestigious regional production. (The show, a musical revival, later transferred to Broadway where it shuttered quickly after negative notices and poor word of mouth.) He was a nice man but fundamentally wrong for the show. For example, he felt that Morris would never take Sarah on a date to Central Park at night, even though he's a cop carrying a gun. He wanted that scene and song ("The First Move") dropped, as well as the Carmella Tocci scene featuring Kit as a dance instructor. And that was just the beginning of the many changes and cuts he was proposing. When I reported back to Bob Straus and Randie, explaining we were incompatible, Bob lit into me: "You need to work with him! He's our last chance!"

"But Bob, he doesn't want the job, can't you see that?"

"You are *this* close," Bob said, indicating a quarter inch between his thumb and index finger. "*This close* to getting the show right!"

"If I'm so close, why do you want me to practically gut my show?" I asked.

"Don't be such a smart ass!" he replied. But he knew as well as I that we were grasping at straws. At some point, Randie interjected, expressing an opinion that was allied with mine. Bob forcefully and disparagingly told her to keep her opinions to herself. (His eruptions were not uncommon.)

Randie and I soon left his office and silently walked to the elevators. She hit the button, then broke down and cried. "This isn't fun anymore," she wept.

I felt badly, as Randie had gotten involved purely out of love for the show. She would try to sell people on *Lady* by saying nothing in theater was a sure thing "but I can promise you'll have the best time at the opening night party." Now we were consoling one another as the elevator doors closed.

I believe theater—or life for that matter—is a game of chutes and ladders. Sometimes you feel you're on a meteoric path, and then the slightest wrong turn sends you in a tailspin, leaving you stranded and bruised.

Clearly, I needed a life. But out of the *Lady* debacle came unexpectedly good news: My wife was pregnant.

14

BIG TIME IN THE BUNKER

Our son Jeremy was born in early April 1995. We had to induce labor, as he was two weeks past his due date with seemingly no interest in making an appearance. At New York Presbyterian, my wife hadn't significantly dilated, so I was encouraged to go to lunch. I remember picking up *The New York Post*—there was a headline about Andrew Lloyd Webber choosing Glenn Close over Patti LuPone for the New York run of *Sunset Boulevard*. It seemed very inconsequential compared to fatherhood, which was only "a heartbeat away."

When I returned to my wife's room, she was starting to feel the contractions. To distract her, I cued the "labor tape" I'd prepared for her with her favorite songs. At one point, her eyes widened, and she started beaming. "How did you get this?!" she exclaimed as she listened to the "Light My Candle" and "Seasons of Love" demos from *Rent*. "Oh, I have connections," I answered slyly, then related how Jonathan Larson had left us the recordings at our building. It was probably the last time I saw Cathy smile over the next few hours, as the contractions became more intense with increasing frequency.

Shortly after we brought Jeremy home, I ran into one of my favorite composers, David Shire, who asked me about projects and life. When I related I had a newborn, David brightened: "Oh, that's wonderful, Doug. You'll find it will also lead to unexpected creativity." David would know—he wrote the music to one of my favorite scores, *Baby*, while raising his children.

And projects *did* follow. Not only did David Evans, Stu Hample, and I begin collaboration on *Children's Letters to God* (a musical adaptation of the bestselling book), but I was also working on *Glimmerglass*, a musicalization of James Fenimore Cooper's *Leatherstocking Tales* with the librettist on *Columbus*, Jonathan Bolt, and lyricist Ted Drachman. Ted was also the nephew of Frank Loesser, a writer I had worshipped since playing Sky Masterson in my high school production of *Guys and Dolls*, so working with Ted was both artistically gratifying and a window into a rich, historical past.

Douglas Carter Beane approached me around this time to ask me if I'd like to collaborate on a musical. Originally entitled *The High Seas* but soon rechristened *The Big Time*, it focused on a third-rate Atlantic City duo, Tony and Donna Stevenitti, who are mistakenly booked on a 1963 North Atlantic Treaty Organization peace-keeping vessel intended for Steve Lawrence and Eydie Gormé. When the ship is taken over by a quartet of Russian rebels, Tony and Donna are placed in the "Useful Not at All" group along with a CIA agent, Big Apple, and UN Undersecretary Penelope Briggs-Hopkins, whom the Russians mistake for a choreographer and English nanny. The Russian rebels' only Achilles' heel is their fascination with Western culture. It's up to our unlikely heroes to save the world—not through violence and gunplay but sure-fire entertainment.

It was a delicious premise, and Doug said he thought of me after seeing *The Gig*. Having originally met at the ASCAP Musical Theater Workshop, Doug was and is a force of nature, an effortlessly funny and endlessly clever playwright who willingly "drives the bus." I often find that I'm the designated driver, actively finding a reading or production with a modicum of support from my collaborators. In many ways, I'm following Bill Goldman's earlier, profane advice: I don't enjoy doing it, but somebody must take the initiative. Doug Beane had a talent for stepping into the driver's seat—or at least co-piloting—and making things happen. And I needed that.

Michael Kerker, the director of Musical Theater at ASCAP, was taking the wheel driving the *No Way to Treat a Lady* bus. He was putting together musical presentations at the Sharon Playhouse in Connecticut with producer Michael Gill. Would I be interested in participating? Nothing was happening with *Lady*, and the Playhouse was a bucolic barn. Why not put on a show . . . or at least a reading?

I don't remember how Scott Schwartz became involved as our director—perhaps through Michael Kerker or the Sharon Playhouse. Either way, I'm grateful. Scott was young at the time, very young: If I was a "yeshiva student," Scott was a "post–Bar Mitzvah boy," but also a wise, old soul. As Stephen Schwartz's son, he came from exceptional genes. It also felt right to be working with the progeny of a man who was instrumental in my getting the rights to Goldman's novel. And like his father, Scott is tremendously perceptive.

Scott also knew we shouldn't reinvent the wheel in twenty-nine hours, the amount of time Actors Equity allocates to learning the music, rehearsing, and presenting a musical. The focus was on some judicious cuts and making sure our cast—Scott Wentworth, John Brady, Alix Korey, and Marguerite MacIntyre—were comfortable with the material. It was a "weekend in the country" without a hitch. James Morgan, then the associate artistic director of The York Theatre Company, and Janet Hayes Walker, the artistic director, made a point to drive up for the reading. Jim is one of the most generous people in the business. He loves musicals, and his passion and profound respect for the art form make him a rarity in the field. Both he and Janet were highly complimentary, and the entire reading was well-received. I left feeling once again euphoric about the piece and cautiously optimistic about its future.

Through Michael Gibson, the remarkable orchestrator of *The Gig* at Goodspeed, I found a new "gig" for *No Way to Treat a Lady*. Michael worked steadily not only on Broadway but also regionally. Since the Signature Theatre in Arlington, Virginia, was producing nearly the entire Kander and Ebb canon, Michael was spending much of his time adapting orchestrations to accommodate their smaller band. When he learned they were looking for an intimate musical and enquired if the rights to *No Way to Treat a Lady* were available, I emphatically replied, "Yes!"

Michael sent the materials off to Eric Schaeffer, the Signature's artistic director, and within a couple weeks word came back they wanted to include it in their upcoming season. Eric was already directing two of the shows, so he declined to helm the production. When I proposed Scott Schwartz for the job, Eric was enthusiastic and invited us to Arlington to see the theater and his production of *The Rink*. Both made a favorable impression.

Then Jim Morgan called. The York Theatre was planning their new season and wanted to present *No Way to Treat a Lady* in their December/January slot. We were already booked for the January/February slot at the Signature. Did it make sense to have another major *No Way to Treat a Lady* production, especially since the Signature Theatre was to act as a springboard?

I proposed *The Gig* to Jim instead: It had yet to make its official New York debut (the Manhattan Theatre Club presentations at City Center had not been reviewed), and the production at the Sacramento Music Circus directed by John DeLuca was a critical and popular success.

The York couldn't make the numbers work for *The Gig* (which had a ten-person cast) without major enhancement. But John and I were offered a January/February slot through Producing Artistic Director James Vagias of the American Stage Company in New Jersey! I reached out to Scott Schwartz and asked him if he wanted to explore directing *Lady* at the York, prior to the Signature. It seemed like putting the cart before the horse, but it was also a bona fide offer from a New York not-for-profit.

When it rains, it pours.

Jim Morgan further enticed me by mentioning that the Citicorp Plaza, a retail bazaar on the ground level of the building that housed the York, was being renovated and expected to re-open in time for the Christmas season. Suddenly I had visions of this beautiful winter wonderland unfolding, attracting throngs with its new stores and dazzling holiday lights. After all, following a forest fire there is renewal and an upsurge in habitation. Why couldn't the same miracle happen on East 54th Street?

You see, I was trying to overlook the fact that The York was three stories below the ground, underneath St. Peter's Church. The theater was affectionately given the moniker "the bunker" by Stu Hample, the book writer of *Children's Letters to God*, and it was an apt one. The York was far removed from daily life: The elevators only sporadically worked, there were no windows, just concrete walls and box-like interiors, and in later years even cell phones didn't operate there. When I was growing up in Connecticut, my family had moved into a house erected in the 1950s that had its own bomb shelter. If we had converted that sealed off room into a theater, it might have resembled a miniature version of the York if not for Jim and company's inviting accessorizing.

Scott and I deliberated and felt it was feasible to do both productions back to back: I wouldn't be needed often at the Signature, as Scott and I will have just worked on the York Theatre production. Even more attractive, I had returned to my job at M. Luca & Associates (the personnel agency), literally two blocks from the York! So far, so good . . .

John DeLuca felt similarly confident remounting *The Gig* in New Jersey without my attending many rehearsals.

Scott and I discussed in some detail the time period of our show. The Hudson Guild production had been set in 1987, the novel in 1964, the film in 1967. (You can even see the construction of Lincoln Center in the film, the locale for Lee Remick's character as a part-time tour guide.)

When Scott and I began rehearsals, however, we were still undecided and openly discussed the issue with our gifted cast, Adam Grupper, Alix Korey, Marguerite MacIntyre, and Paul Schoeffler. Adam recalled that Susan Schulman (with whom he had worked on Broadway's *The Secret Garden*) believed most musicals should not be set in the present. As Adam explained Susan's rationale, "People have a strong connection to the past and understand it more than the present." In other words, audiences are more likely to take the journey if they're stepping into a time machine.

Setting the show in the 1960s or 1970s also solved technical problems. In that era, it would be harder to trace a call, DNA samples weren't analyzed, and surveillance cameras and sophisticated computers didn't exist. You could briefly speak on a phone with a killer and not be able to identify the caller, number, or where the call originated. Scott felt 1970 might be preferable to the 1960s: It was the height of John Lindsay's reign as mayor, and the city was reinventing itself. It wasn't as dark a period as the 1960s, and Scott found an artist who reflected his vision of New York.

Red Grooms, like Warhol, was known for a pop art sensibility. His colorful, multi-media creations had a certain energetic grotesqueness. There was a satirical, exaggerated quality to his work, which often depicted scenes from urban life, particularly New York.

Scott discussed his vision with Jim Morgan: In addition to producing the show, Jim was to design the sets. Jim wrote about the experience in the published Samuel French script:

The production emphasized the musical comedy aspects of the piece; Scott proposed that it be based on the sculptures and environmental constructions of Red Grooms. The audience was surrounded by a very hand-drawn, watercolor version of Manhattan in 1970, with many topical references ("Ethel Merman in Hello Dolly!*," "Zum Zum," etc.). The style was jaunty and colorful, with many mixed scales, all helping to suggest the Lindsay-era phrase "Fun City." The effect was as if the audience was sitting in Central Park, looking south. The West Side, with appropriate landmarks, continued up the right side of the house—all the way to the George Washington Bridge, and the East Side, going up as far as Yankee Stadium, went up the left side of the auditorium. Upstage, the view went out into the harbor and included the World Trade Center—still under construction—and the Statue of Liberty.*

It was an incredibly impressive set and deserved the Drama Desk nomination it received, but its "jaunty and colorful" playfulness suggested a more benign, whimsical New York; it was hard to believe a sinister underbelly existed.

Scott wisely wanted to create visual and aural cues to set up our universe. The show would begin with Morris raising the blinds of his bedroom window, so we, the audience, became voyeurs, like Hitchcock inviting his viewers to peer into Janet Leigh's rented hotel room at the beginning of *Psycho*. We worked on a clock radio announcement that would pierce the dark at the top of the show, following an obnoxious alarm. In that little speech, we were careful to plant themes that would have a significant impact in "Fun City," 1970:

ANNOUNCER'S VOICE: Good morning, you early risers. Expect another muggy, summer day in "Fun City." The Yankees lost their fourth straight to the Senators. *The New York Times* reports that one out of every eighty-two New Yorkers last year was a victim of a violent crime, and Mayor Lindsay has just raised the mass

Berserk over Broadway: Paul Schoeffler (Kit Gill) aloft James Morgan's Drama Desk nominated set in The York Theatre Company's 1996 revival of No Way to Treat a Lady, *directed by Scott Schwartz.* Photofest

transportation fare from 20 to 30 cents. On the lighter side, Zsa Zsa Gabor opens in *Forty Carats* on Broadway . . ."

Scott also felt that Morris and Kit's symbiotic relationship was at the core of the show, and Morris should resist reaching out to *The New York Times* until the end of Act One. This was perhaps one of the most significant changes from previous versions. When Morris finally caves to Kit's demands, he is entering a Faustian pact, elevating not only Kit's status but also his own.

Under Scott's guidance, "You're Getting Warmer," the Act One finale, went on a crash diet, becoming streamlined with greater intent. Instead of four impersonations, Kit adopts only three (there's a reason why most setups find potency in threes). I rewrote many of the lyrics to emphasize Kit's demands for coverage in *The New York Times*. For example, when Kit disguises himself as an employee of New York Telephone, he gains entrée into an unseen, unsuspecting woman's apartment with the following:

"Mrs. Mitchell, I got a printout here that says your phone's on the blink. Mind if I take a look? Oh, here's your problem: Your wires are crossed!"

(Clap of thunder. He flees the scene, leaving a note for MORRIS, which KIT recites rhythmically with rap-like precision:)
THIS USED TO BE THE LINES
OF OUR DEEP COMMUNICATION.
IF YOU'RE HOPIN'
THEY'LL REOPEN,
THE TIMES IS YOUR SALVATION!

I cut sections of music that no longer applied—there were too many musical themes—and Scott encouraged me to reprise "I Need a Life" for Morris to justify his decisive call to *The Times*. Notice how many times the word "time" is used:
MORRIS:
IT'S HIGH TIME I READ THE WRITING ON THE WALL
IT'S MY TIME TO SOUND THE BUGLE, HEED THE CALL.
IN NO TIME I'LL GET MY WISH AND HAVE IT ALL.
OH, I NEED . . .
(Morris sees a payphone in view and begins to dial The New York Times . . .*)*

Wendy Bobbitt Cavett, our uber talented musical director, worked with me on a surprising key change in the middle of this reprise, and it galvanized the piece. We also edited some other pieces, including part of the bridge to "The First Move" (which to this day, I truly miss and hope to restore).

Scott and I cut Morris's "Sarah's Touch," much to my relief. We added a short "Once More from the Top" *pre*prise for Kit to justify disguising himself as Sarah, later performing the song as an eleven o'clock number. That rendition also served Morris, as it evolved into a passionate reprise of "I Need a Life" created under Lonny's guidance.

One of the most important added scenes involved Kit calling Morris with the humiliating news that Sadie, his last intended victim, has escaped. Kit ironically pleads with Morris, "Listen, don't you have any unsolved murders you can give me credit for? If *The Times* gets ahold of this, it could ruin us." Morris, sensing Kit's vulnerability, threatens to feed *The Times* the story "with words like

'failure' and 'weakling,' now that your victim overpowered you."
It's a decisive moment where the tables abruptly turn.

Scott astutely saw Act One as Kit's ascent and Act Two as his
downward spiral. In fact, the whole show became a power play
between two antagonists who collaborate in a dangerous game of
cat and mouse—only to have the mouse eventually defeat the cat.

Which led us to the final showdown. Scott encouraged me to
eliminate the sword fight once and for all, as well as the song "A
Close Call." We still retained Morris overpowering Kit, with not
just force but psychological tactics. After all, the men are two sides
of the same coin . . .

MORRIS: Please, Kit—you don't want to kill Sarah. She doesn't
fit the pattern. You're after your mother, remember?!

*(KIT quickly glances in the direction of his cherished portrait of his
mother. ALEXANDRA'S image is gone. Instead, she appears from the
wings, gradually approaching KIT. Only he sees her.)*

ALEXANDRA: Christopher, time to go now—it's curtain time.

KIT: NO!

MORRIS: You must have loved your mother terribly . . . but
nothing you ever did was good enough for her, was it, Kit?

With Alexandra now tangible to Kit, we were able to create a
ripple of overlapping voices, almost musical in nature, that illus-
trates Kit's descent into madness and infantilization. It culminates
with Morris shooting Kit in the arm and begging Kit to drop his
weapon. Sensing the gig is up, Kit has other plans:

KIT: Do your job, Detective Brummell.

MORRIS: If you drop the gun, I'll see to it that you're given
leniency—

KIT: What? Only three consecutive life terms instead of six?

ALEXANDRA: *(Quietly, near the wings)* Come with me and
you'll be free . . .

KIT: There's a new headline that could blaze across *The New
York Times*: "Detective Saves Girlfriend and Kills Strangler, Christopher Gill."

MORRIS: I can't, Kit.

KIT: *(With feeling)* You can't . . . or you won't, *mon ami*?

In many ways, this echoes Goldman's ending in the novel
where Kit, mortally wounded, begs for mercy. But in the novel,

Morris withholds compassion. In my version, he does the right thing. I won't spoil it for you (although there are spoilers throughout the original cast recording), but let's just say that Kit has one last, great killer surprise up his sleeve having correctly identified Morris's Achilles' heel.

This ending was supremely satisfying, even on the night when Adam Grupper picked up his gun and realized all the blanks had fallen out of their chambers. His faintly audible verbalization, "Bang!" attempted to capture the same impact, although more than a few audience members broke the tension with laughter. Both Paul and Adam, thorough professionals, did not break character.

Even though I was aware this *No Way to Treat a Lady* had less bite in the Big Apple than the sinister version being mounted at the Signature Theatre, it was still a rewarding experience and production. We received an Outer Critics Circle nomination for Best

Sarah (Marguerite MacIntyre) and Flora (Alix Korey) discover they have "So Much in Common," especially their affection for a hapless Moe (Adam Grupper) in The York Theatre Company revival, December 1996, directed by Scott Schwartz. Photofest

Musical Revival (losing to *Chicago*, no surprise there), and Alix Korey earned a well-deserved nomination for Best Featured Actress in a Musical. Reviews were very good—but *The New York Times*, the one review that carried the most weight, was mixed. (The wobbly night *The Times* attended, I applauded so loudly at the curtain call that my wedding band flew off my finger!) Critic Peter Marks had laudatory things to say about my music and lyrics but clearly would have preferred more edge overall. Looking back, I agree but also vividly recall an anonymous elderly woman stopping me after the first preview:

"You wrote this?" she asked.

"Yes, yes I did."

"It's excellent."

"Thank you."

"You wanna know why?" She moved in closer, as if about to reveal the identity of Rosebud. "It's *entertaining*."

Other people must have agreed because we ultimately extended until a revue of Schmidt and Jones's songs entitled *The Show Must Go On*, patiently waiting in the wings, finally debuted. But thanks to an invaluable parting gift and a licensing deal, my show *did* go on . . . and on . . . and on . . .

15

(MIDDLE) GROUND RULES

The production at the Signature Theatre in Arlington couldn't have been more different from The York's. It was like visiting the upside-down world of *Stranger Things*—in fact, it was almost like David Lynch's production of *No Way to Treat a Lady*. It was dark, but then I had faulted the York for not being dark enough. Sometimes it's frightening to be confronted with another aspect of your "baby." Perhaps this *Lady* was closer to what William Goldman had conceived in his novel.

It received an excellent review in *The Washington Post*, the kind of review that would have led to intense New York interest had The York production never materialized. Later, it would be nominated for three major Helen Hayes Awards, winning Best Actor in a Musical for Lawrence Redmond.

I returned to The York in late January 1997, just in time for *No Way to Treat a Lady*'s final week. Based on the mixed *New York Times* review, we didn't commercially transfer, but I did get two lovely consolation prizes: a licensing deal with Samuel French and a CD with intrepid recording producer Bruce Kimmel and Varese Sarabande Records. Bruce had·recorded two songs from *No Way to Treat a Lady* on his *Broadway Bound* CD featuring Liz Callaway and Jason Graae; I can't begin to describe the joy I experienced in hearing those two cuts, beautifully orchestrated by Larry Moore, which represented the very first professional recordings of my work.

We recorded the *No Way to Treat a Lady* revival cast album at Clinton Studios in New York featuring the effective, new orchestrations by David Siegel. Through Mike Rafael, Peter Travers of *Rolling Stone* was asked to write an introduction in the liner notes. Peter had listened to many of the homemade demos of *No Way to Treat a Lady* and was a fan. Not only did he graciously consent to contribute to the booklet but also came up with my favorite quote to date: "How to describe this old-fashioned, new-fangled, thoroughly beguiling musical? Picture the mismatched romantics of *She Loves Me*, hunted by *Sweeney Todd*, and haunted by Mama Rose."

I believe that album is probably the reason *No Way to Treat a Lady* has endured. Raymond Wright, a London producer, found it in the racks at Dress Circle, a London record store, and later produced *No Way to Treat a Lady* (finally) in the West End at the Arts Theatre (which is technically a Fringe theater, but please indulge me). It starred the one and only Donna McKechnie (luminous as Alexandra Gill and memorable as Kit's intended victims), Olivier winners Joanna Riding (a formidable Sarah) and Tim Flavin (a true song and dance man inhabiting Kit), Paul Bowen (an effectively understated detective), and Joan Savage (funny but not "over the top" as Flora). It also benefited from Neil Marcus's respectful direction and Donna's nimble choreography and musical staging. Aside from the most hideous poster design of the Statue of Liberty lying prostrate, it was a first-rate production which deserved a longer run. It also marked the one and only time my parents left the country—aside from our crossing the border into Canada to visit Expo 67 in 1970. And thanks to family friend Wileen Coyne's exceptional generosity, we all stayed in style at London's posh Athenaeum Hotel.

A production at Florida's Coconut Grove Playhouse in February 1998 was memorable for several reasons. Jeffrey Moss helmed, Barbara Siman (Charles Strouse's wife) choreographed, and it featured Broadway veterans Lenny Wolpe, Maureen Silliman, and Ruth Williamson, as well as newcomer, Cordell Stahl. Jim Morgan once again designed the set—a stunner inspired by Andy Warhol lithographs. And it wasn't just a flat stage but also contained levels, as well as a catwalk! With a six-hundred-seat theater, I finally had a chance to see how the show would play in a Broadway-size house.

London Pride: Donna McKechnie (Carmella) and Tim Flavin (Kit as Ramone) begin their dance. Arts Theatre, London, August 1989, directed by Neil Marcus.
Photo by Alastair Muir

A family affair: Cathy, three-year-old Jeremy, and the author at the February 1998 Coconut Grove premiere (captured for posterity by the author's mother).
Photo by Claudia Cohen

It played just fine, receiving seven Carbonell nominations (South Florida's equivalent to the Tony Awards) and surpassing Coconut Grove's second most popular hit that season, *The Sunshine Boys* starring Tony Randall and Jack Klugman.

It probably didn't hurt that Gianni Versace's killer, Andrew Cunanan, ended his reign of terror six months earlier, a scant fourteen miles from the theater. But no one was injured during our run, nor did any other strange mishaps occur during the nearly two hundred productions and concerts that followed.

It's strange, but as productions multiplied, I began to think of myself not as the author but as the author's surviving significant other or progeny, someone called upon to dutifully execute the author's intentions. However, if there were additional rewrites that a producer or theater wished to explore, I suddenly emerged as the author again, excited to take on a new challenge.

I also began to realize that without a commercial hit in New York, I would most likely remain in the middle ground of theater hierarchy. Broadway is an exclusive club, and only people with the right pedigree are invited to play. There are the occasional exceptions, but as you get older, the window begins to close. What's frustrating is that Broadway veterans who are asked to participate often don't boast successful Broadway credits. But the fact they've demonstrated they can play in that arena is enough to qualify. Now, that may sound like sour grapes, but it's just a fact of life I've reluctantly learned to accept.

It means that it's that much harder to get people to attend readings, workshops, and productions. And it's a challenge to get directors or producers to respond to submissions. I wish I had a dime for every submission my agent or I have made to someone I personally know, only to never receive the courtesy of a reply or any additional follow-up. I don't like rejection, but like most people, I prefer it to being virtually ignored. On that issue, there is no middle ground.

There is one thing that all writers have in common: Since our work is constantly evolving, it's not about writing but *rewriting*. Sculptors chip away at a slab of marble until their creation is finally revealed, but they have the advantage of independently controlling their art. Writers must rely on producers, audiences, actors, and theaters while we continue to revise and refine until the true potential of our creation emerges. We often hear of shows getting a mixed or negative reception, and let's face it, most of us believe they must be in their finished state. But often, it's just the beginning of the process. Once upon a time, writers were given the opportunity to learn from their mistakes. It takes a brave producer to buck the trend now and give a failed show another life. But when you see musicals like *Kiss of the Spider Woman* (which won the Tony for Best Musical) and *Next to Normal* (winner of the Pulitzer Prize) rise from the ashes of their problematic premieres and later emerge triumphant, you realize it *can* be done. Not every show is destined for this future, but I passionately believe many shows should be nurtured beyond their initial gestation.

I have great respect for producers: They put a lot on the line and often don't see a penny until the show is in the black, *if* they are fortunate to witness that phenomenon. We desperately need producers, and while they don't often fully understand the artistic process and occasionally fall short on delivering promises, they are emotionally and financially invested. Sometimes I think producers and writers should change jobs as in a Lucy/Desi scenario: Hopefully each party would emerge with a renewed level of empathy.

In 2012, I did have a taste of what it's like to exist on a higher plane when I simultaneously won the Fred Ebb Award and was appointed to the Nominating Committee of The American Theatre Wing's Tony Awards. The former meant I was treated to a lavish party at the top floor of the Roundabout Theatre on 42nd Street with family and friends, as well as revered members of the industry, including my idols John Kander and Sheldon Harnick.

Being appointed to the Tony nominating committee, meanwhile, was a three-year assignment where we were required to see every show on Broadway in a given season to qualify. I use the word "required" loosely as I would have paid *them* for the privilege. Some of my colleagues found it a chore, and I suppose in the last two weeks before the Tony deadline it was challenging attending approximately a show every other night. But I loved every minute of it and took my job very, very seriously. We were asked not to read reviews or discuss our impressions. During the intermission of *On a Clear Day You Can See Forever*, I ran into Craig

With John Kander at the Fred Ebb Awards, November 2010. Photo by Henry McGee

Carnelia, the exceptional songwriter who contributed songs to *Working* and the lyrics to *The Sweet Smell of Success*. In the men's room, Craig commented on how the song "Wait Till We're Sixty-Five" was strangely now in 4/4 when it had always been a jazz waltz. I excused myself, blurted out, "Sorry, I can't comment," and fled. By my third year, I became a bit more relaxed about these things, but only slightly.

What I did notice, however, was that people started treating me with greater respect. Some producers expressed interest in my shows and asked for updates. I even received supportive comments on submissions. It felt like a *Curb Your Enthusiasm* dream sequence, where Larry David projects his secret hopes and desires, and the universe responds in kind. I knew, however, that when my Tony tenure was up, my coach would revert to a pumpkin. It wasn't as if people were no longer cordial, but I could sense there was a difference. And as expected, my theater tickets were not nearly as good: When my wife and I attended a Broadway play and an usher directed us up to our discount mezzanine seats, I joked, "Oh, how the mighty have risen."

With Cathy and Jeremy at the 2015 Tony Awards. Author's collection

Meanwhile, productions of *No Way to Treat a Lady* continued to multiply, giving me the satisfaction that at least this boutique musical was garnering attention. I wasn't present for the Lübeck premiere directed by Stefan Huber, but I did spend a week with this exceptional director and human being when I attended rehearsals for the German premiere of *Der Gig* in Baden-Baden. The Australian premiere at the Darlinghurst Theatre Company—too far down under for this middle grounder to make the journey—inaugurated their new musical series entitled Neglected Musicals, supporting my theory that *No Way to Treat a Lady* is possibly the most showcased "neglected" musical.

I did have the good fortune to attend three significant productions and one reading of special note.

The reading in 2014 (Larry Hirschhorn, producer, Joe Calarco, director, Vadim Feichtner, music director) had a terrific cast of Steve Rosen, Laura Marie Duncan, Cheryl Stern, and featured a brilliant performance by Raúl Esparza as Kit that was so chilling, seductive and mesmerizing that I felt I was witnessing the show anew—the kind of performance that wins Tony Awards.

2013 Tokyo premiere with Natsuki Oh, Kojiro Oka, Ryo Miyauchi, and Rie Miyauchi, directed by Yasuhiko Katsuta.
© Tachi World

Rob Ruggiero, a tremendously intuitive director, struck just the right notes in two explosive productions at Barrington Stage in 2000 and Hartford Theaterworks in 2001. Both boasting the dynamic duo Bradley Dean as Kit and Adam Heller as Morris, they were truly thrilling rides.

Two final productions of note were both abroad. The first was in Saarbrücken, Germany, on the border between Germany and France. It was produced with only piano and acoustic bass, but the cast was incandescent, equally strong, and co-existed in the same world, which can be a rarity.

The other production was at Il Festival Teatrale in the idyllic town of Borgio Verezzi (translated as "where the land meets the sea"). Gianluca Guidi, a brilliant and visionary director, producer, and performer, had discovered the revival cast CD and decided to

"Shhh . . . still": Holger Hauer (Kit) is unmasked and untressed as Bibi Jelinek (Sadie) cowers in the 2000 German premiere, Theater Saarbrücken, directed by Holger Hauer.
Photo by Bettina Stoess

mount a production in August of 2001. Borgio Verezzi sits in the northern part of Italy near the French border. Visitors stay by the water, but when night falls, they navigate their cars up a winding road into the mountains. There, a centuries-old village seems to magically appear with an open courtyard flanked by low-rise apartments. Under the stars, audiences assemble to watch concerts, plays, and musicals unfold.

Having been told events were canceled when it rained, I prayed for good weather. This time Barbara Bonfigli's God of Regional Theater blessed us, and all three performances went smoothly. The show also translated beautifully into Italian thanks to Giorgio Calabrese (who had penned the lyrics to Frank Sinatra's "Softly, As I Leave You") and was sweetened by the enhanced orchestrations of Riccardo Biseo. Retitled *Serial Killer per Signora*, the production

2001 premiere in Borgio Verezzi, Italy, and the first (and so far, only) published folio of my songs. Courtesy of Gianluca Guidi

Douglas J. Cohen

Serial Killer per Signora

MUSICAL

Traduzione italiana delle liriche
Giorgio Calabrese

EDIZIONI CURCI - MILANO

would tour and spawn a cast album and a published folio of my music, the only one that currently exists of the show.

Our premiere was magical. Gianluca created an edgy New York landscape closer to something Jonathan Larson and Michael Greif might have conceived. There were wonderful touches throughout including Morris Brummell making breakfast while skillfully juggling eggs and singing counterpoint in "I Hear Humming." And Morris's Jewish mother successfully morphed into an *Italian* mother. This last observation supported Burton Lane's comment at ASCAP when he related librettist Joe Stein was commended for creating the "perfect Japanese mother" at the Japan premiere of *Fiddler on the Roof.*

At Borgio Verezzi, it is their custom to have the author join the cast for the curtain call. During the thunderous applause, Maria Laura Baccarini, Gianluca's charming and talented girlfriend at the time, excitedly led me to the backstage area. Walking onto that

Now that's a headline! Kit Gill (Gianluca Guidi) and Moe Brummell (Giampiero Ingrassia) are "Front Page News" in the second Italian tour of Serial Killer per Signora, *2017, directed by Gianluca Guidi.* © Luca Vantusso - LKV Photo Agency

stage high above the crowd, it's difficult to describe what I was feeling. It was like sensory overload—a mixture of pride and relief and, yes, gratitude.

I have never admitted this to anyone before, but one night riding home from Leatherhead in the backseat of a car, I was particularly despondent. My left arm was poised on the door handle, and I kept thinking, "Just open the door and you don't have to live with this pain." My world was imploding, I was alone and far away from home, I was trapped in the middle of a vitriolic feud, and my show and my future seemed in shambles. I gripped that door handle the entire time we were on the highway but thankfully never had the audacity to act on the impulse.

At Borgio Verezzi, I looked at the beaming faces of this spectacular company, the hundreds of people crammed into the square, the denizens of the apartments hanging out of their windows to get a closer glimpse. Once my eyes adjusted to the lights, I saw it, there in the distance—the sea! It was brilliantly illuminated by a nearly full moon, and all the moments of despair, the endless rewrites, the false hopes, the thwarted dreams, the passionate and petty arguments suddenly vanished, only to be swallowed up by a vast and bountiful ocean.

EPILOGUE

My son, Jeremy, called me on November 16, 2018, to tell me he read that William Goldman had died. Although I had known Bill was not well, I was greatly saddened to learn he was gone.

We hadn't been in constant touch over the years. He generously treated Cathy and me to a deliciously entertaining dinner on the Upper East Side following our wedding. I brought along my hardback copy of *No Way to Treat a Lady* which he memorably inscribed, "For Douglas Cohen, who is wonderfully talented and tasteful, especially in choosing wives. God bless, Bill." He also attended The York Theatre Company revival, graciously posing for a photo for *The Post* with Marguerite MacIntyre (our Sarah Stone) and took me out to dinner with his new, lovely partner in life, Susan Burden. He couldn't have been more complimentary of the show and the production.

I also ran into Bill through Frank Gilroy. Bill showed up at Goodspeed at Chester for the first performance of *The Gig*, based on Frank's movie, astutely observing, "It's a character-driven musical, like *She Loves Me*. That's why it has such a strong second act." He was at Frank's eightieth and eighty-fifth birthday parties, the latter in 2010 at the home of Tony Gilroy (Frank's oldest son). It was so serendipitous that he and the Gilroys were close. Frank was almost like a father to me, my mentor and inspiration. It blew my mind that two of my literary heroes were such good friends, having created works I later musicalized.

NO WAY
TO TREAT
A *Lady*

WILLIAM
GOLDMAN

7 Nov 87

For Doug Coke
who is wonderfully talented
and tasteful, especially
in choosey wives,
God Bless
Bill

HARCOURT, BRACE & WORLD, INC.

NEW YORK

Bill Goldman inscribes a book. Author's collection

At Tony's dinner party, I greeted Bill outside on Tony's patio. He was in a convivial mood.

"So, I see you're finally consenting to have *The Princess Bride* musicalized," I noted. "You once told me you weren't sure you'd even let Sondheim touch the property."

He smiled sheepishly. "Adam Guettel is good, don't you think?"

Later, Bill and Adam parted company. According to Michael Riedel in the *New York Post*, it was somewhat "acrimonious." Bill reportedly asked for 75 percent of the author's share, but I suspect it wasn't that cut and dried. I also read that Bill had trouble visualizing where Adam was taking the score since Adam would often write the music first, adding lyrics later. It vaguely reminded me of my initial struggle getting Bill to understand my vision. The difference was *No Way to Treat a Lady* was just another novel of Bill's while *The Princess Bride* was, well, *The Princess Bride*.

Many years passed. I delivered a bottle of champagne with a congratulatory note to the stage door when his play *Misery* opened on Broadway. Strangely, I never heard back. Then in the summer of 2017, I realized it had been thirty years since *No Way to Treat a Lady* had debuted at the Hudson Guild. I wanted to do something to celebrate, so I booked Feinstein's/54 Below and assembled not four actors but twenty-four who had participated in the show's history, whether it was productions, workshops, readings, or demos.

I notified Tony Gilroy (his father had passed away two years earlier, but I knew he and Bill were close). Even though Bill was infirm, Tony felt he could convince him to come. Finally, word came back from Tony that Bill would be there . . . only I shouldn't let the audience know. Sound familiar?

It was a wonderfully bittersweet event. My father attended, now a widower after my beloved mother succumbed from a fall four months earlier. Among the photos we projected of various productions was one taken of me with my proud folks on opening night of the Cape Playhouse production six years earlier . . . only twenty minutes from the Cape Cod Melody Tent where my love affair with musicals began.

Local boy makes good: With my proud parents, Claudia and Hirsch Cohen, opening night of No Way to Treat a Lady *at the Cape Playhouse, 2011, directed by Mark Shanahan.* Author's collection

As I arrived at the event, my wife spotted Bill in a banquette nearest the exit, farthest from the entrance but with easy access to make a furtive getaway. I went over to greet him. He was warm but definitely not as vital as I remembered. In addition to Tony and Susan Gilroy, Bill's daughter, Jenny, accompanied him. (She had been immortalized by my first songwriting teacher, Carol Hall, in a haunting tune commemorating her birth entitled "Jenny Rebecca.") It was hard to hear Bill above the din, and he had an even harder time hearing me. But I told him I was touched he came and excited to celebrate our show.

I wish I had asked my son to take a photo. The only pictures I have of us are not great (in the only shot with Bill and Frank Gilroy flanking me, I unfortunately blinked). At 54 Below, I related onstage to Klea Blackhurst (our "hostess with the mostess") how tough it was to convince Bill to give me the rights. I did acknowledge how he obviously said yes and had been supportive of my work. I wish I had had the guts to introduce him from the house. I wish I had shared the story of his returning to the Hudson Guild and exclaiming, "I never thought I'd say this, but it's a fucking musical!"

Those words now mean more to me than any quote in *The New York Times*.

I thought about all these moments as I sat with roughly two hundred invited guests at Bill's memorial at the Ziegfeld Theatre. I laughed at John Kander's reminiscences: He and Bill and Bill's older brother, James, had all shared a spacious apartment together on the Upper West Side during their days as struggling artists. They also shared the same shrink, who was treating them when John won a Tony for *Cabaret*, James won an Oscar for *The Lion in Winter*, and Bill landed his first major book deal. Tony Gilroy, the last to speak, hit it out of the ballpark with an amazingly funny and touching tribute that captured Bill to a fare-thee-well.

But perhaps the most moving part of the program were memories shared by Scott Frank, a successful Hollywood screenwriter Bill had mentored. Like me, Scott had enjoyed a special relationship. He talked about Bill's generosity and asked others in the audience who had benefited from Bill's tutelage to stand. As I rose, I looked around the cavernous Ziegfeld and there were at least forty to fifty people standing.

Clearly, I wasn't an exceptional case; here were many former protégés on whom he'd lavished attention. But it spoke to Bill's heart and mind that he helped so many while making each of us feel like we were one of the chosen few, and indeed we were.

But here's the thing. Bill Goldman may have had a reputation for valuing currency, but at least in my case, I'm prepared to debunk that rumor. Three years after the Hudson Guild production, I wrote Bill a letter explaining that I was losing money on *No Way to Treat a Lady*. Between paying Danny Troob for the continued use of his arrangements (Danny called it "the gift that keeps

Celebrating William Goldman, December 1, 2018. Author's collection

giving"), contributing to my own airfare and meals while attending productions and refining the show, and duplicating and mailing scripts and cassettes to countless theaters, I was always in the red.

A few days later, Bill called me. He was sorry to hear about my travails and offered a solution: "Come up with a reasonable annual figure that you'd like to make from the show. If I approve, you'll have that as a certainty. Anything over it, our deal will be in place."

I thanked him, chose a figure, and he consented. It wasn't a high number—I didn't want to look a gift horse in the mouth—but it gave me a cushion and allowed me to make a sizable dent in my expenses. Bill sent our agreement to his accountant, and for the next twenty plus years, my income was below that figure except for two years when an Italian tour and a major production at The Village Theatre in Issaquah, Washington, gave me a taste of what success-ful writers experience.

That incredible gesture also afforded me the opportunity to keep writing, create new works, and see tangible results from my efforts. John Anderson, the playwright who penned *Tea and Sympa-thy*, once observed "I have always felt it was too bad that you could make a killing, but not a living, in the theater." However, thanks to Bill giving so generously of his time and later withholding his per-centage, I was able to comfortably survive somewhere in between: the middle ground. I've never revealed this until now—Bill likely would have preferred I not go public—but he's not here to tell me otherwise. So even though I couldn't properly acknowledge him from the stage at 54 Below, *this* is the "killer" surprise ending.

Take a bow, Bill, and God bless.

ACKNOWLEDGMENTS

Most of the time when I think of acknowledgments, an acceptance speech comes to mind where one frantically tries to include everyone before the playoff music sounds. What a relief that books offer a real opportunity to give thanks. And I am most thankful to . . .

My agent, Barbara Hogenson, a tireless and passionate supporter who is never more than a phone call or email away. She's also very resourceful for having submitted my manuscript to Rowman & Littlefield, which provides me with a natural segue . . .

Chris Chappell, my deft and experienced editor, offered me a cherished opportunity to tell my story and gently guided me throughout this process. As Chris said at the outset, "I like to believe I leave a campsite better than when I found it." I'm not an avid camper, but this analogy was not lost on me, and it has proven to be accurate. (In return, I'd like to think Chris has benefited in discovering that "hostess with the mostess" is not a misspelling, and "Have an eggroll, Mr. Goldstone" can now be adopted into his lexicon.)

Barbara Claire, Chris's editorial assistant, was invaluable as well, helping me with the art log. (I admit I felt like The Baker in *Into the Woods* collecting permission forms and thumbnail images!) Laurel Myers, Chris's associate, was instrumental in helping me choose the best images, and Ashleigh Cooke, production manager, has skillfully guided me through the final rounds of copy editing, having been tasked with (to quote Sondheim) "putting it together."

I'm very grateful to Bob Marshak's widow, Amy Parks, for generously donating his beautiful photos from the Hudson Guild production. Her daughter, Hila, helped bring us together thanks to Marina Gray's expert research/detective work. Cody Upton, executive director of the American Academy of Arts and Letters, and Virginia Dajani, former executive director, were instrumental in connecting me to Dorothy Alexander, who took the two images of Stephen Sondheim with Jonathan Larson and me, my Holy Grail of photos.

Dan Elish, my great friend and collaborator on *The Evolution of Mann*, was the first person to read this manuscript. It was considerably longer then and in dire need of editing, but Dan, a talented and prolific writer of books as well as musicals, saw past those deficiencies and was very encouraging. Howard Marren, another valued friend and collaborator (*Valentino's Tango*) meticulously noted rules for italicizing titles and using caps, acting as my first copy editor long before Katy Whipple was thankfully assigned.

Author David Margolick recommended I send an early draft to Ron Fassler, an excellent writer who penned *Up in the Cheap Seats*, a fascinating chronicle of indelible Broadway performances that shaped his adolescence. Ron, who reminded me he had auditioned for the world premiere of *No Way to Treat a Lady*, was exceptionally insightful, offering many suggestions, most of which I happily integrated.

Support also came from two dear friends of my parents: Gert Margolick (David's mother and a true inspiration) and Tom Philbrick, an accomplished writer and editor who guided my late father through two of his books and magnanimously shared with me his feedback and support. I also greatly appreciate his son Nathaniel's ringing endorsement, along with those offered by Alex Timbers, Tony Gilroy, Jason Alexander, Jeanine Tesori, and Donna McKechnie, each uniquely gifted and generous at heart.

Special thanks to Concord Theatricals and James Morgan for allowing me to reprint passages from the Samuel French edition of *No Way to Treat a Lady*.

Additional support came from friends, colleagues, and family: Ellen Ziskind and Maggie Brenner, Jan and Peter Cook, Lynn Henderson, Stefan Huber and Alen Hodzovik, Margie Kaplan, Tom Toce, Irene, Glenn and Kara Gordon, Peter and Julie Auster, Ralph and Tobe Sevush, Judy Arons, Nancy Pines, Denise Elmore, Jane Alexander, Jim Hall, Alison and Josh Smith, Colin and Elizabeth Curlee, Paulette and David Kessler, Michele and Bob Perchonok, Howard and Randi Eisen, Dr. Arthur Cohen, Stefanie Steel, Lisa and Shelley Cohen, Jeff and Caren Fogel, Cheryl L. Davis, Peter and Anne Bologna, Miki Murray, Cathy Gale, Mitchell Bernard, Frank Rich, Stephen Schwartz, Charles Strouse, Bettina Weyers, Lori Styler, Paulette Haupt, Robert Jess Roth, Adam Grupper, Stephen Bogardus, Sheldon Epps, Kurt Peterson, Michael Kerker, August Eriksmoen, Larry Hirschhorn, Peter Filichia, Linda Konner, Kevin P. McAnarney, Randie Levine-Miller, Michael Lavine, Steven Howard, Jimmy Smith, M.C. Waldrop, Debbie Toll, Betty Berman, Linda and David Loveman, Anne and Gary Damieki, Caryl and Samantha Steward, Andrea Elish, Parker and Maria Turnage Esse, Emily Loesser and Don Stephenson, Liza Gennaro, Donna Lynn Hilton, Ian Galligan, Richard Hopkins, Jerry Dixon, Margaret Luca, Chip Fabrizi, Walter Marks, Horacio Rojas, Gianluca Guidi, Ghostlight Records, Maria Laura Baccarini, Elena Sanesi, Leyla Lenzi, Amherst College roomies (Peter Kurzweil, Tony Hull, Bruce Gelb, Larry Eichenfield), Amherst Zoomies (Doug Bernstein, Denis Markell, David Kalodner, Beth Rice, David Rubin, Kerry Brennan), and my Godspell family (Kim Heelan, Deirdre Kane, Leslie Fleming-Mitchell, Jenny Campbell, Debra Bloom, Willa Perlmutter, Chris Wells, Jim Vagias, Tony Peck, Jeff Deutsch, Drew Pinsky).

I'm forever beholden to three beloved family pets, Chula, Tic Tac, and Georgie, who played leading roles as support animals.

I'm very grateful to my sister, Debby Hall. We have become quite close in recent years, and her encouraging response to these chapters has meant more to me than I can express.

I'm only sorry my parents are not alive to see this come to fruition. My mother had been such a strong advocate of my keeping a journal. Whenever rehearsals were taking an unexpected turn, she would say, "Are you writing this down? It's important you make the time." I believe she felt it would be therapeutic. Prior to my writing this book, she's the only one who had read the journals, later exclaiming, "I think you've got another play!" Well, I'm not sure about a play, Mom, but definitely a book.

I often thought about my father while writing this book. I began the process in the last months of his life, and he was delighted to know I was in the throes of creativity. I remember he had two questions: Did I see a structure, and was the project bringing me joy? I affirmatively responded to both, and after he passed away, I gained profound solace knowing that this simple act of putting sentences together also gave him enormous pleasure. Like father, like son.

Speaking of sons, I could not have written this if not for my son, Jeremy. Although he didn't immediately impact these pages (he was born more than halfway through the journey), his love and support grounded me in profound ways and made me realize there is indeed life beyond theater. A true renaissance (young) man, it's a shame he didn't get to discuss his love of the New York Knicks with William Goldman, a fellow fan.

And finally, I'm grateful to Jeremy's mother, also known as my wife, Cathy. I realize that I dedicated the book to her, so you might feel she's received sufficient credit. But it's worth noting that she lived through much of what was reported and has been the most authentic sounding board and loving partner imaginable. No rewrite has escaped her eyes, no screams of joy or anguish have escaped her ears. And that is not the stuff of fiction.

Okay, I think that covers it. Let the playoff music begin . . .

APPENDIX

LIST OF NOTABLE PRODUCTIONS

Below is a list of prominent productions of *No Way to Treat a Lady*.

Productions I attended are in bold.

1987
Hudson Guild Theatre, New York City
Cast: Stephen Bogardus, Liz Callaway, June Gable, Peter Slutsker
Director: Jack Hofsiss
Music Director: Uel Wade
Orchestrator: Danny Troob
Choreographer: Christopher Chadman
Assistant Director/Dramaturg: Robert Jess Roth
Producing Director: Geoffrey Sherman
Awards: Winner of a Richard Rodgers Development Grant

1988
Florida Studio Theatre, Sarasota
Cast: Mary Baird, Scott Burkell, Kate Cornell, Adam Grupper
Director/Producer: Richard Hopkins
Music Director: Dan Stetzel

1989
Thorndike Theatre, Leatherhead, UK premiere
Cast: David Burt, Susannah Fellows, Vivienne Martin, Martin Smith, Barbara Young
Director: Vivian Matalon
Music Director: Kate Young
Choreographer: Lindsay Dolan
Additional Orchestrator: Jason Carr

1990
TheatreWorks, Palo Alto, California
Cast: Stephen Frugoli, Annie Kozuch, Darlene Popovic, James Shelby
Director: Randal K. West
Founding Artistic Director: Robert Kelley

1991
Cohoes Music Hall, Cohoes, New York
Cast: Adam Grupper, Kathy Morath, Darlene Popovic, Ray Wills
Director/Choreographer: David Armstrong
Music Director: George Kramer
Executive Director: Joseph McConnell

1992
Unicorn Theatre, Berkshire Theatre Festival, Massachusetts (Staged Reading)
Cast: Adam Grupper, Kay McClelland, Marilyn Pasekoff, James Weatherstone
Director: Bill Castellino

1993
Theatre Club at the Lois Pope Theatre, Manalapan, Florida
Cast: John E. Brady, James Judy, Barbara Tirrell, Ellen Zachos
Director: J. Barry Lewis
Music Director: Michael Lavine
Producing Director: Louis Tyrrell
Awards: Nominated for three Carbonell Awards including Best Musical Production and Best New Musical

Portland Rep, Portland, Oregon
Cast: Richard Bradbury, Kevin Loomis, Zoe McClanahan, Chrisse Roccaro
Director: Geoffrey Sherman

1994
Backer's Auditions at The Friars Club and Lamb's Theatre, New York City
Cast: Tovah Feldshuh, Colleen Fitzpatrick, Jason Graae, Adam Grupper, Kay McClelland, Carole Shelley, Bob Stillman
Director: Lonny Price
Music Director: Tim Weil

1995
Favored Nations Studio Presentations, The Atlantic Theater, New York City
Cast: Brian Stokes Mitchell, Robert Michael Baker, Barbara Tirrell, Karen Ziemba
Director: Gabriel Barre

1996
The York Theatre Company, New York City
Cast: Adam Grupper, Alix Korey, Marguerite MacIntyre, Paul Schoeffler
Director: Scott Schwartz
Music Director: Wendy Bobbitt
Choreographer: Daniel Stewart
Producer: James Morgan
Orchestrations: David Siegel
Awards: Three Outer Critics nominations including Best Revival and Best Featured Actress (Alix Korey); Drama Desk Nomination for Outstanding Set Design for a Musical (James Morgan)

1997
Signature Theatre, Arlington, VA
Cast: Donna Migliaccio, Buzz Mauro, Lawrence Redmond, Peggy Yates
Direction: Scott Schwartz

Musical Direction: Eric Culver
Choreographer: Karma Camp
Artistic Director: Eric Schaeffer
Awards: Nominated for three Helen Hayes Awards: Outstanding Resident Musical, Outstanding Lead Actor, Resident Theatre (Lawrence Redmond), Best Outstanding Supporting Performer, Resident Musical (Donna Migliaccio); Winner: Best Actor (Lawrence Redmond)

1998
Coconut Grove Playhouse, Coconut Grove, Florida
Cast: Maureen Silliman, Cordell Stahl, Ruth Williamson, Lenny Wolpe
Director: Jeffrey B. Moss
Music Director: John Mulcahy
Choreographer: Barbara Siman
Producer: Arnold Mittleman
Awards: Seven Carbonell Award Nominations including Best Musical Production, Best Director, Best Actor (Lenny Wolpe), and Best Actress (Ruth Williamson)

Arts Theatre, London (London Premiere)
Cast: Paul Bown, Tim Flavin, Donna McKechnie, Joanna Riding, Joan Savage
Director: Neil Marcus
Music Director: Christopher Frost
Producer: Raymond Wright/Ballantrae Theatre Productions

Theater LaB Houston, Houston, Texas
Cast: Greg Coles, Jimmy Phillips, Robin Smith, and Jennie Welch
Director: Ed Muth
Musical Direction: Steven Jones
Producing Artistic Director: Gerald LaBita

1999
Phoenix Theatre, Indianapolis, Indiana
Cast: Bill Book, Jeanne Croft, Laura Duvall-Whitson, Stuart Mill
Director: Suzanne Fleenor
Musical Director: Paul Galloway

Village Theatre (second stage)
Cast: David Dollase, Frances King, Leslie Law, David Long
Director/Choreographer: Stephen Terrell
Music Director: Andrew Shields
Executive Producer: Robb Hunt

2000
So Behandelt Man Keine Dame
Saarländisches Staatstheater, Saarbrücken, Germany
Cast: Holger Hauer, Bibi Jelinek, Susanne Marik, Bernhard Stengele
Director/Translator: Holger Hauer

*"Ménage of the Mind":
In the song, "The First
Move,"   Detective
Morris Brummell (Peter
Slutsker) is both fixated
on his date, Sarah Stone
(Liz Callaway) and the
infamous lipstick killer
(Steve Bogardus) in the
1987 Hudson Guild
world premiere directed
by Jack Hofsiss.* Photo by
Bob Marshak

Barrington Stage Company, Massachusetts
Cast: Sandy Binion, Bradley Dean, Adam Heller, Karen Murphy
Director: Rob Ruggiero
Music Director: Darren R. Cohen
Founding Artistic Director: Julianne Boyd

Lyric Stage of Boston
Cast: Robin Allison, Derek Stearns, J.H. Williston, Maryann Zschau
Artistic Director/Director: Spiro Veloudos
Music Director: Jon Goldberg
Awards: IRNE Award: Outstanding Actress: Maryann Zschau (*No Way to Treat a Lady / Sunday in the Park with George*)

2001
Cape Rep Theatre
Cast: Tom Jahnke, Vicki Summers, Susan M. Terner, Tom Wolfson
Director: Robert R. Troie
Musical Director: Nancy Schofield Fadely

2001
Borgio Verezzi Theatre Festival, Italy
Serial Killer per Signora
Cast: Cristina Ginervri, Christian Ginepro, Massimiliano Giovanetti, Crescenza Guarnieri
Director/Producer: Gianluca Guidi
Musical Director: Riccardo Biseo
Choreographer: Stefano Bontempi
Translation and Adaption: Gianni Fenzi
Translation of Lyrics: Giorgio Calabrese

2001–2002, first Italian tour following the successful reception at Borgio Verezzi

TheaterWorks, Hartford, Connecticut
Cast: Bradley Dean, Adam Heller, Eileen Kaden, Cheryl Stern
Director: Rob Ruggiero
Music Director: David Nehls

Kleines Theater, Berlin, Germany
Cast: Marion Musiol, Harald Pilar von Pilchau, Heiko Stang, Gabi Sutter
Director/Musical Director: Christian Struppeck
Director: Gerald Michel

2002
Florida Studio Theatre, Sarasota
Cast: Kevin del Aguila, David Edwards, Kathy Halenda, Lauren Mufson
Director: Fred Weiss
Producer: Richard Hopkins

2004
No Son Maneras de Matar una Dona
Artenbrut Theater, Barcelona, Spain
Cast: Frank Capdet, Ivan Labanda, Elvira Prado, Mercè Martínez
Director: Sílvia Sanfeliu
Awards: Winner Armchair Award (Barcelona's equivalent of the Tony Award): Best Musical and Best Actor (Ivan Labanda)

Theater Lübeck, Germany
Cast: Andreas Hutzel, Martin Schwartengräber, Carolin Soyka, Katja Thiede
Director: Stefan Huber
Music Director: Jan-Peter Klöpfel

2006
North Coast Repertory Theatre
Cast: Susan Denaker, Randall Dodge, Nick Spear, Rebecca Spear
Director: Rick Simas

2007
Broadway Rose Theatre Company
Cast: Adair Chappell, Leif Norby, Luisa Sermol, Joe Theissen
Director: Abe Reybold
Producing Artistic Director: Sharon Maroney
Managing Director: Dan Murphy
Awards: Drammy Award, Outstanding Lead Actor in a Musical (Joe Theissen)

2008
SthlmsMusikTeater, Stockholm, Sweden
Cast: Birgit Carlstén, Joachim Bergström, Mia Poppe, Jonas Samuelsson-Nerbe
Director: Andreas Boonstra
Music Director: Erik Skarby
Translation: Erik Fägerborn, Johan Huldt, Birgit Carlstén

2009
Colony Theatre, Burbank, California
Cast: Heather Lee, Jack Noseworthy, Erica Piccininni, Kevin Symons
Directors: West Hyler and Shelley Butler
Musical Director: Dean Mora
Choreographer: Jane Lanier
Producer: Barbara Beckley
Awards: *Los Angeles Times* Critics Pic. L.A. Drama Critics Award nomination (Heather Lee). Backstage Garland Award for Best Adaptation and Best Score (Douglas J. Cohen) and Best Performance in a (Primarily) Musical Production: Heather Lee.

M-Lab Theatre, Amsterdam, Holland
Cast: Wim van den Driessche, Brigitte Nijman, Frédérique Sluyterman van Loo, Remko Vrijdag
Director: Daniel Cohen

2010
Neglected Musicals, Staged Concert
Darlinghurst Theatre, Sydney, Australia
Cast: Nick Christo, Martin Crewes, Beth Daly, Naomi Livingston
Director: Jason Langley
Musical Director: Michael Tyack
Producer: Michelle Guthrie

2011
Darlinghurst Theatre (Full Production), Sydney, Australia
Cast: Jason Langley, Phillip Lowe, Julie O'Reilly and Katrina Retallick

The dangers of multitasking: Kit (Wim van den Driessche) holds Sarah (Brigette Nijman) hostage while taking aim at Morris (Remko Vrijdag) in Daniel Cohen's stylish production, 2009 at the M-Lab Theatre, Amsterdam. Photo by Bob Bronshoff

Director: Stephen Colyer
Musical Director: Craig Renshaw

2011
Phoenix Theatre, Phoenix, Arizona
Cast: Rusty Ferracane, Lisa Fogel, Jenn Taber, Chris Williams
Director: Richard Roland
Producing Artistic Director: Michael Barnard

2012
Malmö Opera, Sjöbo, Sweden
Cast: Erik Gullbransson, Jan Kyhle, Micaela Sjöstedt, Evabritt Strandberg
Director: Elisabet Ljungar

2013
Tokyo
Cast: Rie Miyauchi, Ryo Miyauchi, Kojiro Oka, Natsuki Oh
Director: Yasuhiko Katsuta

Repertory Philippines, Makati City
Cast: Sheila Francisco, Audie Gemora, Carla Guevara-Laforteza,
Pinky Marquez, Joel Trinidad
Director: Audie Gemora

2014
Landor Theatre, London (off West End)
Cast: Kelly Burke, Simon Loughton, Graham Mackay-Bruce, Judith
Paris,
Director: Robert McWhir
Music Director: Nicholas Chave

Industry Reading, New York City
Cast: Raul Esparza, Laura Marie Duncan, Steve Rosen, Cheryl Stern
Director: Joe Colarco
Music Director: Vadim Feichtner
Producer: Larry Hirschhorn

Cape Playhouse, Dennis, Cape Cod
Cast: Judy Blazer, Bradley Dean, Josh Grisetti, Stacie Morgan Lewis
Director: Mark Shanahan
Music Director: Michael Rice
Artistic Director: Evans Haile

2015
Village Theatre, Issaquah, Washington
Cast: Nick DeSantis, Bobbi Kotula, Jayne Muirhead, Jessica Skerritt,
Dane Stokinger,
Director: Steve Tomkins
Music Director: R.J. Tancioco
Choreographer/Assistant Director: Crystal Dawn Munkers
Producer: Robb Hunt

2016–2017
Serial Killer per Signora, second Italian tour
Cast: Gianluca Guidi, Giampiero Ingrassia, Teresa Federico, Alica
Mistroni

Translation and Adaption: Gianni Fenzi and Gianluca Guidi
Italian Translation of Lyrics: Giorgio Calabrese
Director/Producer: Gianluca Guidi
Music Director: Riccardo Biseo
Producer: Ente Teatro Cronaca Vesuvioteatro in collaboration with
Borgio Verezzi Theatre Festival 2016

2017
54 Below, thirtieth anniversary edition
Cast: Klea Blackhurst and Douglas J. Cohen (co-hosts), Sandy Binion, Stephen Bogardus, Kevin Chamberlin, David Edwards, Tovah Feldshuh, Adam Grupper, Hunter Hoffman, Michael Thomas Holmes, James Judy, Bobbi Kotula, Jillian Louis, Peter Marx (formerly Peter Slutsker), Christiane Noll, Jack Noseworthy, Brad Oscar, Jill Paice, Paul Schoeffler, Maureen Silliman, Cheryl Stern, Kevin Symons, Barbara Tirrell, Karen Ziemba
Director: Bill Castellino
Music Director: Eric Svejkar
Unable to participate: Jason Alexander, Liz Callaway, Bradley Dean, Kevin Del Aguila, Raúl Esparza, June Gable, Jason Graae, Adam Heller, Marin Mazzie, Brian Stokes Mitchell, Mary Testa, Stephanie Umoh, Ruth Williamson, Lenny Wolpe

2023
As we go to press, I'm excited to report that *No Way to Treat a Lady* will appear at the Edinburgh Fringe Festival in August produced by the Clydebuilt Theatre Company. I plan on attending and bringing a new journal along . . .

It takes a village: Alumni from No Way to Treat a Lady *celebrate its thirtieth anniversary at 54 Below, October 2017, directed by Bill Castellino.* Author's collection

INDEX

Note: Page numbers in *italics* refer to photos or images.